National Security, Public Health: Exceptions to Human Rights?

The book deals with the complicated relationships between national security and human rights, and between public health and human rights. Its premise is the fact that national security and public health are both included in human rights instruments as 'exceptions' to the human rights therein sanctioned. However, national security and public health also bear value by upholding, respectively, the security or the health of a population as a whole. In addition, they can be considered human rights themselves. The book therefore asks to what extent the protection of the individual could – or should – be overridden to enable the protection of national security or public health. Through theoretical analysis and case studies of these conflicts, the book examines some of the instances where the concepts of national security and public health are used – and abused – and other rights, including freedom of speech, procedural freedoms, and individual health, are violated as a consequence. It provides many interesting findings on the implications of such conflicts and balancing exercises and seeks to contribute to the ongoing debate on the protection of human rights.

This book was originally published as a special issue of *The International Journal of Human Rights.*

Myriam Feinberg is a Post-Doctoral Fellow at the University of Haifa, Israel. She was previously teaching and conducting research at Tel Aviv University, Israel, and King's College London, UK.

Laura Niada-Avshalom is Learning Adviser at the University of Westminster, London, UK.

Brigit Toebes is an Associate Professor and Rosalind Franklin Fellow at the Faculty of Law, the University of Groningen, The Netherlands.

National Security, Public Health: Exceptions to Human Rights?

Edited by
Myriam Feinberg, Laura Niada-Avshalom and Brigit Toebes

Routledge
Taylor & Francis Group
LONDON AND NEW YORK

First published 2016
by Routledge
2 Park Square, Milton Park, Abingdon, Oxon, OX14 4RN, UK

and by Routledge
711 Third Avenue, New York, NY 10017, USA

Routledge is an imprint of the Taylor & Francis Group, an informa business

British Library Cataloguing in Publication Data
A catalogue record for this book is available from the British Library

ISBN 13: 978-1-138-19378-9

Typeset in Times New Roman
by RefineCatch Limited, Bungay, Suffolk

Publisher's Note
The publisher accepts responsibility for any inconsistencies that may have arisen during the conversion of this book from journal articles to book chapters, namely the possible inclusion of journal terminology.

Disclaimer
Every effort has been made to contact copyright holders for their permission to reprint material in this book. The publishers would be grateful to hear from any copyright holder who is not here acknowledged and will undertake to rectify any errors or omissions in future editions of this book.

Contents

Citation Information vii

Foreword: National security and public health: exceptions to human rights? 1
Myriam Feinberg, Laura Niada-Avshalom and Brigit Toebes

1. International counterterrorism – national security and human rights: conflicts of norms or checks and balances? 6
Myriam Feinberg

2. Protecting 'national security' whistleblowers in the Council of Europe: an evaluation of three approaches on how to balance national security with freedom of expression 26
Dimitrios Kagiaros

3. Resisting accountability: transitional justice in the post-9/11 United States 47
Jonathan Hafetz

4. From the barrier to refugee law: national security's transformation from a balancing right to a background element in the realms of Israeli constitutionalism 65
Solon Solomon

5. The use of incapacitating chemical agent weapons in law enforcement 83
Michael Crowley and Malcolm Dando

6. Human rights and public health: towards a balanced relationship 106
Brigit Toebes

7. WHO International Health Regulations and human rights: from allusions to inclusion 123
Andraž Zidar

8. Some scepticism on the right to health: the case of the provision of medicines 145
Laura Niada-Avshalom

Index 167

Citation Information

The chapters in this book were originally published in *The International Journal of Human Rights*, volume 19, issue 4 (May 2015). When citing this material, please use the original page numbering for each article, as follows:

Foreword
National security and public health: exceptions to human rights?
Myriam Feinberg, Laura Niada-Avshalom and Brigit Toebes
The International Journal of Human Rights, volume 19, issue 4 (May 2015)
pp. 383–387

Chapter 1
International counterterrorism – national security and human rights: conflicts of norms or checks and balances?
Myriam Feinberg
The International Journal of Human Rights, volume 19, issue 4 (May 2015)
pp. 388–407

Chapter 2
Protecting 'national security' whistleblowers in the Council of Europe: an evaluation of three approaches on how to balance national security with freedom of expression
Dimitrios Kagiaros
The International Journal of Human Rights, volume 19, issue 4 (May 2015)
pp. 408–428

Chapter 3
Resisting accountability: transitional justice in the post-9/11 United States
Jonathan Hafetz
The International Journal of Human Rights, volume 19, issue 4 (May 2015)
pp. 429–446

Chapter 4
From the barrier to refugee law: national security's transformation from a balancing right to a background element in the realms of Israeli constitutionalism
Solon Solomon
The International Journal of Human Rights, volume 19, issue 4 (May 2015)
pp. 447–464

Chapter 5

The use of incapacitating chemical agent weapons in law enforcement
Michael Crowley and Malcolm Dando
The International Journal of Human Rights, volume 19, issue 4 (May 2015) pp. 465–487

Chapter 6

Human rights and public health: towards a balanced relationship
Brigit Toebes
The International Journal of Human Rights, volume 19, issue 4 (May 2015) pp. 488–504

Chapter 7

WHO International Health Regulations and human rights: from allusions to inclusion
Andraž Zidar
The International Journal of Human Rights, volume 19, issue 4 (May 2015) pp. 505–526

Chapter 8

Some scepticism on the right to health: the case of the provision of medicines
Laura Niada-Avshalom
The International Journal of Human Rights, volume 19, issue 4 (May 2015) pp. 527–547

FOREWORD

National security and public health: exceptions to human rights?

Myriam Feinberg[a], Laura Niada-Avshalom[b] and Brigit Toebes[c]

[a]*Buchmann Faculty of Law, Tel Aviv University, Israel;* [b]*Student Affairs, University of Westminster, London, UK;* [c]*Department of International Law, Faculty of Law, the University of Groningen, the Netherlands*

In September 2014, the United Nations Security Council adopted two resolutions within a few days of each other, both addressing 'threats to international peace and security': Resolution 2177 (2014), adopted on 18 September, determined that 'the unprecedented extent of the Ebola outbreak in Africa constitute[d] a threat to international peace and security'. Resolution 2178 (2014), adopted on 24 September, addressed the threat of the terrorist freedom fighter and reiterated that terrorism constituted a 'threat to international peace and security'. These resolutions raise questions about the appropriate means to address such threats and how doing so might conflict with human rights obligations. Following Resolution 2178, for example, states have been updating their terrorism legislation, some of which include contentious measures such as administrative bans on leaving or entering the country for suspected jihadis. The controversy over data surveillance, as well as the increase of international human rights instruments and human rights obligations, has renewed the old debate between national security and human rights. In parallel, the resurgence of the Ebola virus and the thousands of deaths attributed to it have again prompted questions about international bodies imposing measures to prevent and protect the population, sometimes at the expense of freedom of movement or other human rights.

A few months before these events, in May 2014, the 'National Security and Public Health: Exceptions to Human Rights?' conference was held at the Institute of Advanced Legal Studies in London. The basis for the conference was the following observation: national security and public health are both included in many human rights instruments as 'exceptions' to the human rights therein sanctioned, yet they can arguably be considered as human rights themselves. Therefore, participants in the conference asked to what extent the protection of the individual could – or should – be overridden to enable the protection of the general public. Both practice and case law have shown that human rights risk being set aside when they clash with the protection of national security or public health; the conference addressed the protection of human rights when faced with other pressing needs and further asked if the language of balance was the appropriate tool to address the relationship between rights and public safety.

This special issue collates articles from the conference and deals with the complicated relationship between national security and human rights and between public health and human rights. Some of the articles focus on the theoretical level and question the use of concepts such as 'balance' and 'proportionality', while others examine, in practical terms, national and thematic examples. The articles that form the content of this special issue all address the tension that arises when the concepts of national security and public health are used – and abused – and other rights, such as freedom of speech, procedural freedoms, freedom of movements, etc., are violated as a consequence.

The opening article, 'International counterterrorism – national security and human rights: conflicts of norms or institutional balance?' discusses the notion of 'conflict' between security and human rights in the context of terrorist sanctions. Feinberg argues that while balancing these two types of norms is the traditional way to include both interests in democratic societies, the focus on the language of 'conflict' that counterterrorism favours too often creates a *choice* between values that should all form the benchmark of counter-terrorism. Using the 2008 *Kadi* case from the European Court of Justice to illustrate the recent trend of judicial involvement in national security matters, Feinberg examines the relationship between United Nations (UN) and European Union (EU) terrorist sanctions as a particular situation where security measures and human rights protection interact. Feinberg contends that the institutional conflict created by the *Kadi* decision, while contributing to the fragmentation of international law and raising a number of legal concerns, has also had some positive consequences on the sanctions regimes. This is because the case law is, in practice, an example of institutional checks and balances, usually absent from international security and which, in effect, enhances the fairness of sanctions regimes by actively criticising executive measures and requesting the protection of fundamental freedoms from those adopting the measures.

In 'Protecting "national security" whistleblowers in the Council of Europe: an evaluation of three approaches on how to balance national security with freedom of expression', Kagiaros focuses on the conflict of values between freedom of information and intelligence sharing and he studies the protection offered to whistleblowers in the intelligence community within the framework of the Council of Europe. In his article, he offers three possible options for such protection by focusing on the concept of public interest: first, an absolute ban on external disclosures for intelligence officials; second, a broad exemption from criminal sanctions or other forms of retaliation when the interest in the information disclosed outweighs national security concerns; and, finally, protection from reprisals provided only for specific disclosures or categories of wrongdoing, which would be exhaustively enumerated in the law. Kagiaros favours the third approach as offering the most reasonable solution to the issue at hand, and as providing concrete protection to whistleblowers while ensuring that security concerns are adequately addressed. Yet, Kagiaros stresses that this approach needs to be supported by strengthened regional standards on whistleblower protection and vigilance on behalf of the judiciary.

The next two articles deal with case studies on the tension between national security and human rights at the national level in the United States (US) and in Israel. This tension often features in these two states, yet, in this special issue, the authors use novel angles to examine it.

In 'Resisting accountability: transitional justice in the post-9/11 United States', Jonathan Hafetz examines US national security considerations post 9/11 through the lens of transitional justice in order to assess whether it could pave the way towards accountability for human rights violations. With the release of the Senate Select Committee on Intelligence report about the CIA interrogation programme, these issues have become even more pressing. In his article, Hafetz stresses how 'resistance to accountability can take root and spread in a stable, advanced democratic society'. He demonstrates how the legal framework on national security was altered to, in effect, limit risks of liability in cases where allegations of torture could be raised. His analysis also suggests that such opposition to any future accountability process can effectively decriminalise categorical norms. Hafetz claims that this kind of reframing in the narrative on torture can happen even in societies with a strong rule-of-law foundation and sophisticated legal system such as the US. For Hafetz, the US experience in the war on terrorism further shows how changes of administration must be accompanied with specific legal measures to address crimes committed by previous administrations in order to promote accountability and to avoid future violations of human rights.

In 'From the barrier to refugee law: national security's transformation from a balancing right to a background element in the realms of Israeli constitutionalism', Solon Solomon examines the role of the Israeli Supreme Court in adjudicating cases of national security. Drawing both from cases in which the court considered the legality of governmental actions that infringed upon human rights for the purpose of enhancing national security, and from citizenship and immigration law cases where the national security nexus was less apparent, he observes how Israeli constitutionalism unfolds in its treatment of national security issues: Solomon notes that while the court defined national security as a decisive factor when adjudicating a balance between various human rights, it appeared less willing to award national security an equally significant role in cases where security did not constitute the main legal argument. Solomon concludes that, in doing so, the Israeli Supreme Court aligned its jurisprudence with that of other supreme courts, as well as with the international thematic constitutionalism model, by interpreting the different fields of laws and various provisions under the concept of the right to dignity.

In 'The use of incapacitating chemical agent (ICA) weapons in law enforcement', Michael Crowley and Malcolm Dando examine cases where states have resorted to weapons utilising chemical agents outside the context of wars and conflicts. The article surveys contemporary chemical and life science research potentially applicable to the study or development of ICA weapons, and highlights reported possession or use of such weapons by states. The authors also explore contemporary advances in relevant science and technologies, and the potential implications for ICA weapons development. Their empirical analysis consequently provides a summary of the obligations upon states under relevant international law – specifically the Chemical Weapons Convention and applicable regional and international human rights instruments. Crowley and Dando argue that although existing international law certainly constrains and arguably prohibits the development, acquisition and use of ICA weapons for law enforcement, there are areas of contested interpretation. The authors highlight the policy and regulatory lacunae that exist in this area and argue that this situation must be urgently addressed by the international community in order to prevent the potential proliferation and misuse of such weapons.

As the Ebola crisis evidences, there is an urgent need to clarify the links between efforts to protect the health of the public whilst securing human rights. The last three entries to this special volume address these matters from different perspectives and lead to different results and conclusions.

In 'Human rights and public health: towards a balanced relationship', Toebes discusses the complex relationship between public health, human rights and international law which, according to Toebes, is still ill-understood. Toebes explains that in international law there are many references to the protection of public health contrasting with other interests, including the interests of trade, commerce, intellectual property protection, transportation and warfare. Potentially, in such contexts, the 'right to health' as an economic and social right can be used as an additional collective claim to advance the health of the public, thus counterbalancing such interests as international and domestic trade and the conduct of warfare. While this approach has potential, Toebes warns that public health measures may potentially infringe on the civil and political rights of individuals, including their rights to privacy and freedom of movement. The author concludes that an integrated approach to human rights, taking into account both civil and political and economic, social and cultural rights, is the most balanced response to public health concerns.

In 'Some scepticism on the right to health: the case of the provision of medicines', Niada-Avshalom analyses the duties relating to the provision of medicines envisaged by the right to health included in the International Covenant on Economic, Social and Cultural Rights (ICESCR). Niada-Avshalom closely studies the problem of rationing scarce resources, a necessary exercise considering that health and medicine needs are virtually infinite while resources are limited. Her study leads to the finding that the covenant and its monitoring body, the Committee on Economic, Social and Cultural Rights, do not clearly indicate which interventions are to be prioritised – and therefore do not conclusively answer the problem of limited resources. The ICESCR framework only refers to duties of providing public health as well as interventions that would benefit groups of vulnerable people or the individual's medical needs. Niada-Avshalom concludes that such lack of clarity, and a slight penchant for public health, both contribute to engender legal, moral and political flaws such as discretion for states to determine what action – if any – to take on access to medicines and the tendency to focus on numbers rather than individuals.

In 'WHO international health regulations and human rights: from allusions to inclusion' Zidar investigates what limitations and derogations human rights can be subject to during international public health emergencies, when these are declared by the World Health Organisation (WHO) Director-General according to WHO International Health Regulations. Zidar remarks that references to human rights in these regulations are 'scant and general', yet they state that their implementation shall be guided by the Charter of the United Nations, which Zidar considers includes the UN corpus juris of human rights. Thus he calls for integrating the Universal Declaration of Human Rights (UDHR) and the International Covenant on Civil and Political Rights (ICCPR) legal regimes into the legal framework of the regulations. Zidar's approach is constructive in that he argues that the UN international human rights framework includes satisfactory guidance to deal with the limitation and derogation of human rights during public health emergencies. For example, it includes tests that ensure that such limitations and derogations to human rights are 'in conformity with human rights', and procedural safeguards. Zidar concludes that the regulations are 'fully compatible with international human rights standards', but that these standards need to be included in the training and education of public health officials and, more significantly, that it has to be ensured that these standards will be applied in practice.

Thus, the articles of the special issue reflect particular instances in which human rights are considered as obstacles or challenges to national security and public health and can thereby be side-tracked or, on the contrary, where national security and public health are considered to constitute an integral part of human rights protection and will therefore contribute to its enhancement. For example, Toebes carefully argues that, while conflicts between public health and human rights exist, the right to health can be used for public health claims in order to form a collective right. For Zidar, human rights law includes satisfactory guidance to deal with the limitation and derogation of human rights during public health emergencies but he stresses implementation issues. Kagiaros envisages the various ways in which the concept of public interest could solve the conflict between freedom of speech and national security. For Niada-Avshalom, instead, public health represents utilitarian argument when it is opposed to individual care – and thus it is a distortion of the right to health, which states will use to include and endorse public health. Feinberg argues also that placing national security in conflict with human rights can lead to the abuse of the concept. Instead, she suggests that transposing the language of conflict to institutions will provide the checks and balances that are necessary to combine security interests with the protection of fundamental freedoms. Hafetz also shows the negative consequences of placing national security in conflict with human rights with his tale of the use of torture in the US after 11 September 2001. Hafetz recalls how torture was conducted based on the ends justifying the means. Further warning is provided by Solomon, who argues that national security should not be used in a broad and vague sense.

This special issue focuses on debates that are not new, but it aims to reconsider them in light of recent events. These articles contribute to the analysis of the relationship between national security and human rights and between public health and human rights in very specific contexts. Yet they also aim to theorise this relationship more generally in order to identify and avoid the abuses that can arise in emergency situations. The first five articles stress the crucial need for review, transparency and for fair processes for the protection of the democratic nature of states as the emergence of human rights violations caused in the name of security and the strengthening of executive measures prove how fragile the concept of human rights is. The last three entries emphasize the importance of paying attention to the relation between public health matters and human rights protection at an international level, and whilst filling certain normative gaps they are also evidence of the enormous momentum this topic currently faces.

This special issue is a testimony of the importance and need to re-examine these issues as they, once again, raise new legal questions. It provides many interesting findings on the values that states are ready to protect – and forego – to ensure their safety, which can contribute to the ongoing debate on the protection of human rights.

International counterterrorism – national security and human rights: conflicts of norms or checks and balances?

Myriam Feinberg

Buchmann Faculty of Law, Tel Aviv University, Israel

Security and human rights norms usually require a balancing act for their contemporaneous application but are often considered to conflict with one another. This is the case, especially when terrorism threats lead the executive branch to temporarily suspend or reduce its human rights obligations. Yet this presumption that these two norms inherently conflict is increasingly criticised. International terrorist sanctions regimes, such as that of the European Union and United Nations, are a prime example of this conflict because these organisations have been concurrently adopting counterterrorism measures, often through their executive branch and without any human rights protections. This article will use the 2008 *Kadi* case of the European Court of Justice as a framework to provide a contextual analysis of the term 'conflict' and provide criticism for the use of the conflict label to describe the relationship between national security policies and human rights, when norms of security and human rights should *all* form the benchmark of counterterrorism. This article will examine the legal issues created by the *Kadi* case and suggest that, despite the legal and normative uncertainties it raised, in practice, the case is an example of institutional conflict, or checks and balances that, in effect, actually enhances the fairness of sanctions regimes.

Introduction

Current discourse on international counterterrorism places security and human rights in conflict with each other. While this perspective is hardly new as security and human rights need to be balanced on a regular basis in democratic societies, the norms are increasingly conflicting, due both to the global nature of the terrorist threat, which requires wider-reaching security measures, and to the numerous human rights obligations imposed on states by international and regional instruments. This article questions the assumption that security and human rights should be seen as opposing values and attempts to map out the concept of 'conflict' in the specific context of terrorist sanctions.

Using the 2008 *Kadi* case adjudicated before the European Court of Justice (ECJ) as a framework to analyse the language of 'conflict', I critique the focus on the notions of balance generally and 'conflict' (between national security and human rights) more specifically, as triggering a choice between norms that should all form the benchmark of counterterrorism. I suggest that, despite the many legal and normative uncertainties raised by the

Kadi case, the recent regional case law on terrorist sanctions is, in practice, an example of institutional checks and balances, usually absent from international security and which, in effect, enhances the fairness of sanctions regimes by actively criticising executive measures and requesting the protection of fundamental freedoms from those adopting the measures.

1. Security and human rights: the language of balance

Numerous moral, legal and political justifications exist, either for the complete or partial derogation of human rights. In cases of public emergencies or war, states are entitled to derogate from and completely suspend certain existing human rights protections, thereby making them inoperative. Similarly, public health, national security, or other considerations, are considered to be legal justifications for the partial limitation of human rights in non-emergency situations. Of course, even in situations of emergencies, not all human rights are necessarily suspended and some rights are non-derogable, in which case, no exception or limit is acceptable. A definition of these peremptory norms, which create non-derogable rights, is included in the Vienna Conventions for the Law of Treaties,[1] but the exact list of these rights is unclear. As the recent December 2014 release of the 528-page executive summary of the United States (US) Senate Select Committee on Intelligence's 6300-page report on the CIA torture programme[2] shows, freedom from torture, usually considered a non-derogable human right, has been spurned.

These derogations and limitations are included in various human rights instruments or policies: article 4 of the 1966 International Covenant on Civil and Political Rights[3] allows states to derogate from their obligations under the convention for reasons of 'public emergency'. Conversely, the European Convention on Human Rights includes a limitation clause for some of its protected rights, which then leads the court to conduct a balancing exercise between the right and its limitation:

> The exercise of these freedoms, since it carries with it duties and responsibilities, may be subject to such formalities, conditions, restrictions or penalties as are prescribed by law and are necessary in a democratic society, in the interests of *national security*, territorial integrity or public safety, for the prevention of disorder or crime, for the protection of health or morals, for the protection of the reputation or rights of others, for preventing the disclosure of information received in confidence, or for maintaining the authority and impartiality of the judiciary.[4]

In the context of national security, the political discourse often oscillates between reassurances that human rights are respected and support for a security apparatus. In a 1977 case in the United Kingdom (UK), Lord Denning said:

> It is a case in which national security is involved; and our history shows that, when the state itself is endangered, our cherished freedoms may have to take second place.[5]

When it comes to the specific case of terrorism, many counterterrorism measures are considered a necessary evil aimed at protecting the security of a population, sometimes at the expense of an individual or a group, leading to a language of balance between various norms. This balance between norms of security and of human rights – a necessary feature of democratic societies – becomes problematic if it leads government entities to make an exclusive choice between the norms. In this context, the events of 11 September 2001, and the nature of terrorism subsequently, have definitely shifted this so-called balance discourse to a discourse of choice.[6] The language on counterterrorism itself changed drastically after 11 September 2001 when President Bush declared that the US was at war against terrorism.[7] In the US, this new view formed the basis of the Patriot Act 2001 and for the 2001 Authorisation for Use of Military Force (AUMF) against terrorism[8] and, more broadly, of a whole new legal discussion on the laws of war and their application to terrorism.[9] The attacks of 11 September 2001 also resulted in the adoption of Resolution 1373 by the United Nations (UN) Security Council, which required its member states to adopt legislation to address terrorism.[10] The resolution was adopted under Chapter VII of the UN Charter, which makes its obligations binding on member states. Following the attacks, many argued that an entirely new approach to counterterrorism should be adopted to reflect the new nature of the terrorist threat.[11] This new approach generally prioritises security and can be seen in the US' political rhetoric about counterterrorism:

> First, our highest priority is – and always will be – the safety and security of the American people. As President Obama has said, we have no greater responsibility as a government.[12]

Such security discourse is not isolated and has been summarised as follows: 'in this world; security (hence order) is prior to justice'.[13] For Thomas Poole, 'in the political realm, human rights are not considered as a useful weapon against the enemy but as a dangerous constraint against effective action'.[14] An approach that focuses on security will often come at the expense of personal freedoms and that has been the case in the post-11 September 2001 legal context.[15]

Yet, against this backdrop, which prioritises national security as atop the hierarchy of needs for the protection of citizens, it is justifiable to question the actual rationale of placing security and human rights in *conflict* with one another, when both are such fundamental needs of our societies. Some authors and practitioners wisely challenge the practice of inserting conflict between these two societal features,[16] stating that 'we must reject the false choice between our values and our security'.[17] In particular, human rights experts have determined that it is a 'mistaken belief… that the protection of human rights and the protection of national securities (which are both a state responsibility) are mutually exclusive, when in fact they are not'.[18] Attacking the idea of balance itself, Daniel Moeckli actually considers that this balancing approach is 'inadequate and misleading' because it focuses on the relationship between the two concepts at one particular point in time, and not on a general basis.[19] For Stavros Tsakyaris, 'the very imagery of balancing unavoidably carries with it connotations of mathematical precision or at any event alludes to some kind of quantification',[20] which is problematic when it applies to such values as security, liberty, privacy, etc. Gugliemo Verdirame similarly discusses the value of the concept of proportionality in the context of human rights.[21]

As a result of the criticism rejecting a conflict between security and human rights, a new concept termed 'human security' even posits that individual liberty and human rights are not in opposition, but rather, at the very heart of security.[22] While there is a controversial aspect to human security,[23] this concept has definitely led to a 'shift in focus of various security issues for a much greater spectrum than national security'[24] and provides the theoretical foundation for the 'responsibility to protect'.[25] The concept of human security, and more generally the responsibility to protect movement implies that the protection and security of citizens has become a state obligation, and not merely a feature of state power. Indeed it is recognised, in the specific context of counterterrorism, that

> all human beings have a right to security and to life. All governments have a responsibility to respect, ensure, and fulfil these rights and, to that end, to employ effective strategies to prevent

and to punish acts of mass murder and destruction. No human rights advocate would deny this responsibility.[26]

It therefore seems counterproductive to place security in opposition to human rights. Yet, in practice, it appears that lawmakers, practitioners and judges are constantly faced with having to choose between, or balance, these two needs. The balance between the two values is not inherently problematic because both values need to be present at all times and balancing these two values allows – in theory – both values to coexist. Yet, in practice, it is the language of 'conflict' that seems prevalent in most counterterrorism theories, fostering an emergency environment without the necessary safeguards. Focusing on the term 'conflict' too often leads to a choice between security and human rights, instead of a healthy combination. This article will therefore examine terrorist sanctions regimes such as the UN and the European Union (EU) in order to determine whether it is possible to move the focus beyond the conflict between security and human rights. I will focus here on the idea that a conflict *does* occur, but at a different level, that of institutions, and assert whether that conflict can be useful in order to enhance the fairness of sanctions regimes.

2. The international legal order: a new dimension to the conflict?

In one given legal order, the balance between security and human rights is usually clearly defined, whether they apply to derogations of human rights or legitimate limitations of human rights. In the example mentioned above, the European Convention on Human Rights lists a variety of limitations to the application of rights within the instrument. Most national constitutions will include specific powers allocated to the executive branch in cases of emergency, which might lead to the suspension or limitation of human rights.[27] This does not mean that these emergency measures are always adopted without any controversy or without judicial review, or that the exceptions are always easily identifiable. Moreover, it becomes an issue when the 'emergency' nature of security measures is replaced by a de facto status quo.[28]

Yet, the situation becomes inherently problematic when different legal orders create parallel, and sometimes conflicting, obligations, which is the current situation in international counterterrorism. In effect, this crowded market of international counterterrorism actors exacerbates two other conflicts, beyond the 'conflict' between security measures and human rights, and which I consider to be conflicts of authorities.

First, international counterterrorism creates a conflict between legal orders. This is because more and more international organisations are involved in addressing the terrorist threat and this in turn may impact on a state's sovereignty in its capacity to deal with the phenomenon. Indeed, actors other than states might adopt the necessary measures to deal with the threat and therefore supplement – or replace – the state in one of its core powers. More generally, the increasing role of international organisations is at the core of the challenge that international organisations present for state sovereignty, as some competences are transferred to non-state actors and obligations are imposed on member states by international or regional organisations.

Second, there is a conflict between the various branches of governance *within* these legal orders themselves. Certainly, where security is involved, there is a tendency to favour action by the executive branch, which can adopt emergency measures, without going through the necessary parliamentary routes and by avoiding the possibility of judicial review.[29] Moreover, when asked to adjudicate on security matters, courts have traditionally chosen to defer to the executive.[30]

These two conflicts collude in international counterterrorism because the creation of international law through treaties enhances the role of the executive since it is that branch that negotiates these agreements (although treaties generally have to be implemented at the national level, often through approval by or an act of parliament) and in general, because 'foreign policy is made almost entirely by governments'.[31] Membership of both international and regional organisations enhances the role of the executive arm of that organisation, sometimes at the expense of other branches because 'conducting foreign policy is – both within the EU and at the national level – first and foremost a task of the executive'.[32] For instance, binding decisions of the UN can be adopted by the Security Council, composed of 15 member states, including five permanent members with a right of veto, and not by the General Assembly. In the EU, the legislative process has traditionally been shared between its council and commission. There is a 'consensus' that the EU has

> strengthened executive power, because it is the executive which has direct access to European policy-making and policy-makers in the Council, in the European institutions and other Member States.[33]

The central role of the executive in international law is exacerbated by the fact that the role of the international judiciary is limited because its decisions are not easily enforceable.[34] Moreover, in the specific context of counterterrorism, cases from the International Court of Justice are limited, partly due to its lack of universal and compulsory jurisdiction, but mostly due to the fact that there is no agreed-upon international definition of terrorism[35] and that the phenomenon is addressed via a variety of measures. Benvenisti summarizes this move as follows: 'all too often, the move to international institutions has to varying degrees eroded the traditional constitutional checks and balances found in many democracies ... as well as monitoring mechanisms of executive discretion'.[36] Therefore, because of the 'absence of a fully fledged centralised judiciary within the international legal order, domestic and regional courts play a key role in the enforcement and balancing of various international obligations'.[37] This new balancing role, by regional courts, has become crucial in international counterterrorism and has shifted the focus of emergency measures. For instance, David Bonner considers that the 'rules of the game' have not actually changed since 11 September 2001. For him, what is different is that courts 'have started applying an enhanced level of scrutiny in an area they once characterised as too sensitive for judicial involvement'.[38]

This change can be traced back to the adoption, by the Security Council, of targeted sanctions in the 1990s: targeted sanctions and asset freezing measures raise human rights issues because they are aimed at individuals, where traditional counterterrorism measures adopted through treaties did not directly affect individuals' rights. Indeed, in the context of terrorism measures, and more generally targeted sanctions, the increasing role of courts has brought some considerable changes, and in this article I will therefore be using the example of counterterrorism sanctions as a case study of this change and of the conflicts I previously identified: the conflict between national security and human rights, the conflict between legal orders and the conflict between branches of government.

3. Terrorism sanctions: conflicts of authorities

Today, there are two types of UN sanctions regimes that specifically target terrorism, which have then been replicated at the EU level, as well as by UN member states. The first regime was created by Resolution 1267 (1999), in which the UN Security Council determined that the failure of the Taliban authorities to comply with Security Council Resolution 1214 regarding support for terrorism constituted a threat to international peace and security.[39] Consequently, the resolution called on member states to take a variety of measures in order to force compliance, in particular, a freezing of assets of individuals and groups included in a list.[40] The list currently consists of 231 individuals and 69 entities that are regularly updated.[41] The member states are obligated to implement the measures imposed by the Security Council and enforce this list. I note here that, in 2011, the Security Council divided the 1267 sanctions regime, which 'was split up into two separate regimes, one targeting the Taliban as a nationalist movement (the 1988 sanctions regime), and the other targeting al-Qaeda as a global actor (the 1989 al-Qaeda sanctions regime)'.[42] However, for the purposes of this article, I will be referring to the 1267 regime for simplicity.

Second, and as part of Resolution 1373 (2001) mentioned previously, the Security Council required member states to freeze assets of individuals and groups who 'commit, or attempt to commit, terrorist acts or participate in or facilitate the commission of terrorist acts'.[43] In this resolution, there is no specific list of individuals or groups to which these obligations apply, or even a definition of terrorism. Instead, it is left to member states to decide whose assets should be frozen and to decide what the definition of terrorism should be in their own jurisdiction. Resolution 1373, therefore, creates an obligation for member states to act against terrorism, but gives them the discretion as to the means of this action. States therefore have an obligation to create their own sanctions lists independent of the 1267 list.

Most UN member states have therefore adopted two sets of sanctions regimes. For instance, France has created two sets of sanctions through its financial and monetary code[44]: 'Terrorists linked to Al-Qaeda', under an order signed 18 January 2011 and a decree from December 2009, applying various Articles of the Code Monétaire et Financier, and 'Other terrorist organisations', under an order from January 2012, applying various Articles of the Code; under the United Nations Act 1946, the UK has adopted a series of Orders in Council giving effect to the UN Resolutions, including the Afghanistan (United Nations Sanctions) Order 1999 (SI 1999/3133) and the Terrorism (United Nations Measures) Order 2001 (SI 2001/3365), which were each amended by later Orders to reflect changes at the UN levels.[45]

However, and while the EU is not required to implement UN obligations because it is not a member state of the UN, Declaration 13 to the Lisbon Treaty states that 'the European Union and its Member States will remain bound by the provisions of the Charter of the United Nations and, in particular, by the primary responsibility of the Security Council and of its Members for the maintenance of international peace and security'.[46] Moreover, under article 5 of the Treaty on the Functioning of the European Union, the EU is responsible for ensuring the coordination of economic policies of the organisation[47] and is therefore required to define the broad direction and guidelines to be followed by member states. In practice, the EU made a choice to transpose the Security Council sanctions regimes in its legal order and stated that it is 'committed to the systematic implementation of sanctions decided on by the UN Security Council'.[48] In effect, this creates another discrete level of counterterrorism measures: the EU has adopted sanctions which are the direct application of UN sanctions imposed through the Al-Qaida Sanctions Committee resulting from the 1267 sanctions regime: a series of common positions and regulations were adopted that implemented the various resolutions taken by the Security Council. Council Decision 2011/487/CFSP[49] and EC Regulation 881/2002[50] contain the main current obligations for member states and include the 1267 list of individuals and groups from the UN regime. On the other hand, and in the context of Security Council Resolution 1373, the EU created an independent sanctions regime through Common Position 2001/931/CFSP[51] and EC Regulation 2580/2001.[52] This means that the EU, like member states of the UN, has drawn up its own list of terrorist suspects against which to apply sanctions. While this is normal procedure for member states, here it means that the EU has added a level of specific obligations to its own member states in addition to that specified by the UN and national entities.

The consequence of this EU sanctions regimes list is that member states that belong to both the UN and the EU now tend to implement both EU lists, whereas non-EU member states will follow the UN model. This variety of sanctions regimes has created legal conflicts because various – and potentially conflicting – regimes exist, creating potential basis for litigation. Moreover, the targeted nature of the sanctions coupled with their lack of human rights protection have prompted regional courts that *do* have a mandate for human rights protection to address these issues.

In international law, there is a 'presumption against normative conflicts'[53] and courts are therefore generally 'expect[ed] … to exhaust the limits of interpretation in order to avoid a conflict'. To this end, courts display a tendency to strive for consistent interpretation. But when consistent interpretation is not possible and where UN binding obligations are involved, courts have traditionally given precedence to the binding obligations, according to Article 103 of the UN Charter.[54] One early example of this deference to the executive in the context of counterterrorism is the *Lockerbie* case where the International Court of Justice (albeit at the stage of provisional measures) gave precedence to a UN Security Council Resolution over a UN Convention, even though the resolution had been adopted after the start of the proceedings.[55]

However, a variety of regional courts have challenged this traditional conflict resolution and, by actively becoming involved in terrorism cases, have introduced the protection of human rights into the core of sanctions regimes. A number of regional courts have handed down decisions on the issue. European cases include the 2006 *Organisation des Modjahedines du peuple d'Iran* v. *Council of the European Union and UK* case from the EU and the 2012 *Nada* v. *Switzerland* case decided by the European Court of Human Rights (ECtHR).[56] Non-EU cases include a decision by the Human Rights Committee of the International Covenant on Civil and Political Rights[57] and a number of national cases.[58] Despite more recent cases from the ECJ, I will focus on the *Kadi* case law from the EU, because it was the impetus for the change in the procedural fairness of terrorist sanctions.

Beyond the conflict of norms that this case raises between security needs and the protection of human rights, it represents a paradigmatic shift in the traditional relationship between various organisations and questions the authority of member states. Yet, I note that they also contributed to increasing the fairness of sanctions regimes, by actively criticising executive measures and requesting the protection of fundamental freedoms from those adopting the measures.

4. The *Kadi* case: a landmark decision, a complex solution

Yassin Abdullah Kadi, a Saudi resident, was placed on the US assets freezing list in October 2001 as a 'specially designated global terrorist'.[59] Days later, he was added to the UN 1267 Sanctions Committee list and consequently put on the EU list based on Council Regulation 881/2002.[60] Mr Kadi filed an appeal with the Court of First Instance of the EU (CFI) arguing that the EU Regulation should be annulled because it infringed his fundamental rights, namely, the right to be heard, the right to respect for property, and the right to effective judicial review.[61] In 2005, and following article 103 of the UN Charter, the CFI ruled that it could not review the legality of the EU's Council Regulation because doing so would mean reviewing the legality of the Security Council's decisions.[62] With this decision, the court followed the traditional norm conflict resolution that gives precedence to UN obligations. The CFI held, however, that the EU judicial system was able to review the legality of the European Regulation in the light of *jus cogens*, because even the UN could not derogate from these rights.[63]

Mr Kadi appealed to the ECJ against the decision of the CFI. In a landmark decision dated 2008, the ECJ overruled the judgment of the CFI and annulled Council Regulation 881/2002, because it found a breach of fundamental rights of the EU.[64] The ECJ held that fundamental rights are an integral part of the general principles of the EU law[65] and that the lawfulness of European measures depends on their respect for human rights, despite the parallel obligation on the organisation to respect international law, which might impose conflicting obligations. It is important to note that the ECJ stressed that the decision concerned the EC Regulation and not the Security Council's Resolution 'as such'.[66] The ECJ specifically recalled that it did not have jurisdiction to review decisions from the UN body.[67] However, the ECJ's main view was that, since the UN regime did not provide an adequate legal mechanism to protect individuals against sanctions, the court could not refrain from exercising its jurisdiction. In its judgment, the ECJ accepted that the success of sanctions lies partly on an element of surprise.[68] Yet, it held that after having imposed sanctions on suspects, the authorities should then provide the suspects with information and reasons for their listing.[69] Therefore, the ECJ annulled the listing on procedural grounds and stressed the need for procedural fairness, while recognising the security needs of the international community and the relevance of sanctions. The decision in effect strikes a balance between these two interests. However, I will examine later how the court's legal basis for its argument was problematic.

Despite the ECJ judgment in *Kadi*, the European Commission included Mr Kadi on another listing after providing him with a statement of reasons[70] and therefore Mr Kadi filed an action with the General Court on 30 January 2009 against the renewed listing. On 30 September 2010 the General Court delivered its decision in what became known as *Kadi II*.[71] In that case, the General Court noted that criticism had been expressed against the decision of the ECJ because it questioned traditional international law, which gives deference to UN resolutions,[72] a point I will return to. However it also stressed that it had to follow decisions of the ECJ. Consequently, the General Court had to analyse the legal nature of the listing of Mr Kadi. It did consider that the review system of the sanctions regime of the Security Council was still unsatisfactory[73] and 'so long as the re-examination procedure operated by the Sanctions Committee clearly fails to offer guarantees of effective judicial protection',[74] the General Court had to exercise the principle of full review decided by the ECJ in *Kadi*.[75] In that context, the court noted that the commission had not granted the applicant access to evidence against him[76] and he, therefore, did not have any way to challenge the decision to list him. The General Court concluded that maintaining the freeze of Mr Kadi's assets was unlawful and should, for that reason, be annulled.[77]

The commission appealed the 2010 judgment and the ECJ handed down its decision in July 2013,[78] even though the UN delisted Mr Kadi in October 2012 and the EU itself delisted him a few days later.[79]

The core legal issue of the 2013 case was the scope of judicial review that the EU is willing or expected to conduct in cases of asset freezing and listings. In fact, and for the purpose of this analysis, the scope of the EU's choice in implementing UN listings is at stake: as I mentioned, under the 1373 regime, the EU has discretion regarding the list of individuals and groups it chooses to list. And in a series of cases, the EU affirmed that this discretion obligated the EU to respect human rights.[80] In *Kadi* I, the ECJ stated that the EU had the obligation to provide the same human rights protection for the 1267 regime[81] although the 1267 regime does not technically provide the same leeway to member states (and the EU) and in its 2013 decision, the ECJ reiterated this argument and requested a substantive review on the part of the EU.[82] Technically however, the EU has no discretion when it comes to the individuals or groups that are listed by the 1267 regime. I contend that the ECJ stating it has authority to – in effect – review sanctions imposed by the Security Council can be problematic as it can create conflicts between the various actors of the international community, or exacerbate existing conflicts.

5. Conflicts of authorities

When a situation is identified as a threat to international peace and security, the UN Security Council is the competent authority to adopt binding obligations on its member states in order to address the threat.[83] In the event of a conflict between various measures adopted in international law, article 103 of the UN Charter will resolve this conflict by giving precedence to the UN obligations.[84] Whether this is the best way to deal with conflicts of norms is questionable – in particular when human rights norms are involved – but, it allows a form of judicial consistency, and courts have traditionally used it in order to avoid norm conflict.[85] With the *Kadi* jurisprudence, this hierarchy of measures is questioned. Here, I will attempt to map out the legal consequences – both positive and negative – of the decision, in the context of the conflicts I identified, in order to move from a conflict of norms to a conflict of institutions.

From a general perspective, the *Kadi* decision may compromise compliance with international obligations.[86] Although the case law on sanctions has increased the due process profile of sanctions regimes, the *Kadi* case has, in effect, created a standard that is different from that of the UN, and this might therefore 'threaten to place States in breach of their Chapter VII obligations'.[87] Member states that belong to both the UN and the EU face the complex problem of trying to accommodate two different sets of norms, while trying to deal with security within their own territory: the onus is on states to 'adopt new legislation to transpose the UNSC resolutions' in a way that will also satisfy the European courts.[88]

The participation of states in international institutions is further complicated by the new dynamics created by the case law, as was noted in a review of the case:

> Should other countries or regional groups also decide that the application of Security Council decisions is dependent on their compatibility with national or regional values, and in particular their own view on human rights issues, this could endanger the authority of the Security Council in the maintenance of international peace and security.[89]

In effect, such an argument has the potential to be abused by states in the name of regional specificity. The issue here is that in *Kadi* the EU only referred to its own human rights standards and *jus cogens*, and did not discuss 'the obligations of States as regards human rights derived from international law in general and its principal instruments in particular, among which the Universal Declaration of Human Rights occupies a prominent place',[90] which the CFI did. To do so would have strengthened the EU's argument because it would have moved the focus from the limited scope of European human rights to international human rights that apply more widely.

The ECJ was further criticised for not paying 'sufficient attention to the source of the violation; it did not allow any leeway to the Security Council'[91] even though the Security Council is one of the main actors in counterterrorism and it allows a global effort to address terrorism. It is also interesting to note here that the *Kadi* case did not refer to the declaration on the common foreign and security policy of the Treaty on the European Union mentioned above and the duty of the EU to 'remain bound by the provisions of the Charter of the United Nations and, in particular, by the primary responsibility of the Security Council and of its Members for the maintenance of international peace and security'.[92]

Over the years, the EU has built its own constitutional order by reference to its member states through the principles of primacy and subsidiarity.[93] It has been generally considered that EU law is directly applicable into national systems, based on monism.[94] And in the *Kadi* case, the ECJ even stated the existence of a 'basic constitutional charter, the EC Treaty'.[95] Yet, in the same *Kadi* case, the ECJ treated international norms as external norms emanating from 'distinct legal orders'.[96] Still, the EU sanctions precisely copy those of the UN, even when the EU is not requested to do so. The ECJ's case law, therefore, contributes to the 'fragmentation in the implementation of sanctions',[97] in that states now face different requirements for the sanctions regimes of the various orders. This dual approach has been criticised[98] and it runs the risk of making the sanctions regimes, originally coherent, ineffective.

In addition, the decision further creates confusion in international law because it creates a division between EU member states that have human rights requirements different from non-EU states. The EU and the Council of Europe are strong legal systems, and their decisions have had a major impact on the legislation taken in the context of terrorist sanctions regimes. However, many states do not belong to the EU or the Council of Europe and, therefore, the individuals and groups that are listed by these non-member states do not have access to the aforementioned regional courts. Hence, they do not have the possibility of challenging their listing, especially since many national courts might be unable or unwilling to review the executive action of their own government.

Finally, the case raises issues of responsibility. According to the decision, violations of EU human rights will be attributed to the organisation if individuals or groups are listed without the necessary safeguards. However, and for the 1267 regime, states implement obligations directly imposed by the UN.[99] In a 2010 case, the ECtHR stressed that states have leeway in the way they implement terrorist sanctions[100] although this approach was criticised, including by the concurring judges, as unconvincing.[101] On the other hand, the EU held in *Kadi II* that a European judicial review would be necessary as long as the UN did not include the necessary safeguards in its regime.[102] Thus, whereas the ECtHR approach, rightly or wrongly, puts the onus on states to protect the human rights of those subjects in their jurisdiction, the EU approach in *Kadi* aimed at directly criticising the UN's sanctions regimes. Erika de Wet considers that states are thereby 'forced to disobey either a decision of the CJEU or a UNSC resolution, which will trigger state responsibility under either the one or the other regime'.[103] Antonios Tzanakopoulos further suggests that action by states refusing to comply with UN obligations could amount to countermeasures and might therefore be justifiable, if one considers that the Security Council's actions are illegal.[104] This particular argument raises further issues of whether the UN is under international obligations to protect human rights in the same manner as states in order for its actions to amount to international wrongful acts, but these are too complex to analyse here.[105]

Yet, precisely this last point of criticism regarding responsibility outlines the positive consequences of the cases. Indeed, the mechanisms that emerge from this case law might 'fill the vacuum that was created in the place where the [State] is no longer accountable and the international organization operates de facto'.[106] Certainly, in many national cases, states have argued that it is their obligation to follow the Security Council Resolutions,[107] even if it means violating some human rights standards.[108] With *Kadi*, the ECJ excludes 'more clearly than previously that Member States can use the UN as a forum to circumvent EU law'.[109] In future cases, article 103 might therefore not be accepted as the basis for national action violating human rights.

Thus, despite the legal concerns expressed here, the foremost positive consequence of the case is the pressure it actually put on the UN Security Council and other organisations, including the EU itself: as a result of the 2008 *Kadi* case, the European Commission proposed amendments to regulations on sanctions and EU Regulation 1286/2009 introduced procedural and due process reforms to the implementation of the UN 1267 regime in the EU.[110] Furthermore, the Lisbon Treaty of the EU now contains an express provision empowering the EU to take 'restrictive measures against natural or legal persons and groups or non-State entities'[111] that includes a provision stating that the ECJ has jurisdiction to review 'the legality of decisions providing for restrictive measures against natural or legal persons' adopted on the basis of the EU's common and foreign security policy.[112] Thus this jurisdiction that was first developed by the court in *Kadi* was recognised a posteriori by the EU in the new treaty.[113]

At the UN level, changes have also been introduced to improve the sanctions systems following the *Kadi* case. Originally, the Security Council had created, in 2006, a 'Focal Point', a contact mechanism established by the UN Secretary-General within the Secretariat (Security Council Subsidiary Organs Branch) that coordinates all delisting requests.[114] This delisting procedure was created in order to receive delisting requests from anyone affected by UN sanctions. However, because of its procedure, this Focal Point was criticised for being no more than a 'mailbox',[115] without authority to review the legality of the listings because it still places the last word in the hands of the states, and is dependent on the Security Council, thereby lacking any independence. To date, the Focal Point procedure is still in place for some sanctions regimes.[116] More significantly, to remedy criticisms raised by the Focal Point and '*taking note* of challenges, both legal and otherwise, to the measures implemented by Member States',[117] the Security Council, through Resolution 1904, created the Office of the Ombudsperson charged with assisting the Sanctions Committee with the delisting procedures for the 1267 regime.[118] This change was aimed at addressing 'shortcomings' of the listing process[119] by creating an office that is 'independent and impartial'.[120] The creation of the Ombudsperson office was a direct consequence of the *Kadi* case and it is the Ombudsperson report which finally led to the delisting of Mr Kadi. Yet, discussions abound on whether this new office completely remedied the fairness issues in sanctions regimes. The creation of the Ombudsperson's office is obviously an improvement for the particular sanctions regime of 1267 but, in general, courts have considered this to be insufficient. In *Ahmed*,[121] the UK Supreme Court 'rejected this introduction of an Ombudsperson as a radical step towards creating a regime that would deserve its deference'.[122] While the Supreme Court welcomed this new mechanism,[123] it still maintained that the 1267 sanctions regime does not offer any access to effective judicial remedies.[124] This ineffectiveness was echoed in *Kadi II* where the EU General Court held that 'the Security Council has still not deemed it appropriate to establish an independent and impartial body responsible for hearing and determining, as regards matters of law and fact, actions against individual decisions taken by the Sanctions Committee'.[125] Moreover, in the 2013 *Kadi* decision, the ECJ listed the reasons for which the Ombudsperson's office still does not amount to the necessary judicial review expected, by the EU, for individuals and groups that are listed by the 1267 regime.[126] Finally, it is crucial to note that the office is only mandated to act under the 1267 regime and does not apply to any of the other UN sanctions regimes, thereby creating legal differences in treatment between individuals targeted by sanctions.

The *Kadi* case is clearly concerned with whether the security needs of the international community allow states to forego or limit some of their human rights obligations, and in response the court focused on procedural issues surrounding the listing, rather than decide on the rationale of the listing: the court did not pronounce itself on whether the Council of the EU had rightly listed the claimants, but rather, whether the listing was done legally and whether the rule of law had been respected. More deeply therefore, it questions the relationship between international organisations and states and between various international organisations themselves. In that respect, it created a number of legal issues, which I was only able to refer to briefly. However, and for the purpose of this specific analysis, *Kadi* also questions the traditional monopoly of the executive branch in matters of security by empowering courts to ensure human rights are protected. In this context, we must note that the EU or the ECtHR are much more likely to act against non-compliant states than the UN, because of the possibility of judicial action and their focus on human rights issues.

6. Conclusions

Is conflict a good thing? Conflict is certainly not helpful if it means states have to – or can – choose between security needs and the protection of human rights at the expense of the other. Human rights should form the backdrop of counterterrorism rather than constitute a conflicting and cumbersome interest. This is true, all the more so because it is likely that a security discourse could prevail, since a language of emergency does not prevent strong executive measures from being applied for an unlimited time.

The European Convention on Human Rights, in its exceptions clauses, provides a framework for the balance between national security and the protection of human rights, by stating that the rights it protects 'may be subject to such formalities, conditions, restrictions or penalties as are prescribed by law and are *necessary in a democratic society*'.[127] This last expression forms the theoretical basis for the correct balance between the two conflicting needs before the ECtHR. In its case law – both generally, and in terrorism cases[128] – that court has traditionally used the principle of proportionality in order to give practical effect to this clause.[129] However, this principle still remains at the level of a balancing exercise between norms, with all the issues that I pointed to, and has therefore been criticised for its lack of objectivity and moral basis.[130]

Therefore, I raise here the possibility that the 'formalities, conditions, restrictions or penalties that are present and necessary in a democratic society' could refer to another requirement, in particular that of the separation of power, which is a 'way to foster a system of checks and balances necessary for good government'.[131] Indeed, while I reject the language of conflict between being safe and being free, the *institutional* conflict which happened in *Kadi* is, in practice, a good thing, in this particular context: while judicial decisions that challenge measures adopted by another branch create the normative uncertainties that I mentioned and can be strongly criticised, it means, in effect, that checks and balances exist in an international community that is traditionally the prerogative of the executive.

Whether this factual finding can be translated into a normative way to approach security and human rights is debatable and this article does not advocate such a normative change: we saw that one criticism of the *Kadi* case is that the European decisions only affect European states. They are not binding over organs of the UN, or over non-EU states. Therefore, even if a listing is annulled at the EU level, it will remain intact at the UN level itself (and in other states) and this 'will remain the case until such a time as the UNSC sanctions committee itself de-lists the affected individual or entity'.[132] Bennoune similarly rejects a conflict between security and human rights and states

> The real challenge today is to find ways to move beyond these binary oppositions between human rights and effectiveness, and between liberty and peace/security. Instead, the contemporary moment requires a holistic understanding of both security and rights on the part of governments, international organizations and human rights advocates. Such an approach requires reconciling the international legal regimes that govern peace and security on the one hand, and the protection of persons on the other.[133]

To remedy such a focus on conflict of norms, fairer sanctions regimes with judicial review at the UN level itself would, therefore, be the ideal option: they would allow a similar protection across all member states and would avoid being a system where an individual that has been delisted in one country, does not have similar remedies to challenge his or her listing by a different country. Moreover, it would bring normative coherence to international counterterrorism if all sanctions systems contained the same safeguards as the 1267 regime. Yet, I question whether there is a risk that the Sanctions Committee, or the Security Council in general, would grow complacent if the ECJ *did* consider that the office of the Ombudsperson allowed a sufficient remedy for sanctions regimes. I noted above that the most crucial improvements to sanctions regimes came from outside the UN, or outside of the executive branch at least. Therefore, the possibility must be raised that if the executive organ competent to adopt terrorist sanctions is not challenged on its human rights record, would it actually feel the need to improve it?

I note here that contrary to the resolutions studied here, Resolution 2178 adopted by the Security Council in September 2014 contains the obligation to protect international human rights within its operative paragraphs.[134] For Marko Milanovic, 'this at least will serve to blunt overly extravagant arguments relying on the primacy clause in Article 103 of the UN Charter'.[135] Resolution 2178 definitely constitutes a move to include human rights at the international institutional level as an aspect of counterterrorism rather than an obstacle to it. As the Attorney General of the UK argued in the recent hearing of the *Al-Dulimi* case in the ECtHR,[136] a 'UN Security Council Resolution should trump the European Convention of Human Rights when a country is expected to comply with both'[137] the protection of these human rights by Security Council resolutions removes the conflict and allows instead a balance of interests.

In the meantime, the challenges from the EU courts have already brought some necessary changes and they continue to challenge the sanctions regimes: in a March 2014 case, the ECJ said that the commission's principal error, in the case concerned, was in failing to follow the procedures set down by the European court in the *Kadi* cases and that 'instead of reviewing the reasons given by the Sanctions Committee carefully and impartially, the Commission had incorrectly continued to regard itself as being strictly bound by the findings of the Sanctions Committee'.[138]

A normative way to balance sanctions against individuals and their human rights should be devised in order to provide similar protection to every individual: checks and balances should ideally occur at the UN level through the existence of procedural remedies, in order to apply in all member states but, in the current state and until judicial review is possible at the UN level, this conflict between legal orders has the potential to bring positive changes to international counterterrorism, where a conflict of norms too often forces actors to choose one at the expense of the other. This is true especially as the courts have focused on procedural rights, which are necessary for democratic societies to thrive. Security and human rights will always have to be addressed together and they should, in order to protect both values. But focusing on the *conflict* between norms because of their goal (i.e. the protection of a population's security versus the protection of individuals' human rights) has generally led to the adoption and implementation of executive measures without necessary fundamental human right protections. Focusing instead on the roles and competences of each of the institutions involved in the process, and fostering a balance of institutions, while creating an imperfect solution at this stage because it only happened in one region, has the merit of challenging this monopoly of the executive and it means that the actors involved in international counterterrorism cannot escape the necessary scrutiny for security norms.

Acknowledgements

The publication of this special issue of the *International Journal of Human Rights* was based on a conference organised in May 2014 at the Institute of Advanced Legal Studies, London. I would like to thank in particular my colleague and friend Dr Laura Niada, co-organiser of the conference, the editor in chief of the *IJHR*, Dr Damien Short, the reviewers for their comments, as well as Shifra Goldberg for her editing.

Disclosure statement

No potential conflict of interest was reported by the author.

Notes on contributor

Myriam Feinberg is a Post-Doctoral Fellow of the Global Trust Project at the Buchmann Faculty of Law of the Tel Aviv University. She was previously Visiting Lecturer at King's College London. Her research interests include counterterrorism, human rights, international organisations and conflicts of norms.

Notes

1. Article 54 of the convention reads: 'Treaties conflicting with a peremptory norm of general international law (jus cogens): A treaty is void if, at the time of its conclusion, it conflicts with a peremptory norm of general international law. For the purposes of the present Convention, a peremptory norm of general international law is a norm accepted and recognized by the international community of States as a whole as a norm from which no derogation is permitted and which can be modified only by a subsequent norm of general international law having the same character', United Nations, *Vienna Convention on the Law of Treaties*, 23 May 1969, United Nations, Treaty Series, Vol. 1155, p. 331.
2. Senate Select Committee on Intelligence, Committee Study of the Central Intelligence Agency's Detention and Interrogation Program (Executive Summary) (3 December 2014), http://www.washingtonpost.com/wp-srv/special/national/cia-interrogation-report/document/ (accessed January 2015).
3. UN General Assembly, International Covenant on Civil and Political Rights, 16 December 1966, United Nations, Treaty Series, Vol. 999, p. 171.

4. Council of Europe, European Convention for the Protection of Human Rights and Fundamental Freedoms, as amended by Protocols Nos 11 and 14, 4 November 1950, ETS 5, article 10(2). Emphasis mine. Unless stated otherwise, all emphases are added by the author.
5. *R.* v. *Secretary of State for Home Affairs ex. Parte Hosenball*, [1977] 1 WLR 766, 778.
6. Jeremy Waldron, 'Security and Liberty: The Image of Balance', *The Journal of Political Philosophy* 11, no. 2 (2003): 191–210.
7. President Bush, 20 September 2001, Address to a Joint Session of Congress and the American People, http://www.washingtonpost.com/wp-srv/nation/specials/attacked/transcripts/bushaddress_092001.html (accessed January 2015).
8. United States, Uniting and Strengthening America by Providing Appropriate Tools Required to Intercept and Obstruct Terrorism (USA Patriot Act) 107–56–OCT. 26, 2001 and Authorization for Use of Military Force § 2(a), 115 Stat. 224, 224 (codified at 50 U.S.C. § 1541 note) (2001).
9. It is too complex or lengthy to detail here but many authors have written about the consequences of the phrase 'war on terror' and the question of use of force in counterterrorism, see for instance Jonathan I. Charney, 'The Use of Force against Terrorism and International Law', *The American Journal of International Law* 95 (2001): 835; David Abramowitz, 'President, the Congress, and Use of Force: Legal and Political Considerations in Authorizing Use of Force against International Terrorism, *Harvard International Law Journal* 43 (2002): 71; Michael Byers, 'Terrorism, the Use of Force and International Law after 11 September', *International Relations* 16 (2002): 155–70; Christopher Greenwood, 'International Law and the Pre-emptive Use of Force: Afghanistan, Al-Qaida, and Iraq', *San Diego International Law Journal* 4 (2003): 7; Christine D. Gray, *International Law and the Use of Force* (Oxford: Oxford University Press, 2008); and Christian J. Tams, 'The Use of Force against Terrorists', *European Journal of International Law* 20 (2009): 359–97.
10. UN Security Council, *Security Council Resolution 1373 (2001) [On Threats to International Peace and Security Caused by Terrorist Acts]*, 28 September 2001, S/RES/1373 (2001), §1(b) and 2.
11. 'Blair Vows Hard Line on Fanatics', BBC News, 5 August 2005: Former British Prime Minister Tony Blair said, at a press conference following the terrorist attacks in London in July 2005 'the rules of the game are changing', http://news.bbc.co.uk/2/hi/uk_news/4747573.stm (accessed January 2015).
12. Remarks of John O. Brennan (Director of the Central Intelligence Agency) – As Prepared for Delivery, Program on Law and Security, Harvard Law School, Cambridge, Massachusetts, Friday, 16 September 2011, http://www.whitehouse.gov/the-press-office/2011/09/16/remarks-john-o-brennan-strengthening-our-security-adhering-our-values-an (accessed January 2015).
13. Daniel Moeckli, *Human Rights and Non-discrimination in the 'War on Terror'* (Oxford: Oxford University Press 2008), Oxford Monographs in International Law 7.
14. Thomas Poole, 'Sovereign Indignities: International Law as Public Law', *European Journal of International Law* 22, no. 2 (2011): 351.
15. For general discussions on the link between security and human rights post 9/11, read Kent Roach, *The 9/11 Effect – Comparative Counter-Terrorism* (Cambridge: Cambridge University Press, 2011); Kent Roach, 'Uneasy Neighbors: Comparative American and Canadian Counter-Terrorism', *William Mitchell Law Review* 38, no. 5 (2012): 1701–1803.
16. Goold and Lazarus, 'Introduction Security and Human Rights: The Search for a Language of Reconciliation', in *Security and Human Rights*, ed. Goold and Lazarus, 2.
17. Remarks of John O. Brennan (Director of the Central Intelligence Agency).
18. Milena Costas-Trascasas, 'Terrorism, State of Emergency and Derogation from Judicial Guarantees', in *International Legal Dimension of Terrorism*, ed. Pablo Antonio Fernández Sánchez (Leiden: Brill, 2009), International Humanitarian Law Series, 471.
19. Moeckli, *Human Rights and Non-discrimination in the 'War on Terror'*, 11.
20. Stavros Tsakyrakis, 'Proportionality: An Assault on Human Rights?', *International Journal of Constitutional Law* 7 (2009): 477.
21. Guglielmo Verdirame, 'Rescuing Human Rights from Proportionality', King's College London Dickson Poon School of Law, Legal Studies Research Paper Series, paper no. 2014–14, forthcoming in *Philosophical Foundations of Human Rights*, ed. Rowan Cruft, S. Matthew Liao, and Massimo Renzo (Oxford: Oxford University Press, April 2015).

22. Sandra Freedman, 'The Positive Right of Security' and Liora Lazarus, 'Mapping the Right to Security', in *Security and Human Rights*, ed. Goold and Lazarus, 307. For a history of how the concept evolved, see Rhoda E. Howard-Hassmann, 'Human Security: Undermining Human Rights?', *Human Rights Quarterly* 34, no. 1 (2012): 88.
23. Moufida Goucha and John Crowley, *Rethinking Human Security* (Chichester: John Wiley & Sons 2009), 5; Mark Duffield, *Development, Security and Unending War: Governing the World of Peoples* (London: Polity, 2007), 114.
24. Nasu Hitoshi, 'The Expanded Conception of Security and International Law: Challenges to the UN Collective Security System', *Amsterdam Law Forum* 3 (2001): 3.
25. Ibid.
26. Paul Hoffman, 'Human Rights and Terrorism', *Human Rights Quarterly* 26, no. 932 (2004): 949.
27. For instance, article 16 of the French Constitution of 1958 gives, in time of crisis, 'extraordinary powers' to the president – Constitution of 4 October 1958. The American Constitution does not expressly grant the president additional powers in times of national emergency but the courts will recognise a right of the executive branch to use emergency powers if congress has granted such powers to the president (Legal Information Institute, Cornell Institute Law School, 'War Powers'), *United States of America: Constitution* [United States of America], 17 September 1787.
28. It is important to note for example that the US has formally been in a state of emergency for a number of years now in relation to the terrorist threat: President Barack Obama extended several times George W. Bush's Declaration of Emergency regarding terrorism, more recently in September 2013: 'Letter to the Congress of the United States', 10 September 2013, http://www.whitehouse.gov/the-press-office/2013/09/10/letter-continuation-national-emergency-message (accessed January 2015).
29. See notes 2, 3, 4 and 26 above, as well as Roach, *The 9/11 Effect – Comparative Counter-Terrorism*, for an analysis of counterterrorism post-9/11.
30. See for instance the *United States* v. *Reynolds*, 345 U.S. 1 case of 1953 where the court upheld 'the privilege against revealing military secrets, a privilege which is well established in the law of evidence'; or more recently *R* v. *Secretary of State for the Home Department, ex parte Cheblak* [1991] 2 All ER 319 (CA) where the court held that national security was exclusively the responsibility of the executive.
31. Adam Tomkins and P. P Craig, eds, *The Executive and Public Law: Power and Accountability in Comparative Perspective* (Oxford: Oxford University Press, 2006), 1.
32. Christina Eckes, 'Protecting Supremacy from External Influences: A Precondition for a European Constitutional Legal Order?', *European Law Journal* 18 (2012): 233.
33. William Phelan, 'Does the European Union Strengthen the State? Democracy, Executive Power and International Cooperation' (Center for European Studies, Working Paper No. 95 2003), 5.
34. Jure Vidmar and Erica de Wet, eds, *Hierarchy in International Law* (Oxford: Oxford University Press 2012), 1.
35. The issue of the definition of terrorism is too complex to include here. For a discussion on the question of whether terrorism is defined at the international level, see Antonio Cassese, 'Terrorism is Also Disrupting Some Crucial Legal Categories of International Law', *European Journal of International Law* 12, no. 5 (2001): 993; Ben Saul, 'Reasons for Defining and Criminalising "Terrorism" in International Law', *Mexican Yearbook of International Law* 6 (2006): 419; and Rosalyn Higgins and Maurice Flory Maurice, *Terrorism and International Law* (London: Routledge, 1997).
36. Eyal Benvenisti and George W. Downs, 'Democratizing Courts: How National and International Courts Promote Democracy in an Era of Global Governance', *Journal of International Law and Politics* 46, no. 3 (Spring 2014): 749.
37. Vidmar and de Wet, *Hierarchy in International Law*, 4.
38. David Bonner, *Executive Measures, Terrorism and National Security: Have the Rules of the Game Changed?* (Aldershot: Ashgate Publishing, Ltd., 2007), ix.
39. UN Security Council, *Resolution 1267 (1999) Adopted by the Security Council at its 4051st Meeting on 15 October 1999*, 15 October 1999, S/RES/1267 (1999), Preamble.
40. Ibid., §4.
41. Details of the list can be found on http://www.un.org/sc/committees/1267/aq_sanctions_list.shtml (accessed January 2015).

42. Larissa Van den Herik and Nico J. Schrijver, 'Introduction: The Fragmented International Legal Response to Terrorism', in *Counter-Terrorism Strategies in a Fragmented International Legal Order, Meeting the Challenges* (Cambridge: Cambridge University Press, 2015), 16.
43. Resolution 1373, §1(c).
44. Article L151-2, Article L562-1 and Article L562-2 of the Code Monétaire et Financier. For a full list of financial sanctions imposed by the French government, see the right tab on http://www.tresor.economie.gouv.fr/sanctions-financieres-internationales (accessed January 2015).
45. For updated instruments on both al-Qaida and terrorist groups in general, see the UK government website and in particular http://www.legislation.gov.uk/all?title=al-qaida and http://www.legislation.gov.uk/all?title=terrorist (accessed January 2015).
46. 'Declaration Concerning the Common Foreign and Security Policy', Consolidated version of the Treaty on European Union, OJ C 326, 26.10.2012, 13–390.
47. Article 5(2), Consolidated version of the Treaty on the Functioning of the European Union, OJ C 326, 26.10.2012, 47–390.
48. European Parliament Resolution, 'The Evaluation of EU Sanctions as Part of the EU's Actions and Policies in the Area of Human Rights' (2008/2031 (INI), September 4, 2008), para. F.
49. Council Decision 2011/487/CFSP of 1 August 2011 amending Common Position 2002/402/CFSP concerning restrictive measures against Usama bin Laden, members of the al-Qaida organisation and the Taliban and other individuals, groups, undertakings and entities associated with them, OJ L 199, 2.8.2011, 73.
50. Council Regulation (EC) No. 881/2002 of 27 May 2002 imposing certain specific restrictive measures directed against certain persons and entities associated with Usama bin Laden, the al-Qaida network and the Taliban, and repealing Council Regulation (EC) No. 467/2001 prohibiting the export of certain goods and services to Afghanistan, strengthening the flight ban and extending the freeze of funds and other financial resources in respect of the Taliban of Afghanistan, OJ L 139, 29.5.2002, 9–22.
51. Council Common Position of 27 December 2001 on the application of specific measures to combat terrorism, OJ L 344, 28/12/2001 P. 0093–0096.
52. Council Regulation (EC) No. 2580/2001 of 27 December 2001 on specific restrictive measures directed against certain persons and entities with a view to combating terrorism, OJ L 344, 28/12/2001 P. 0070–0075 and updated annexes available at http://europa.eu/legislation_summaries/justice_freedom_security/fight_against_terrorism/l24402_en.htm#Amendingacts (accessed January 2015).
53. Antonios Tzanakopoulos, 'Collective Security and Human Rights', in *Hierarchy in International Law: The Place of Human Rights*, ed. Erika de Vet and Jure Vidmar (Oxford: Oxford University Press 2012) 51.
54. United Nations Charter article 103 declares that 'In the event of a conflict between the obligations of the Members of the United Nations under the present Charter and their obligations under any other international agreement, their obligations under the present Charter shall prevail.'
55. International Court of Justice, Question of Interpretation and Application of the 1971 Montreal Convention arising from the Aerial Incident at Lockerbie, Order-Request for the Indication of Provisional Measures (*Libyan Arab Jamahiriya* v. *United Kingdom*), 14 April 1992, §39. It must be noted here that in its order on provisional measures, the court repeatedly indicated that this did not prejudge questions of law and fact to be decided in further proceedings, although the question of conflict was never solved per se, following a compromise between the UK, the US and Libya.
56. See Case T-228/02, *Organisation des Modjahedines du Peuple d'Iran* v. *Council* [2006] ECR II-4665 (OMPI I) (12 December 2006); Case T-256/07, *People's Mojahedin Organization of Iran* v. *Council* [2008] ECR II-03019 (OMPI (II)) (23 October 2008); Case T-284/08, *People's Mojahedin Organization of Iran* v. *Council* (OMPI (III) (4 December 2008) and *Nada* v. *Switzerland*–10593/08 – HEJUD [2012] ECHR 1691.
57. Human Rights Committee (HRC), Communication No.1472/2006, *Nabil Sayadi and Patricia Vinck* v. *Belgium* (29 December 2008).
58. See for instance *HM Treasury* v. *Mohammed Jabar Ahmed and ors (FC)*; *HM Treasury* v. *Mohammed al-Ghabra (FC)*; *R (on the application of Hani El Sayed Sabaei Youssef)* v. *HM Treasury* [2010] UKSC 2.

59. The US Department of State and Department of the Treasury both compile lists of individuals and groups to be sanctioned. The Foreign Terrorist Organisations list is compiled by the Department of State and the Specially Designated Nationals List is by the Department of Treasury, under which Mr Kadi and Al Barakaat were listed. The current list is available at http://www.State.gov/j/ct/rls/other/des/123085.htm (accessed January 2015).
60. See European Commission Regulation 2062/2001/EC of 19 October 2001.
61. Case T-315/01 *Kadi* v. *Council* [2005] ECR II-3649, §233.
62. Ibid., §222.
63. Ibid., §226. In the case in point, the CFI held that no *jus cogens* has been violated, §240 and 242.
64. Joined Cases C-402/05 P & C-415/05 P, *Kadi & Al Barakaat* v. *Council of the European Union and EC Commission*, 3 C.M.L.R. 41 (2008).
65. Ibid., §283.
66. Ibid., §286.
67. Ibid., §283.
68. Ibid., §340.
69. Ibid., §346. European Commission Regulation 1190/2008/EC of 28 November 2008. The statement of reason provided to Mr Kadi was provided originally to the French government by the UN Sanctions Committee. The French government then passed it on to the EU. See online updates of Trevor Hartley, *The Foundations of European Union Law*, 7th ed. (Oxford: Oxford University Press, 2010),
70. http://global.oup.com/uk/orc/law/eu/hartley7e/resources/updates/ (accessed January 2015). The statement of reason is also included in Case T-85/09 *Kadi* v. *Commission* [2010] OJ C317, §49. The statement focuses on Mr Kadi's involvement with the Muwafaq Foundation. It did not however provide any evidence of this.
71. Case T-85/09 *Kadi* v. *Commission* [2010] OJ C317.
72. Ibid., §114.
73. Ibid., §128.
74. Ibid., §127.
75. Ibid., §126.
76. Ibid., §173.
77. Ibid., §29.
78. Joined Cases C-584/10 P, C-593/10 P and C-595/10 P *European Commission & the Council of the European Union* v. *Yassin Abdullah Kadi* [2013] ECR.
79. European Commission Implementing Regulation (EU) No. 933/2012 of 11 October 2012 amending for the 180th time Council Regulation (EC) No. 881/2002 imposing certain specific restrictive measures directed against certain persons and entities associated with the al-Qaida network, OJ L 278 , 12/10/2012 P. 0011–0012.
80. See Case T-228/02, *Organisation des Modjahedines du Peuple d'Iran* v. *Council* [2006] ECR II-4665 (OMPI I) (12 December 2006); Case T-256/07, *People's Mojahedin Organization of Iran* v. *Council* [2008] ECR II-03019 (OMPI (II)) (23 October 2008); Case T-284/08, *People's Mojahedin Organization of Iran* v. *Council* (OMPI (III) (4 December 2008).
81. *Kadi & Al Barakaat* v. *Council of the European Union and EC Commission*, (2008), §298-299.
82. *European Commission & the Council of the European Union* v. *Yassin Abdullah Kadi*, [2013], §111–130. These paragraphs contain a full analysis of the scope of the review.
83. United Nations Charter articles 25 and 39.
84. See note 54 above.
85. For instance, the UK court relied on article 103 in many of its counterterrorism cases. See *R (on the application of Al-Jedda)* v. *Secretary of State for Defence, House of Lords* [2007] UKHL 58.
86. Mehrdad Payandeh and Heiko Sauer, 'European Union: UN Sanctions and EU Fundamental Rights', *International Journal of Constitutional Law* 7, no. (2009): 306, 312.
87. Roach, *The 9/11 Effect – Comparative Counter-Terrorism*, 37.
88. Takis Taki Tridimas and José A. Gutiérrez-Fons, 'EU Law, International Law and Economic Sanctions against Terrorism: The Judiciary in Distress?' (College of Europe 2008), Research Papers in Law, 704.

89. Juan Santos Vara, 'The Consequences of Kadi: Where the Divergence of Opinion between EU and International Lawyers Lies?', *European Law Journal* 17, no. (2011): 252, 265.
90. Ibid., 266.
91. Chatham House International Law Discussion Group, 'UN and EU Sanctions: Human Rights and the Fight against Terrorism – The Kadi Case', January 22, 2009.
92. See note 46 above.
93. *Flaminio Costa* v. *ENEL* [1964] ECR 585 (6/64) for the first occurrence and more recently Declaration No. 17 Concerning Primacy, Declarations annexed to the Final Act of the Intergovernmental Conference, which adopted the Treaty of Lisbon, signed on 13 December 2007.
94. Lando Kirchmair, 'The "Janus Face" of the Court of Justice of the European Union: A Theoretical Appraisal of the EU Legal Order's Relationship with International and Member State Law', *Goettingen Journal of International Law* 4, no. 677 (2012): 679.
95. *Yassin Abdullah Kadi and Al Barakaat International Foundation* v. *Council of the European Union and Commission of the European Communities* (2008), §81.
96. Ibid., §285 et seq., 326–7.
97. Misa Misa Zgonec-Rozej, 'Kafka, Sisyphus, and Bin Laden: Challenging the Al-Qaida and Taliban Sanctions Regime Rights', *Essex Human Rights Review* 8 (2011): 97.
98. Kirchmair, 'The "Janus Face" of the Court of Justice of the European Union', 677.
99. Antonios Tzanakopoulos, 'Sharing Responsibility for UN Targeted Sanctions', *EJIL Talk*, 14 February 2013, http://www.ejiltalk.org/sharing-responsibility-for-un-targeted-sanctions/ (accessed January 2015).
100. *Nada* v. *Switzerland* (2010), §180.
101. *Nada* v. *Switzerland* (Joint Concurring Opinion of Judges Bratza, Nicolau and Yudkivska), §1, 3 and 5.
102. *Yassin Abdullah Kadi* v. *European Commission* (2010), §128.
103. Erica de Wet, 'From Kadi to Nada: Judicial Techniques Favoring Human Rights Over United Nations Security Council Sanctions', *Chinese Journal of International Law* 12 (2013): 14.
104. Antonios Tzanakopoulos, *Disobeying the Security Council: Countermeasures against Wrongful Sanctions* (Oxford: Oxford University Press, 2011).
105. For a recent analysis of the human rights obligations of the Security Council, see Karima Bennoune, 'All Necessary Measures? Reconciling International Legal Regimes Governing Peace and Security, and the Protection of Persons, in the Realm of Counter-Terrorism', in *Counter-Terrorism Strategies in a Fragmented International Legal Order, Meeting the Challenges* (Cambridge: Cambridge University Press, 2015), 680 and following.
106. Shelly Danosh, 'The Kadi Case: The International Position of the European Union after the Ruling' (Working Paper, European Forum at the Hebrew University 2009), 42.
107. See *R (on the application of Al-Jedda) (FC)* v. *Secretary of State for Defence*, [2007] UKHL 58, United Kingdom: House of Lords (Judicial Committee), 12 December 2007, §34.
108. Ibid., §35.
109. Eckes, 'Protecting Supremacy from External Influences', 245.
110. Council Regulation (EU) No. 1286/2009 of 22 December 2009 amending Regulation (EC) No. 881/2002 imposing certain specific restrictive measures directed against certain persons and entities associated with Usama bin Laden, the al-Qaida network and the Taliban, OJ 2009 L 346 of 2009-12-23, 42–6.
111. Consolidated Version of the Treaty on the Functioning of the European Union (TFEU), 2008 OJ C 115/47, Article 215.
112. Article 275 TFEU: this is one of the exceptions under which the court has jurisdiction with respect to the provisions relating to the common foreign and security policy.
113. The importance of due process and legal control were also recognised in a declaration attached to the treaty: Declaration 25 on Article 75 and 275 on the TFEU.
114. UN Security Council, *Security Council Resolution 1370 (2001) on the Situation in Sierra Leone*, 18 September 2001, S/RES/1370 (2001).
115. Clemens A. Feinäugle, 'The UN Security Council Al-Qaida and Taliban Sanctions Committee: Emerging Principles of International Institutional Law for the Protection of Individuals?', *German Law Journal* 11, no. 9 (2008): 1530.
116. See the website of the Focal Point at http://www.un.org/sc/committees/dfp.shtml (accessed January 2015).

117. UN Security Council, *Security Council Resolution 1904 (2009) [on Continuation of Measures Imposed against the Taliban and Al-Qaida]*, 17 December 2009, S/RES/1904 (2009), Preamble.
118. UN SC Resolution 1904 (2009), §20. It must be noted that the Ombudsperson only has a mandate for sanctions under the 1267 Committee, but not for sanctions under Resolution 1373, which are still examined through the Focal Point procedure.
119. UN Security Council 6247th Meeting, 17 December 2009, S/PV.6247.
120. Ibid.
121. *HM Treasury* v. *Mohammed Jabar Ahmed and ors (FC)*; *HM Treasury* v. *Mohammed al-Ghabra (FC)*; *R (on the application of Hani El Sayed Sabaei Youssef)* v. *HM Treasury* [2010] UKSC 2.
122. Antonios Tzanakopoulos, 'The UK Supreme Court Quashed Domestic Measures Implementing UN Sanctions', *EJIL Talk*, 23 February 2010, http://www.ejiltalk.org/the-uk-supreme-court-quashes-domestic-measures-implementing-un-sanctions/ (accessed January 2015).
123. *HM Treasury* v. *Mohamed Jabar Ahmed* (2010), §78.
124. Ibid., § 78, 80, 239.
125. *Yasin Abdullah Kadi* v. *European Commission*, 2010, §128.
126. *European Commission & the Council of the European Union* v. *Yassin Abdullah Kadi*, 2013, §96.
127. See note 2 above.
128. For instance, *Handyside* v. *The United Kingdom*, ECHR, 07.12.1976, *Klass and others* v. *Germany*, ECHR 06.09.1978, *Mccann and Others* v. *The United Kingdom* (21 ECHR 97 GC), *Osman* v. *United Kingdom* [1998] EHRR 101, and *Finogenov and Others* v. *Russia*, Judgment 20.12.2011.
129. R.A. Lawson and H.G. Schermers, eds, *Leading Cases of the European Court of Human Rights* (Nijmegen: Ars Aequi Libri, 1997), 28–42.
130. See for instance Tsakyrakis, 'Proportionality'; and Verdirame, 'Rescuing Human Rights from Proportionality'.
131. Richard Benwell and Oonagh Gay, 'The Separation of Powers' (Parliament and Constitution Centre, House of Commons Library, 15 August 2011), http://www.parliament.uk/briefing-papers/sn06053.pdf (accessed January 2015).
132. de Wet, 'From Kadi to Nada', 16.
133. Bennoune, 'All Necessary Measures?', 668.
134. UN Security Council, Resolution 2178 (2014) [On Foreign Terrorist Fighters], 24 September 2014, S/RES/2178 (2014), §5.
135. Marko Milanovic, 'EJIL: Talk! – UN Security Council Adopts Resolution 2178 on Foreign Terrorist Fighters', 24 September 2014, http://www.ejiltalk.org/un-security-council-adopts-resolution-2178-on-foreign-terrorist-fighters/ (accessed January 2015).
136. *Al-Dulimi and Montana Management Inc.* v. *Switzerland* (No. 5809/08), Grand Chamber Hearing – 10 December 2014 Hearing.
137. 'Attorney General Appears before European Court of Human Rights', 10 December 2014, https://www.gov.uk/government/news/attorney-general-appears-before-european-court-of-human-rights (accessed January 2015).
138. Case T-306/10 *Yusef* v. *Commission* (21 March 2014).

Protecting 'national security' whistleblowers in the Council of Europe: an evaluation of three approaches on how to balance national security with freedom of expression

Dimitrios Kagiaros

The University of Edinburgh Law School, Edinburgh, UK

In its recent case law, the European Court of Human Rights has extended freedom of expression protection to whistleblowers, including those who work for the intelligence and security sector. Thus, contracting parties to the European Convention on Human Rights are required to balance any damage to national security caused by the disclosure, with the public interest in the information revealed, before handing down sanctions to the whistleblower for a breach of official secrecy. The article will identify, and critically evaluate, three possible approaches to balancing national security with the whistleblower's right to freedom of expression and the public interest in the disclosure of the information. These approaches are first, an absolute ban on external disclosures for intelligence officials; second, a broad exemption from criminal sanctions or other forms of retaliation when the interest in the information disclosed outweighs national security concerns; and finally, protection from reprisals provided only for specific disclosures or categories of wrongdoing, which are exhaustively enumerated in the law. It will examine the compatibility of each approach with nascent Council of Europe whistleblower protection standards and conclude that the final approach, in spite of its deficiencies, can best guarantee the whistleblower's right to free speech while ensuring that security is protected.

Introduction

Institutions often fail us. Public or private institutions can go wrong due to maladministration, incompetence or deliberate attempts to abuse power to achieve illegitimate aims. Such instances of misconduct are often revealed through whistleblowers – individuals who in the course of their work come across information relating to wrongdoing and decide to speak out about it.[1] Such individuals have begun to enjoy protection from retaliation on an international and regional level under freedom of expression provisions in recognition of the fact that, in certain cases, the public interest (PI) in the disclosure of certain information can be so compelling as to outweigh a legally binding duty of confidence.[2] Whistleblowers who work for the security or intelligence sector however, remain disadvantaged under this burgeoning protection scheme. In both the United States (US) and the United Kingdom (UK) for instance, individuals from the intelligence world[3] who have proceeded to unauthorised disclosures of wrongdoing, have been met with severe penalties and prosecutions[4] more akin to 'spies committing treachery'.[5] National security whistleblowers are in many cases 'separate and immune'[6] from domestic whistleblower protection laws[7] and are instead usually expected to rely exclusively on internal procedures provided by the executive to report instances of wrongdoing they have uncovered.[8]

Yet, recent developments in whistleblower protection call for a re-evaluation of the protection provided to the national security whistleblower. In the Council of Europe (COE), the Parliamentary Assembly and the European Court of Human Rights (ECtHR) in its recent case law, have been setting standards for the protection of whistleblowers under freedom of expression that have included protection for members of the military and the security and intelligence community.[9] The free speech protection from reprisals that is afforded to good-faith whistleblowers in the COE is the result of a balancing exercise between the public interest in disclosure and the public interest in maintaining secrecy. When the former outweighs the latter, restrictions to the whistleblower's free speech rights cannot be justified, if the whistleblower acted in good faith.[10] When applied in the context of whistleblowing that affects national security, however, this balancing exercise presents a series of complications. If contracting parties to the European Convention on Human Rights (ECHR) are to take this balancing into consideration in order to secure compliance with the convention, their secrecy laws pertaining to the unauthorised public disclosure of security-related information must be framed in a way that allows them to take into account the possible PI in an unauthorised disclosure before handing down any sanctions to the intelligence official.

It is important to note however, that in spite of these developments on the COE level, whistleblower protection legislation is a rarity among European states. In the European Union (EU) for instance, only four states[11] have comprehensive whistleblower protection laws, a further 16 only have 'partial provisions and procedures',[12] while the remaining states have no form of protection for whistleblowers. The situation for intelligence sector employees is worse, as the framework for their protection remains entirely inchoate, even among the EU and COE member states with more advanced whistleblower protection frameworks. For instance, the UK's Public Interest Disclosure Act 1998 excludes members of the security and intelligence community,[13] while in Sweden, the general rule that any employee in the public or private sector can pass on information to the media is not applicable in relation to official secrets and national security information.[14] Similarly, the Romanian Whistleblower Protection Act of 2004 provides particularly broad protection from retaliation to government employees who blow the whistle, however penalties under official secrets legislation in relation to security-sensitive disclosures have been passed down to whistleblowers.[15] Furthermore, some states do not clearly differentiate between the disclosure of state secrets and acts of espionage.[16] For instance, while Swedish legislation makes a clear distinction between the two, by requiring the involvement of a foreign power for the commission of espionage,[17] the UK's Official Secrets Act 1989 simply penalises any public disclosure of information for members of the security and intelligence community.[18] Thus, while whistleblower protection for security sector employees is virtually nonexistent, COE member states have robust legislation penalising the disclosure of state secrets.[19] This varies in form, especially in relation to how an 'official secret' is defined.[20] However, national security consistently appears as a reason to bar disclosure,[21] and coupled with the lack of whistleblower protection for security sector employees, creates an almost impenetrable fortress of secrecy in security matters.

This lack of standards for whistleblower protection in general on the domestic level, prompted the COE Committee of Ministers to release a recommendation[22] encouraging member states to adopt whistleblower protection legislation that allows for a balancing of the public interest in non-disclosure with the public interest in an informed citizenry. Therefore, what the article aims to explore, is how secrecy laws or whistleblower protection instruments can incorporate this balancing exercise in order to protect security sector whistleblowers and thus to secure the compatibility of their legislation with freedom of speech standards on the one hand, while ensuring that national security will not be compromised on the other. The article identifies three possible avenues for this public interest exercise to be included in the law.

The first approach considers public disclosures, to the media for instance, as incompatible with the role of the intelligence official. It thus altogether disposes of the balancing exercise between the interest in disclosure of the specific information and national security. Consequently, this approach does not require proof of damage to security interests in order to justify retaliation against the whistleblower. In order to ensure the compatibility of such a law with emerging COE freedom of expression standards, the article argues that a robust system that would permit internal disclosures to official mechanisms for raising concern would be required. If these mechanisms were genuinely independent of the line management chain and could ensure that individuals approaching them would be protected and that their concerns would be effectively addressed, free speech restrictions to public whistleblowers could be justified. The article will argue however, that such internal mechanisms have their inherent limitations and the COE standards allow for public disclosures even when such mechanisms exist in specific circumstances that will be examined in detail. Thus, an absolute ban on external reporting would be difficult to reconcile with ECHR freedom of expression standards.

The second approach would be for the law to include a rebuttable presumption that public disclosures from intelligence officials are damaging to national security. If the whistleblower was nonetheless able to prove that, as a means of last resort, the interest in publicly disclosing the information outweighed security concerns, protection would be provided. While this approach would require an ad hoc assessment of whether any freedom of expression restrictions that the whistleblower experienced were justified based on the damage caused by the disclosure, the lack of a definition as to what would constitute wrongdoing could result in 'opening the floodgates' and in allowing overzealous intelligence sector employees to make assessments on particularly sensitive national security issues, thus 'usurping' the role of their superiors. If the intelligence official's duty of confidentiality was conditional in this sense, the intelligence services would not be able to function effectively, and whistleblowers would face the risk that their own interpretation of the public interest, a notoriously nebulous concept, would not be confirmed by the courts.

The final approach includes specific definitions or categories of wrongdoing that would allow the whistleblower to proceed to public disclosures as a means of last resort, either in the form of specific exemptions to secrecy or as categories of protected disclosures in a whistleblower protection instrument. This approach, where the balancing exercise between national security and the interest in disclosure is enshrined in law, allows whistleblowers a greater degree of certainty that their disclosures will be protected and ensures that they will not proceed to arbitrary PI assessments. However, this has the drawback that whistleblower protection becomes conditional on the generosity of lawmakers in their interpretation of the public interest in the law. Therefore, if lawmakers follow a particularly narrow approach, there is a risk that whistleblowers' free speech rights will not be upheld. Furthermore, the lack of consensus on the international level as to which specific disclosures would be deemed important enough to outweigh national security concerns and allow for public disclosures, would make the implementation of such a system questionable as to its feasibility in the security sector. However, the article will conclude that this approach offers the most reasonable solution to the issue at hand, and along with strengthened regional standards on whistleblower protection and vigilance on behalf of the judiciary, would provide concrete protection to whistleblowers while ensuring that security concerns are adequately addressed.

Before proceeding with the examination of each of these approaches and their impact on whistleblowers' free speech rights, it is necessary to examine how the freedom of expression of whistleblowers has been protected on the COE level, followed by a short analysis of how the whistleblower becomes, in essence, an assessor of the PI when deciding to proceed to a public disclosure. The article will then proceed to examine the aforementioned approaches before providing some thoughts on the status of the intelligence official whistleblower.

Protection for whistleblowers in the COE

Free speech in contracting parties to the convention is largely informed by Article 10 of the ECHR and the case law of the ECtHR, which domestic courts are expected to take into account when deciding on cases that involve human rights.[23]

When faced with the challenge of assessing whether a restriction to a right is in line with convention standards, [24] the court will examine whether the measure that interferes with the right is prescribed by law and whether it is 'necessary in a democratic society'.[25] This requires the state to prove that 'action taken is in response to a pressing social need, and that the interference with the rights protected is no greater than is necessary to address that pressing social need'.[26]

Articles of the convention that provide for restrictions to rights are to be narrowly construed; however, states enjoy 'a certain but not unlimited margin of appreciation in the matter of the imposition of restrictions'.[27] The margin of appreciation doctrine, which appears prominently in national security related cases, maintains that state parties are 'entitled to certain latitude in resolving the inherent conflicts between individual rights and national interests'.[28] This translates in practice to a 'judicial self-restraint'[29] – at times significant – on the part of the ECtHR.

In relation to state secrecy, the ECtHR has recognised in its case law that 'a consensus appears to exist among the member States of the Council of Europe on the need for appropriate criminal sanctions to prevent the disclosure of certain confidential items of information'.[30] It is also common practice for intelligence officials to sign agreements that they will never reveal or publish any information relating to their work in the services, without seeking prior authorisation.[31] However, the COE Parliamentary Assembly, in Resolution 1551 (2007), called on the court 'to find an appropriate balance between the state interest in preserving official secrecy on the one hand, and freedom of expression [...] and society's interest in exposing abuses of power on the other hand'.[32] In a similar vein, Resolution 1507 (2006) had called for member states to 'ensure that the laws governing state secrecy protect the whistleblowers, that is persons who disclose illegal activities of state organs from possible disciplinary or criminal sanctions'.[33] The Parliamentary Assembly has also consistently argued that '[c]rimes such as murder, enforced disappearances, torture or abduction committed by state agents do not deserve to be protected as "state secrets"'.[34] It was Resolution 1729 (2010) on the protection of whistleblowers however, that went further to encourage member states to adopt whistleblower protection legislation for individuals who in good faith 'sound an alarm in order to stop wrongdoings that place fellow human beings at risk'.[35] The resolution included members of the security services and armed forces in its ambit of protection.[36] In defining which disclosures should enjoy protection the resolution provided that:

> The definition of protected disclosures shall include all bona fide warnings against various types of unlawful acts, including all serious human rights violations which affect or threaten the life, health, liberty and any other legitimate interests of individuals as subjects of public administration or taxpayers.[37]

It urged state parties to adopt whistleblower legislation that would 'protect anyone who, in good faith, makes use of existing internal whistle-blowing channels from any form of retaliation'.[38] Thus it is safe to deduce that internal mechanisms are viewed as the initial avenue for whistleblowers to raise concern. The resolution however, went further to stress that:

> [W]here internal channels either do not exist, have not functioned properly or could reasonably be expected not to function properly given the nature of the problem raised by the whistle-blower, external whistle-blowing, including through the media, should likewise be protected.[39]

Therefore, the mere fact that internal whistleblowing mechanisms exist does not suffice to argue that an absolute prohibition on external reporting can be justified. This view was reinforced through the Committee of Ministers' recommendation to COE member states, which noted that 'the individual circumstances of each case will determine the most appropriate channel'[40] for raising concern.

The view that alerting the media should be a viable avenue even for national security whistleblowers was further solidified in the COE's Parliamentary Resolution 1838 (2011), which provided that:

> The media play a vital role in the functioning of democratic institutions, in particular by investigating and publicly denouncing unlawful acts committed by state agents, including members of the secret services. They rely heavily on the co-operation of 'whistle-blowers' within the services of the state. The Assembly reiterates its calls for adequate protection ... for whistleblowers.[41]

Similarly, Resolution 1877 (2012) provided that in relation to secrecy laws, 'member States must not curtail the right of the public to be informed by restricting the right of individuals to disclose information of public concern, for example by applying ... national security and anti-terrorist laws in an overly broad and non-proportional manner'.[42] Finally, Parliamentary Assembly Resolution 1954 (2013), provided that '[a] person who discloses wrongdoings in the public interest (whistle-blower) should be protected from any type of retaliation, provided he or she acted in good faith and followed applicable procedures'.[43] Applicable procedures would therefore refer to the use of internal mechanisms when these are available and public disclosures only in cases where these mechanisms fail.

Turning to the court, the primacy of free speech in a democratic society is well established in the ECtHR case law.[44] For the ECtHR, the function of the press as a 'public watchdog' is central to a democracy,[45] and 'the national margin of appreciation is limited when the author of the expression in question is a journalist'.[46] Press freedom has indirectly protected anonymous whistleblowers, as the court has consistently held that compelling a journalist to reveal the source of an information leak constitutes a free speech violation.[47] However, in more recent cases, Article 10 protection has not been limited to protecting the dissemination of leaked information through the press, but was extended to include the source of the leak: the good faith whistleblower.

The landmark case of *Guja* v. *Moldova*[48] was the 'first to deal explicitly with the practice of whistleblowing'.[49] In *Guja*, the ECtHR allowed for Article 10 protection for whistleblowers by asserting that 'the interest which the public may have in particular information can sometimes be so strong as to override even a legally imposed duty of confidence'.[50] In the case of *Bucur and Toma* v. *Romania*,[51] the ECtHR examined PI disclosures by intelligence officials. The court seemed to differentiate between leaks of state secrets with no discernible PI[52] (where states retain a wide margin of appreciation in assessing whether their release could damage national security)[53] and whistleblowing in the public interest. The court held that retaliation against a good faith whistleblower who publicly disclosed instances of illegal surveillance by the Romanian services, after unsuccessfully attempting to address the issue using internal means, was in fact a violation of Article 10. The national security arguments against disclosure in *Bucur* led the court to argue that protecting national security cannot come at the price of destroying democracy[54] and it proceeded to criticise the domestic courts for not taking into account the applicant's arguments relating to the public interest of the information disclosed.[55]

Before proceeding to examine how these developments could affect secrecy legislation in the contracting parties to the ECHR however, it is worthwhile to briefly examine the process under which the whistleblower, by deciding that certain information is in fact deserving of exposure, becomes in fact an assessor of the PI. By conducting a PI test to ascertain whether the interest in releasing the information at hand outweighs competing security considerations, national security whistleblowers become engaged in a complex balancing exercise, the outcome of which is not necessarily objective.

The whistleblower as an assessor of the public interest

The article submits that an act of an unauthorised public disclosure can be further analysed into a two-step process. Initially, the whistleblower makes an evaluation that certain information he or she has come across relates to wrongdoing.[56] Subsequently, the whistleblower decides, after finding that an internal report would be ineffectual, that it would be beneficial to make this instance of misconduct public. Both these steps, however, contain an assessment that relates to the public interest.

In the first step, according to the whistleblower's understanding, there is a specific activity of an organisation that contravenes the PI. In the national security context, such a balancing exercise, when conducted by the whistleblower, is fraught with dangers. Although in some cases it is self-evident that the information the whistleblower comes across relates to wrongdoing – for instance where there is clear evidence of corruption or state complicity in gross human rights violations – this is not always the case. In the context of national security especially, the work of the intelligence community or the war against terrorism, it may not be simple for the potential whistleblower to discern between legitimate conduct of a public authority, and wrongdoing.[57] The services, by their nature, infringe on human rights, namely the right to privacy protected under Article 8 ECHR, when they monitor communications, for instance in order to collect intelligence.[58] For a whistleblower to ascertain whether specific instances of such monitoring constitute misconduct, he or she must perform a balancing exercise to assess whether in these 'suspicious' cases the intelligence agency is acting within the remit of the law or not. Thus, a PI balancing exercise between security and the privacy of the monitored individual must take place before the whistleblower decides to proceed with a disclosure.

The second step involves a decision on whether the perceived wrongdoing is so severe as to warrant a public disclosure. The whistleblower therefore decides to disclose the information in an act that in fact 'overrides the judgment of the executive authority'.[59] This means that the whistleblower asserts, contrary to the judgement of his or her superiors, that the PI will be best served by full disclosure of the information at hand and that this interest outweighs conflicting interests in security.[60] Although the decision to 'go public' could in many cases be motivated by the fact that the whistleblower was unable to address the issue using less extreme measures, an assessment of the PI is required, as the whistleblower would be reluctant to breach his or her duty of confidentiality to reveal information that is trivial and of little importance to the public discourse. As Morse notes, 'not all violations of law are equally important to make public'.[61] Therefore the balancing exercise between the interest in security and the interest in the disclosure is in such circumstances entrusted to the individual whistleblower.

Due to the PI being a particularly nebulous concept which lacks a concrete and universally accepted definition that can be applied in every case,[62] it is an arduous task for the whistleblower to assess whether this evaluation and judgement that leads to a disclosure is indeed in the PI.[63] This could result in problems when granting free speech protection, as any restrictions to the whistleblower's free speech that are due to damage caused to national security by the disclosure could be justified under Article 10 (2). Therefore, it is vital for secrecy laws or whistleblower protection instruments pertaining to national security whistleblowers to take this balancing exercise into account and to examine ways to protect the whistleblower while ensuring that overzealous employees are not encouraged to proceed to complicated PI and national security assessments that result in harmful disclosures.

The question that the article aims to answer therefore, in relation to the intelligence community whistleblower, is how official secrecy legislation can be framed in light of the recent developments in whistleblower protection mentioned above, in order to ensure first, that the whistleblower's assessment on the PI is less of an instinctual process, and second, that security is not harmed to a disproportionate extent when weighed against the public interest in disclosure.

After these clarifications the article will proceed to examine the first possible avenue for secrecy legislation to be framed.

The first approach: a blanket ban on disclosures

The first method to frame secrecy legislation or confidentiality agreements of the intelligence official seeks to exclude discussion of a possible PI in public disclosures, by using criminal law or other retaliatory measures to prosecute those who proceed to any unauthorised disclosures of information. This approach is premised on the idea that it is the act of publicly disclosing security-related information *itself* that is contrary to the PI, regardless of whether or not the specific disclosure actually endangered national security.[64] Furthermore, the ECtHR has held that information relating to security and intelligence can legitimately be withheld from the public.[65] This is the system currently favoured by the Official Secrets Act 1989 (OSA 1989) in the UK, for instance, which does not allow for public disclosure of information by members of the intelligence and security community, even if it relates to wrongdoing.[66] The OSA 1989 does not include a *damage test* for intelligence officials, which means that the prosecution is not required to prove that there was some damage caused to national security or other state interests in order to hand down penalties against the whistleblower under criminal law.[67] Furthermore the act does not include a PI defence, which would allow the whistleblower to argue that the public interest in disclosure outweighs the public interest in security. Thus, the irrebuttable presumption that disclosures emanating from the services are damaging[68] results in prohibiting the judiciary from making an ad hoc assessment of the national security considerations that could be endangered by a specific disclosure, in order to assess the legitimacy of the free speech restriction.

For those supporting this line of argument, the role of the intelligence official should be limited to providing support to the government of the day and not to assume the role of an 'impartial umpire' in political disputes.[69] The work of civil servants in general requires them to support and not hinder the government of the day and thus they assume a particularly strong duty of loyalty.[70] Furthermore, since for intelligence officials 'their official job duty is protecting the country's national security interests',[71] more stringent free speech restrictions are permissible. This approach ensures that the whistleblower will not proceed to PI assessments, particularly in issues that touch upon the security of the state. An absolute restriction on disclosures relies on the idea that the interests of maintaining public confidence in these institutions, the fact that such disclosures carry with them a particularly strong credibility, and the heightened duty of secrecy of intelligence officials, all outweigh any potential benefit from a public disclosure.[72] Thus the value of the information disclosed to the PI is not part of the proportionality equation, and any information, however trivial, when disclosed can justify criminal sanctions or other forms of retaliation if the authorities decide to prosecute. Thus the 'balancing exercise' of the interest in the information and national security is altogether discarded as 'the protection of secrets is synonymous with the public interest'.[73]

This approach seems to be irreconcilable prima facie with the established COE whistleblower and free speech standards examined above. However, the fact that *public* whistleblowing to the media is protected only when more discreet means of remedying the situation are not available to the whistleblower,[74] could provide contracting parties with the necessary justification to ban external disclosures. If a state chooses to follow such an approach in order to secure the compatibility of the law with free speech, it would have to counterbalance the absolute ban on external disclosures by establishing a robust system of independent and effective internal mechanisms, where whistleblowers could report their concerns and be protected from reprisals while also be assured that the issues they have raised will be addressed appropriately.[75]

The exclusive reliance on internal mechanisms or official channels of reporting however can be said to have significant drawbacks. Sagar argues that internal whistleblowing carries the danger that the wrongdoing may remain unaddressed. As he stresses, 'senior officials may ignore or suppress a whistleblower's complaint in order to hide their complicity or to avoid a scandal'[76]; an internal report could leave the whistleblower without 'external support in the event that her colleagues and managers retaliate against her'[77]; and finally, using official channels without external pressure 'could provide wrongdoers with the opportunity to destroy incriminating evidence'.[78] Internal reporting 'may also result in superficial fixes without deep reform',[79] fixes meant to placate the whistleblower but lacking in bringing about genuine results to rectify the misconduct. Research into whistleblowing has also consistently shown that external whistleblowing has been more successful in eliciting change.[80]

Relying on the ECtHR case law,[81] one could argue that the existence of effective internal mechanisms that could be approached by whistleblowers without fear of retaliation would negate the need for a whistleblower to approach the media. However, in recognition of the inherent limitations of official reporting channels, the court has found the fact that such mechanisms are in place does not suffice to justify an absolute ban on internal disclosures. If the nature of the information at hand made it unlikely for internal mechanisms to respond appropriately, if the internal mechanisms have a history of not addressing instances of such internal whistleblowing, or if they refuse to examine the whistleblower's allegations, external disclosures are permitted under the ECtHR whistleblowing protection regime.[82] In *Heinisch* and *Bucur* for instance, the whistleblowers had approached their superiors to report the illegal activity they had uncovered, but no concrete action was taken to address the issue. When they subsequently proceeded to a public disclosure they were provided with free speech protection.[83] Therefore, even if such mechanisms exist, they do not suffice to bar the whistleblower from proceeding to a public disclosure and courts from proceeding to the ad hoc test of whether they functioned properly in that particular instance and whether the disclosure was in the PI.[84] The first approach therefore, does not provide an adequate solution to the problem of balancing the interests of security and disclosures.

Second approach: the introduction of a public interest test or defence where wrongdoing is not defined in the legislation

As the article has argued, the lack of a PI defence in a contracting party's secrecy legislation, would make such legislation suspect as to its compatibility with free speech. This part seeks to discuss how the inclusion of a PI exception to secrecy would affect national security whistleblowers.

Supporters of such an approach argue that official secrecy laws should make for an exception for disclosures emanating from a breach of secrecy that are in the PI.[85] This would allow the intelligence official whistleblower that is facing criminal proceedings for an unauthorised disclosure, for instance, to employ a PI defence, and to argue that the interest in the disclosure outweighs the interest in keeping the information secret. Such a defence, which would exonerate national security whistleblowers where they could prove their disclosures were in the PI, would also ensure that the state was in line with freedom of expression standards on whistleblower protection. An example of this approach can be found in Canada, where the Security and Information Act 1985[86] provides that 'no person is guilty of an offence … if the person establishes that he or she acted in the public interest'.[87] The Act does not contain a definition of wrongdoing but allows judges to make assessments on whether to grant protection based on the whistleblower's conduct and good faith, the gravity of the reported offence, the PI in the disclosure and the possible harm it caused.[88] This approach has the added benefit that it allows for a future expansion of the understanding of the types of conduct that constitute wrongdoing, as courts can take into account novel developments without being restricted to a stringent definition of wrongdoing in the law. Similarly, in Slovenia, while there is no specialised whistleblower protection instrument, public and private employees are protected for reporting 'all forms of illegal or unethical behaviour'.[89]

Such a system would require courts to balance the whistleblower's free speech rights and the public interest in the information disclosed on the one hand, with the potential harm the disclosure may cause to national security on the other, by applying the test of proportionality. Since proportionality 'seeks to police the justification of state interference with human rights',[90] it would thus require courts to consider whether any retaliation against a security whistleblower could be defended based on the damage caused to national security by focusing on the content of the disclosure. As the ECtHR has stressed, 'the Court must look at the "interference" complained of in the light of the case as a whole and determine whether the reasons adduced by the national authorities to justify it are relevant and sufficient'.[91]

In order to gain a better understanding of how such a PI defence would work in practice for the national security whistleblower, it is worthwhile to examine the case law of the ECtHR with regard to whistleblower protection and disclosures in the public interest in general. The court has provided a useful illustration of how the balancing of the interest in the disclosure and competing concerns that favour non-disclosure can be exercised when assessing whether there has been a freedom of expression violation.

In *Guja*, the ECtHR held that the PI involved in the information disclosed is a determining factor in assessing the proportionality of an interference with a whistleblower's free speech rights.[92] The court took a broad approach in its interpretation of the PI in this instance, by arguing that 'in a democratic system the acts or omissions of government must be subject to the close scrutiny not only of the legislative and judicial authorities but also of the media and public opinion'.[93] In assessing whether freedom of expression protection would be extended to the applicant in this particular case, which involved a public disclosure of information that showed evidence of political interference in the administration of justice from the Moldovan Prosecutor General's Office, the ECtHR proceeded with the usual proportionality test. In order to make the calculation on whether the disclosure had an important benefit to the public at large, the court looked into the background of the disclosure and the overall political context under which it was made[94] before concluding that '[t]here is no doubt that these are very important matters in a democratic society which the public has a legitimate interest in being informed about and which fall within the scope of political debate'.[95] In the view of the court these concerns overrode the interests in maintaining public confidence in the Prosecutor General's Office.[96]

In *Bucur and Thoma* v. *Romania*, a case concerning the disclosure of information by a member of the Romanian security services to a newspaper, the ECtHR held that 'the general interest in the disclosure of information revealing illegal activities ... was so important in a democratic society that it prevailed over the interest in maintaining public confidence in that institution'.[97] In *Voskuil* v. *Netherlands* the court stressed that 'in a democratic state governed by the rule of law the use of improper methods by a public authority is precisely the kind of issue about which the public has the right to be informed',[98] while in *Heinisch* it argued for an even broader understanding of the PI by stating that 'there is little scope under Article 10 § 2 of the Convention for restrictions on debate on questions of public interest'.[99] Similarly, in *Dupuis*, the ECtHR took into account the fact that, in France, the revelation of extensive wiretapping of political figures in the media, revealed in a book published by two journalists, had already 'aroused a considerable degree of emotion and concern among public opinion'.[100] Thus, the interest already expressed in France over the revelations was a factor to be considered by the ECtHR in its balancing of the interest in disclosure with competing interests.

It is important to note that proof of the court's case-by-case approach is found in the fact that the circumstances of every contracting party are taken into account during the proportionality test when assessing the public interest in the disclosure. This is prevalent in issues concerning national security. As Cameron observes, security in the COE is 'both dynamic and relative: what "vulnerability" is will vary from state to state and from time to time'.[101] In *Bucur* for instance, the court stressed that illegal surveillance by the security services was undeniably a matter of public interest,[102] especially in a state that had experienced extensive surveillance under the previous communist regime. Thus, Romania's historical past was viewed as a contributing factor to accept that there was a pressing PI need in the disclosure, a PI that was viewed as compelling enough to override the intelligence official's duty of secrecy.

This type of assessment, on a case-by-case basis, seems to be the optimum way for domestic courts to establish the proportionality of an interference with free speech, in cases where a national security whistleblower has experienced retaliation. However, when examined from the viewpoint of domestic legislation regarding national security, whistleblowing and official secrecy, a 'general' PI exception to the duty of confidentiality, which does not define in a more broad or narrow manner what disclosures would be in the public interest and would outweigh security considerations, could result in jeopardising national security and the safety of the whistleblower. Without interpretation or guidelines of what the PI is, such legislation would not provide any assurances to the potential whistleblower that their disclosures will be protected. In political terms, the PI is a highly divisive standard. What recent national security-related disclosures have confirmed is that 'people disagree fundamentally over what the public interest is',[103] as evidenced by the fact that whistleblowers are, in many cases, simultaneously labelled as heroes or traitors.[104] Thus, when the whistleblower becomes an assessor of the PI, there is no guarantee that the courts will confirm his or her interpretation of the concept.[105]

Such disputes, when transferred to the context of a disclosure emanating from the intelligence community, can undermine national security. If the whistleblower's disclosures are the result of an instinctual response that perceived wrongdoing should be reported in the PI, there is no certainty that irreparable damage will not be caused. It would in fact be impossible for the intelligence community to function effectively under such an environment where PI decisions on disclosure are made at every level by any and every employee with access to information.

Furthermore, even in cases where one could argue that whistleblowers were prudent in their interpretation of the PI, it is questionable whether this would be accepted by the judiciary. Domestic courts have, to a great degree, shown reluctance to question the executive on matters of national security. As Popelier and Van De Heyning note, constitutional and supreme courts in Europe tend to 'readily accept public safety and security concerns proposed by public authorities as legitimate objectives with a considerable weight, without scrutinizing the danger ... threats actually pose'.[106] Thus, a great degree of deference is given to decision-makers or the executive in assessing which information should remain secret.

As many proponents of whistleblowing propose, a way to overcome these potential problems is to set the threshold for protection based on whether the whistleblower acted under the 'reasonable belief' that he or she was uncovering wrongdoing that was in the PI.[107] Protection, it is argued, should also cover disclosures made 'in honest error'[108] when the information on wrongdoing that is publicly revealed is inaccurate but the whistleblower acted in good faith with the disclosure. This has the benefit of disengaging protection from whether the information was in fact in the PI. Yet, when applied to national security whistleblowers, it could be said to create more problems than it solves. First, setting the bar at reasonable *belief* that wrongdoing was committed would require the whistleblower to proceed to a more thorough examination of the wrongdoing he/she is alleging was committed. This in many cases would not be possible to do or could potentially be harmful to the whistleblower and could thus further dissuade concerned individuals from proceeding to the disclosure. As Lewis proposes, requiring reasonable *suspicion*, as opposed to reasonable *belief*, would be a better approach as 'the great advantage of this would be that it would highlight the fact that it is the recipient's job to investigate concerns and not that of the potential whistleblower'.[109] However, it is questionable that in the context of national security whistleblowers this approach would be realistic. Keeping in mind the heightened demands for secrecy the services function under,[110] extending free speech protection to disclosures where the concerns for national security would outweigh the interest in disclosure would be difficult to reconcile with Article 10(2) ECHR. These are the dangers inherent in legislation that would not enumerate specific areas of concern, which would guide the whistleblower during his or her PI assessment.

Thus, providing protection for PI disclosures without defining the PI in the law ensures that the law will allow for a balancing of national security and competing interests on a case-by-case basis and thus will not collide with free speech standards. At the same time however, such an approach has the potential to prove more damaging for the whistle-blowers, who will have to navigate the nebulous concept that is PI without guidance, and also to national security as the duty of secrecy will become conditional on the PI assessments of any employee that handles confidential information.

This leads us to the examination of the third approach to whistleblower protection – official secrecy laws.

Third approach: a list of specific PI disclosures contained in the whistleblower protection instrument

Providing whistleblower protection for only specific types of disclosures enumerated in the whistleblower protection instrument or in official secrecy legislation has the benefit of giving the whistleblower greater certainty that his/her disclosure will be perceived to be in the PI, a PI that will override competing security concerns. In this approach, the balancing between national security and the public's right to know is included in the legal instrument and the function of the judiciary is limited to examining whether a specific disclosure falls under one or more pre-determined categories.

The inclusion of a prescribed list of disclosures, especially in relation to national security, raises the obvious and important question of *which* types of wrongdoing should qualify for protection. It is first advisable to examine whether there is an international consensus on how whistleblowing and secrecy laws deal with definitions on wrongdoing and the public interest in disclosures. Second, one must assess whether there are developing international standards on when national security related disclosures would be in the PI. Finally, it should be asked whether nascent ECHR and COE standards on whistleblowing could provide contracting parties with the necessary guidelines to draft their secrecy legislation.

According to Banisar, there are more than 30 countries around the world that have adopted some form of whistleblower protection,[111] and most 'create comprehensive definitions of what constitutes wrongdoing'.[112] Others limit it to one area, usually crimes related to corruption, while others provide protection for the disclosure of 'a wide variety of issues including violations of laws, good practises, and ethics'.[113] Furthermore, due to the fact that 'the definition of "public interest" varies across different jurisdictions',[114] there are no established international standards or a consensus as to what qualifies as a public interest disclosure.[115]

States possess a degree of flexibility in deciding which areas are most important to protect. Circumstances that are specific to certain states seem to play an important part in deciding which areas of wrongdoing will be included in a whistleblower protection instrument. As Banisar[116] observes, the South African Act 'includes unfair discrimination'[117] as a category where PI disclosures apply, while the Japanese equivalent 'specifically names food and health laws, clean air and waste disposal, and personal information laws'.[118] The US approach seems particularly all encompassing[119] as the federal Whistleblower Protection Act of 1989 protects government employees from sanctions for reporting violations of 'law, rule and regulation' or 'gross mismanagement, a gross waste of funds, an abuse of authority, or a substantial and specific danger to public health or safety'.[120] Furthermore, in the US there are whistleblower protection schemes found in laws relating to a more specific context. As Dworkin explains, 'an individual who reports illegal water pollution, for instance, is protected from retaliation by the Safe Water Drinking Act'.[121] As Banisar observes, there is agreement, however, in that states 'typically require that the action is not trivial in nature and has not previously been disclosed or addressed'.[122]

How could such categories of protected disclosures, however, be framed in the context of national security? In the search for international standards on the reasons that would allow for public disclosures of wrongdoing in national security cases, Transparency International has made a significant contribution to the discussion in its 2013 International Principles for Whistleblower Legislation by arguing that:

> External disclosure (i.e. to the media, civil society organisations) would be justified in demonstrable cases of urgent or grave threats to public health, safety or the environment; if an internal disclosure could lead to personal harm or the destruction of evidence; and if the disclosure was not intended or likely to significantly harm national security or individuals.[123]

In a similar vein, the Tshwane Principles on National Security and Access to Information (2013) attempted to deal with the issue of national security whistleblowers and the balancing between national security concerns and their free speech rights. The principles were endorsed by the UN and OSCE Rapporteurs on Freedom of Expression and formed the basis for the COE's Parliamentary Assembly Resolution 1954 (2013) which will be examined below.

The principles provide a more specific list as to which types of wrongdoing could trigger *public* disclosures when left unaddressed by internal mechanisms and would allow for protection based on the whistleblower's freedom of speech. The list includes violations of international human rights and humanitarian law, such as the prevention of torture, violations of the right to life, decisions to use military force or acquire weapons of mass destruction, mass surveillance, mismanagement or waste of funds, constitutional and statutory violations, abuses of power and issues relating to public health, public safety or the environment.[124]

Adapting these principles to the COE level, the Parliamentary Assembly in its 2013 Resolution on National Security and Access to Information stated that an overriding PI can typically be found where the publication of the information in question would make 'an important contribution to an ongoing public debate, promote public participation in political debate, expose serious wrongdoings, including human rights violations, other criminal offences, abuse of public office and deliberate concealment of serious wrongdoing, … benefit public health or safety'.[125] The resolution added that 'information about serious violations of human rights or humanitarian law should not be withheld on national security grounds in any circumstances'.[126]

The obvious focus of these provisions is the violation of human rights. The reporting of gross human rights violations would in all cases seem to trump national security concerns and allow for the national security whistleblower to be protected from retaliation. The Tshwane Principles in particular are drawn in a way that validates recent high-profile security-related whistleblowing cases[127]; however, they could be viewed as overly ambitious, as one would expect from a document aiming to provide broad international guidelines on whistleblower protection. A strikingly bold step for instance, is the inclusion of decisions on the use of military force as a protected category, where there would be a 'high presumption'[128] in favour of disclosure. This, according to the Tshwane Principles, would include protection for disclosure of 'information relevant to a decision to commit combat troops or take other military action, including [...] its general size and scope'.[129] Thus according to the principles, reporting general information on size and scope would suffice, and a disclosure need not contain 'all of the details of the operational aspects of the military action'[130] to satisfy the PI in accessing the information. Without doubt, disclosing information during the decision-making process leading up to combat would be valuable to the PI if there were deliberate attempts from the executive and the intelligence services to mislead the legislature and the public[131] on the necessity of combat or its rationale. A more realistic approach however would argue that it would be destructive to make combat-related decisions under the glaring eye of publicity and to allow anyone with access to the specific information to make assessments on which of the operational details could be reported in the PI.

This example of information on the use of military force as a protected category of disclosure, illustrates the fact that the existence of a prescribed list of disclosures does not relieve the whistleblower from the responsibility of proceeding to complicated PI assessments, much like in the second approach we described. Is it feasible to expect every intelligence official to be able to discern which operational aspects of an upcoming or ongoing combat are worth reporting or whether specific 'suspicious' conduct constitutes 'a constitutional or statutory violation'[132] which the Tshwane Principles regard as a legitimate reason for public disclosures? Although this is true of every whistleblower, in security-related cases the adverse results of an incorrect assessment are arguably more profound. Consequently, a list of protected disclosures as broad as the Tshwane Principles or the ones cited in Parliamentary Assembly Resolution 1954, can be further criticised for being ambiguous and vague in nature. This is compounded by the fact that, for security whistleblowers it is 'impossible [...] to obtain independent legal or other advice before making a disclosure'.[133] However, highly specific and unambiguous categories of wrongdoing would have the drawback of being too limited and providing protection that is too narrow and is not adaptable to newer developments.

Thus it is questionable whether, in the realm of the intelligence community, where decisions are made on sometimes fragmented intelligence in a highly compartmentalised environment, this approach in essence manages to overcome the problems of the whistleblower making sensitive PI assessments cited in the second approach we described. Furthermore, it is important to note that since 'hard' data, purely factual information, are not always sufficient to make security-related decisions, intelligence agencies also have to rely on *speculative* intelligence in order to determine which people 'are probably or possibly, threatening national security'.[134] This is a highly subjective exercise and a degree of deference to agency decisions is required, because when it comes to striking these balances, the optimum way to deal with a potential threat 'is not always straightforward, and reasonable people can differ on how to do it'.[135] Thus, this final method to frame secrecy laws does not entirely resolve the dangers that can arise from well-meaning, yet overzealous, national security whistleblowers.

Furthermore, the fact that the principles mentioned above are derived from non-binding instruments means that they can only serve as an indication or suggestion for legislators. Therefore, when allowing the types of wrongdoing that warrant public disclosure as a means of last resort to be enumerated in the law, whistleblower protection in national security cases becomes conditional on how generous lawmakers will be in their interpretation of the PI in the whistleblower protection instrument or the secrecy law. This problem is not limited to national security whistleblowers. For instance, and in stark opposition to the broad protection provided to federal whistleblowers in the US mentioned above, in France, the French Labour Law Code provides protection only for disclosures relating to allegations of corruption.[136] Although corruption is a particularly broad term, such legislation would still preclude a significant number of whistleblowers whose disclosures are arguably in the PI from seeking protection from retaliation. Although the extent to which legislators will agree that certain national security disclosures warrant specific protection can be indicated by their free speech obligations, they would still be permitted great latitude when translating free speech standards for national security whistleblowers into the domestic context.

In spite of these drawbacks, however, this seems to be the most reasonable approach for national legislators. To ensure the compatibility of domestic laws with Article 10 without weakening the secrecy that is necessary for the intelligence community to function, there would need to be a strict prohibition on disclosures, with exemptions where the PI would override secrecy requirements, in line with COE and ECtHR free speech standards and COE guidelines; combined with the strengthening of the independence of intelligence oversight bodies and official reporting mechanisms; as well as adequate training of officials as to what the responsible whistleblowing procedures are. Further development of standards in whistleblower protection on the COE level, through the Parliamentary Assembly and the ECtHR, would allow the judiciary in contracting parties to challenge overly restrictive domestic laws that provide for an excessively narrow list of protected public disclosures. It would also ensure that the ECtHR retains its supervisory role in cases where unwarranted retaliatory measures were taken against whistleblowers whose disclosures are not damaging to national security and contain information that makes a significant contribution to the public interest.

Conclusion

Technological developments and the advent of the digital age have made it significantly easier to leak and share security-related information.[137] Therefore, the need to find an appropriate way to balance national security with the public's 'right to know' is more pressing than ever. The article has attempted to highlight the problems that occur when attempting to regulate national security whistleblower exceptions to state secrecy in a manner that is compatible with emerging freedom of expression standards of the COE. The COE adheres to the view that whistleblowers are 'part of society's alarm and self-repair system, bringing attention to problems before they become far more damaging',[138] and it has, in recent years, significantly extended free speech protection for unauthorised public interest disclosures. The impact this will have on the domestic context remains to be seen, as courts and legislators will have to grapple with the task of balancing security interests with the need for an informed citizenry. Out of three possible avenues for the PI to be incorporated into secrecy laws or whistleblower instruments, the article has argued that, in relation to national security, broad categories of wrongdoing must be included in the law to ensure that intelligence officials who proceed to PI disclosures will enjoy free speech protection. This will also allow for greater guarantees that the public interest in the information disclosed will outweigh the potential harm to national security. The judiciary will be vital in ensuring that legislators include a list of protected disclosures that are in line with ECHR demands on restrictions to freedom of expression, while the ECtHR, civil society and the broader international community can continue to establish standards for balancing of the national security with the public accountability of intelligence institutions for their actions. The fundamental role of freedom of expression in combating corruption and wrongdoing must thus be strengthened and not sacrificed at the altar of national security rhetoric in the intelligence community.

Acknowledgements

The author would like to thank Prof. Patrick Birkinshaw, Dr. Elisenda Casanas-Adam and Dr. Myriam Feinberg.

Disclosure statement

No potential conflict of interest was reported by the author.

Notes on contributor

Dimitrios Kagiaros is Teaching Fellow in Public Law and Human Rights Law at the University of Edinburgh Law School.

Notes

1. Whistleblowing is 'the reporting by employees or former employees of illegal, irregular, dangerous or unethical practices by employers'. International Labour Organisation, 'ILO Thesaurus', http://www.ilo.org/thesaurus/defaulten.asp. Also see Transparency International, 'International Principles for Whistleblower Legislation', Report published 5 November 2013, http://www.transparency.org/whatwedo/pub/international_principles_for_whistleblower_legislation; OECD, 'G20 Anti-Corruption Action Plan: Protection for Whistleblowers, Study on Whistleblower Protection Frameworks, Compendium of Best Practices and Guiding Principles for Legislation (2011)', http://www.oecd.org/g20/topics/anti-corruption/48972967.pdf; and David Lewis, *A Global Approach to Public Interest Disclosure: What Can we Learn from Existing Whistleblowing Legislation and Research?* (Cheltenham: Edward Elgar, 2010).
2. On the United Nations (UN) level, protection is provided through the UN Convention against Corruption (2003) Article 33. Protection afforded in the Council of Europe (COE) will be examined in detail below.
3. The scope of the article is limited to individuals who are employed in the intelligence community and the security sector and are bound by secrecy laws or confidentiality agreements relating to the disclosure of intelligence information. For an analysis and definitions of security services and intelligence agencies in the COE context, see European Commission for Democracy through Law (Venice Commission), 'Report on the Democratic Oversight of the Security Services' (2007), http://www.europarl.europa.eu/meetdocs/2009_2014/documents/libe/dv/3_cdl-ad%282007%29016_/3_cdl-ad%282007%29016_en.pdf.
4. As in the convictions of David Shayler and Katharine Gun in the UK, and Chelsea Manning and Edward Snowden in the US.
5. Palmer Stephanie, 'Tightening Secrecy Law: the Official Secrets Act 1989', *Public Law* (1990): 252.
6. G. Robert Vaughn, *Successes and Failures of Whistleblower Laws* (Cheltenham: Edward Elgar Publishing, 2012), 314.
7. For a thorough examination of the reprisals whistleblowers experience see Alford Fred, *Whistleblowers: Broken Lives and Organizational Power* (Ithaca, NY: Cornell University Press, 2001); and P.B. Jubb, 'Whistleblowing: A Restrictive Definition and Interpretation', *Journal of Business Ethics* 21 (1999): 77.
8. Vaughn, *Successes and Failures*, 314.
9. These will be examined in detail in below.
10. For an analysis of the good faith requirement in the ECtHR case law see John Bowers and others, *Whistleblowing: Law and Practice* (Oxford: Oxford University Press, 2012), para. 11.140.

11. These are Luxembourg, Romania, Slovenia and the UK. See Transparency International, *Whistleblowing in Europe: Legal Protections for Whistleblowers in the EU* (Transparency International, 2013), 10, http://www.transparency.org/whatwedo/publication/whistleblowing_in_europe_legal_protections_for_whistleblowers_in_the_eu.
12. Ibid.
13. Employment Rights Act 1996 s43B (3).
14. Transparency International, *Whistleblowing in Europe*, 14.
15. Article 3 and Article 10 of law No. 51/1991 of 29 July 1991 on official secrecy. For prosecutions of whistleblowers see ECtHR, *Bucur and Toma* v. *Romania* (App. No. 40238/02, 8 January 2013).
16. Iain Cameron, *National Security and the European Convention on Human Rights* (The Hague: Kluwer International Law, 2000), 382.
17. Swedish Criminal Code, chapter 19, sections 5 and 7.
18. Official Secrets Act 1989 s1.
19. See COE Parliamentary Assembly, 'Fair Trial Issues in Criminal Cases Concerning Espionage or Divulging State Secrets', 25 September 2006, Report by Christos Pourgourides, http://assembly.coe.int/ASP/Doc/XrefViewHTML.asp?FileID=9149&Language=EN#P391_61374.
20. Ibid., at [57] and [58].
21. Ibid. The report by Rapporteur Pourgourides contains an exhaustive analysis and comparison on the regulation of official secrecy in the COE region in paras [56]–[68].
22. Recommendation CM/Rec(2014)7 of the Committee of Ministers to member states on the protection of whistleblowers. Adopted by the Committee of Ministers on 30 April 2014, at the 1198th meeting of the Ministers' Deputies.
23. Steve Foster, 'Are We Becoming Afraid of Free Speech?', *Coventry Law Journal* 18 (2013): 93.
24. Francis Jacobs, Robin White and Clare Ovey, *The European Convention on Human Rights* (Oxford: Oxford University Press, 2010), 312.
25. Ibid.
26. Ibid., 325.
27. ECtHR, *Silver and Others* v. *United Kingdom*, (Application No. 5947/72; 6205/73; 7052/75; 7061/75; 7107/75; 7113/75; 7136/75, 25 March 1983) at [97]. On the use of proportionality see Julian Rivers, 'Proportionality and Variable Intensity of Review', *Cambridge Law Journal* 65 (2006): 174.
28. Eyal Benvenisti, 'Margin of Appreciation, Consensus and Universal Standards', *NYU Journal of International Law and Policy* 31 (1998–1999): 843.
29. Paul Mahoney and Lawrence Early, 'Freedom of Expression and National Security: Judicial and Policy Approaches under the European Convention on Human Rights and Other Council of Europe Instruments', in *Secrecy and Liberty: National Security, Freedom of Expression and Access to Information*, ed. Sandra Coliver et al. (The Netherlands: Kluwer International, 1999), 116. See also Leigh Ian, 'Case Comment: Spycatcher in Strasbourg', *Public Law* (1992): 200, 203. On the abuse of national security see Yutaka Arai-Takahashi, *The Margin of Appreciation Doctrine and the Principle of Proportionality in the Jurisprudence of the ECHR* (Oxford: Intersentia, 2002), 104; Jonas Christophersen, *Fair Balance: Proportionality, Subsidiarity and Primarity in the European Court of Human Rights* (Brill, 2009); Peter Noorlander, 'Fighting Words – The War on Terror and Media Freedom', in *Freedom of Expression and the Media*, ed. Merris Amos, Jackie Harrison and Lorna Woods (The Netherlands: Martinus Nijhoff Publishers/Brill Academic, 2012) 229. In the court's case law see ECtHR, *Leander* v. *Sweden* (App. No. 9248/81, 26 March 1987), ECtHR, *Klass and others* v. *Germany* (App. No. 5029/71, 6 September 1978), ECtHR, *A. and others* v. *United Kingdom* (App. No. 3455/05, 19 February 2009).
30. ECtHR, *Stoll* v. *Switzerland* (App. No. 69698/01, 10 December 2007), at [155].
31. Paul Hoffman and Kate Martin, 'United States', in *Secrecy and Liberty: National Security, Freedom of Expression and Access to Information*, ed. Sandra Coliver et al. (The Netherlands: Kluwer International, 1999), 496.
32. Council of Europe Parliamentary Assembly, Resolution 1551 (2007) 'Fair Trial Issues in Criminal Cases Concerning Espionage or Divulging State Secrets', 19 April 2007 at [9].
33. Council of Europe Parliamentary Assembly, Resolution 1507 (2006) 'Alleged Secret Detentions and Unlawful Inter-State Transfers of Detainees Involving Council of Europe Member States', 27 June 2006 at [19.5.].

34. Council of Europe, 'Call for Protection of Whistleblowers Who Reveal State Wrongdoing', 2 October 2013, http://www.assembly.coe.int/nw/xml/News/News-View-EN.asp?newsid=4669&lang=2&cat=8.
35. Council of Europe Parliamentary Assembly, Resolution 1729 (2010) 'Protection of Whistle-blowers', 29 April 2010 at [1].
36. Ibid., at [6.1.2.].
37. Ibid., at [6.1.1.]. For an in-depth analysis of Resolution 1729 see David Lewis, 'The Council of Europe Resolution and Recommendation on the Protection of Whistleblowers', *Industrial Law Journal* 39 (2010): 72.
38. Resolution 1729 at [6.2.1.].
39. Ibid., at [6.2.3.].
40. Recommendation CM/Rec(2014)7 of the Committee of Ministers.
41. Council of Europe, Parliamentary Assembly Resolution 1838 (2011) 'Abuse of State Secrecy and National Security: Obstacles to Parliamentary and Judicial Scrutiny of Human Rights Violations', 6 October 2011 at [8].
42. Council of Europe, Parliamentary Assembly Resolution 1877 (2012) 'The Protection of Freedom of Expression and Information on the Internet and Online Media', 25 April 2012 at [4].
43. Council of Europe, Parliamentary Assembly Resolution 1954 (2013) on 'National Security and Access to Information', 2 October 2013 at [9.7.].
44. See for instance ECtHR, *Handyside* v. *United Kingdom* (App. No. 5493/72, 7 December 1976), ECtHR, *Steel and Morris* v. *United Kingdom* (Application No. 68416/01, 15 February 2005), *Lingens* v. *Austria* (Application No. 9815/82, 8 July 1986), *Vogt* v. *Germany* (App. No. 17851/91, 26 September 1995).
45. ECtHR, *Goodwin* v. *United K*ingdom (App. No. 17488/90, 27 March 1996), at [39].
46. Jacobs, White and Ovey, *The European Convention*, 433; and ECtHR, *Prager and Oberschlick* v. *Austria* (App. No. 15974/90, 26 April 1995), at [38].
47. ECtHR, *Financial Times Ltd and Others* v. *UK* (App. No. 821/03, 15 December 2009).
48. ECtHR, *Guja* v. *Moldova* (App. No. 14277/04, 12 February 2008).
49. Jacobs, White and Ovey, *The European Convention*, 442.
50. *Guja* v. *Moldova* at [74]. This position was reiterated in the subsequent cases of ECtHR, *Heinisch* v. *Germany* (App. No. 28274/08 21 July 2011); and ECtHR, *Sosinowska* v. *Poland* (App. No. 10247/09, 18 October 2011).
51. ECtHR, *Bucur and Toma* v. *Romania* (App. No. 40238/02, 8 January 2013).
52. See for instance ECtHR, *Hadjianastassiou* v. *Greece* (App. No. 12945/87, 16 December 1992); and ECtHR, *Pasko* v. *Russia* (App. No. 69519/01, 22 October 2010).
53. *Hadjianastassiou* at [47].
54. *Bucur* at [102].
55. Ibid.
56. Near and Miceli refer to this step as the 'triggering event' and define it as 'an activity that is considered *wrongful*, rather than an acceptable but not optimal organizational activity' in Marcia Miceli and Janet Near, *Blowing the Whistle: The Organizational and Legal Implications for Companies and Employees* (New York: Lexington Books, 1992), 17 (emphasis added).
57. For further analysis on this process see Rahul Sagar, *Secrets and Leaks: The Dilemma of State Secrecy* (Princeton, NJ: Princeton University Press, 2013), 103–26.
58. Venice Commission Report, 'Oversight of Security Services', 4.
59. Rahul Sagar, 'On Combating the Abuse of State Secrecy', *The Journal of Political Philosophy* 15 (2007): 424.
60. See also Sissela Bok, 'Whistleblowing and Professional Responsibility', in *Ethical Issues in Business: Inquiries, Cases, and Readings*, ed. Peg Tittle (Ontario: Broadview Press, 2000), 70.
61. Mika Morse, 'Honor or Betrayal: The Ethics of Government Lawyer Whistleblowers', *Georgetown Journal of Legal Ethics* 23 (2010): 448.
62. Richard Flathman, *The Public Interest: An Essay Concerning the Normative Discourse of Politics* (New York: Wiley, 1966), 13.
63. One could argue that this assessment on the public interest in public disclosure is made by the whistleblower in conjunction with the medium that will publish it.
64. See for instance Stella Rimington, *Open Secret* (London: Arrow Books, 2002), 186; and Rahul Sagar, 'Wikileaks and Democracy', in *Wikileaks and the Consequences: Internet, Media, Politics*, ed. Heinrich Geiselberger (Frankfurt: Suhrkamp, 2010), 201–223.

65. See ECtHR, *Murray* v. *United Kingdom* (App. No. 14310/88, 28 October 1994); *Vereniging Weekblad Bluf* v. *The Netherlands* (App. No. 16616/90, 9 February 1995); and ECtHR, Telegraaf Media Nederland and others v. Netherlands (App. No. 39315/06, 22 November 2012).
66. UK Official Secrets Act 1989, s 1 (1). The Espionage Act 1917 in the US makes for a similar 'broad and sweeping prohibition'. Stephen Vladeck, 'The Espionage Act and National Security Whistleblowing after *Garcetti*', *American University Law Review* 57 (2007–2008): 1534.
67. See Ann Rogers, *Secrecy and Power in the British State: A History of the Official Secrets Act* (London: Pluto Press, 1997); Laurence Lustgarten and Ian Leigh, *In From the Cold* (Oxford: Clarendon Press, 1994); Christopher Moran, *Classified: Secrecy and the State in Modern Britain* (Cambridge: Cambridge University Press, 2013).
68. A.T.H. Smith, 'Security Services, Leaks and the Public Interest' *Cambridge Law Journal* 61 (2002): 515.
69. UK House of Commons Public Administration Select Committee, 'Leaks and Whistleblowing in Whitehall: Tenth Report of Session 2008-09', HC 83 11.
70. See ECtHR, *Ahmed and Others* v. *United Kingdom* (App. No. 22954/93, 2 September 1998).
71. Jamie Sasser, 'Silenced Citizens: The Post-Garcetti Landscape for Public Sector Employees working in National Security', *University of Richmond Law Review* 41 (2006–2007): 760.
72. Helen Fenwick, *Civil Liberties and Human Rights* (Oxford: Routledge-Cavendish, 2007), 597.
73. William Freivogel, 'Publishing National Security Secrets: The Case For Benign Indeterminacy', *Journal of National Security Law and Policy* 3 (2009): 98.
74. *Guja* at [73]. See also ECtHR, *Morissens* v. *Belgium* (App. No. 11389/85, Commission decision 3 May 1988).
75. The existence of internal mechanisms was the justification used in *R* v. *Shayler* [2002] UKHL 11 by the Law Lords in the UK to justify the compatibility of the OSA with Article 10. The Lords argued that there was no need to examine the efficiency of such mechanisms. This justification seems weak in light of the COE standards that were subsequent to the *Shayler* judgment, thus putting into question the compatibility of the OSA with free speech. This is the system also currently followed in New Zealand where the particularly broad Protected Disclosures Act 2000 does not cover national security whistleblowers. Security sector employees can only approach an Ombudsman, the Inspector-General of Intelligence and Security. David Banisar, 'Whistleblowing: International Standards and Developments', in *Corruption and Transparency: Debating the Frontiers between State, Market and Society*, ed. I.E. Sandoval World Bank-Institute for Social Research (Washington, DC: UNAM, 2011, http://papers.ssrn.com/sol3/papers.cfm?abstract_id=1753180 45. In the US, intelligence officials are allowed to approach the House and Senate Intelligence Committees with national security disclosures under the Military Whistleblower Protection Act 1988, and the Intelligence Community Whistleblower Act 1998. See Louis Fisher, 'National Security Whistleblowers' (Report for the Congressional Research Service, Library of Congress 2005), http://www.fas.org/sgp/crs/natsec/RL33215.pdf at 45.
76. Sagar, *Secrets and Leaks*, 133.
77. Ibid.
78. Ibid.
79. Morse, 'Honor or Betrayal', 449.
80. Janet Near and Marcia Miceli, 'Organizational Dissidence: The case of Whistle-Blowing', *Journal of Business Ethics* 4 (1985): 11; Terry Dworkin and Melissa Baucus, 'Internal vs. External Whistleblowers: A Comparison of Whistleblowing Processes', *Journal of Business Ethics* 17 (1998): 1295. For a more recent study conducted in the UK, see Public Concern At Work, 'Report on "Whistleblowing: The Inside Story", http://pcaw.org.uk/files/Whistleblowing%20-%20the%20inside%20story%20FINAL.pdf at 5.
81. *Guja* [80–4]; *Heinisch* [72–6]. Also see dissenting opinion in ECtHR, *Kudeshkina* v. *Russia* (App. No. 29492/05, 14 September 2009).
82. Resolution 1729 [6.2.3.].
83. *Heinisch* [72–6]; *Bucur* [97].
84. An ideal internal mechanism would include: 'a clear statement that malpractice is taken seriously in the organisation ... respect for the confidentiality of staff raising concern ... an opportunity to raise concern outside the management structure and effective follow up mechanisms that will provide the whistleblower with information on how their concern has been

addressed'. See Guy Dehn, 'Whistleblowing and Integrity: A New Perspective' , http://www.cfoi.org.uk/pdf/corruptiongd.pdf.

85. Palmer, for instance, argues that if internal mechanisms fail, intelligence officials should be permitted to use a public interest defence if prosecuted. Palmer, 'Tightening Secrecy Law', 252.
86. (R.S.C., 1985, c. O-5)
87. Ibid., s15.
88. Ibid.
89. Transparency International, *Whistleblowing in Europe*, 79.
90. Andrew Legg, *The Margin of Appreciation in International Human Rights Law: Deference and Proportionality* (Oxford: Oxford University Press, 2012), 178.
91. ECtHR, *Dupuis and others* v. *France* (App. No. 1914/02, 7 June 2007), [37].
92. *Guja* at [74].
93. Ibid.
94. Ibid., at [87]
95. Ibid., at [88].
96. Paul Latimer and A.J. Brown, 'Whistleblower Laws: International Best Practice', *UNSW Law Journal* 31 (2008): 782.
97. Dirk Voorhoof, *The Right to Freedom of Expression and Information under the European Human Rights System: Towards a More Transparent Democratic Society* (European University Institute, 2014), 18, http://cadmus.eui.eu/bitstream/handle/1814/29871/RSCAS_2014_12.pdf?sequence=1.
98. ECtHR, *Voskuil* v. *Netherlands* (App No. 64752/01, 22 November 2007).
99. *Heinisch* [66]; *Dupuis* [40]; ECtHR, *Surek* v. *Turkey (no. 1)* (App. No. 26682/95, 8 July 1999) [61].
100. *Dupuis* [41]. See also ECtHR, *Fressoz and Roire* v. *France* (App. No. 29183/95, 21 January 1999).
101. Cameron, *National Security*, 42.
102. *Bucur* [101].
103. David Luban, 'Taking Out the Adversary: The Assault on Progressive Public-Interest Lawyers', *California Law Review* 91 (2003): 210.
104. See Marion Hersh, 'Whistleblowers – Heroes or Traitors? Individual and Collective Responsibility for Ethical Behaviour', *Annual Reviews in Control* 26 (2002): 244; and Martin Brian, 'Illusions of Whistleblower Protection', *UTS Law Review* 5 (2003): 122.
105. In the Snowden case for instance, a federal judge held that the policy of the intelligence agencies that Snowden disclosed was lawful. See *ACLU* v. *Clapper* (No. 13-3994, S.D. New York, 28 December 2013).
106. Patricia Popelier and Catherine Van De Heyning, 'Procedural Rationality: Giving Teeth to the Proportionality Analysis', *European Constitutional Law Review* 9 (2013): 238.
107. See Open Society Foundations, The Global Principles on National Security and the Right to Information 2013 (Tshwane Principles), http://www.opensocietyfoundations.org/sites/default/files/global-principles-national-security-10232013.pdf . Principle 40 argues that 'the "reasonably believed" test is a mixed objective-subjective test. The person must actually have held the belief (subjectively), and it must have been reasonable for him or her to have done so (objectively) … [I]t is ultimately for an independent court or tribunal to determine whether this test has been satisfied so as to qualify the disclosure for protection'.
108. Transparency international, 'Whistleblower Laws', 7.
109. David Lewis, 'Enterprise and Regulatory Reform – Whistleblowing Aspects', *Employment Law Bulletin* 110 (2012): 5.
110. See note 74 above.
111. Banisar, 'Whistleblowing', 2.
112. Ibid., 23.
113. Ibid. For a specific list of countries and an exhaustive state-by-state analysis see David Banisar, *Freedom of Information around the World: A Global Survey of Access to Government Information Laws* (Privacy International, 2006), http://www.freedominfo.org/documents/global_survey2006.pdf; and Banisar 'Whistleblowing'.
114. Latimer and Brown, 'Whistleblower Laws', 785.
115. However, the UN Rapporteur on Freedom of Opinion and Expression has attempted to define certain areas where disclosures ought to enjoy free speech protection. The 2000 report stated

that: 'Individuals should be protected ... for releasing information on wrongdoing, viz. the commission of a criminal offence or dishonesty, failure to comply with a legal obligation, a miscarriage of justice, corruption or dishonesty or serious failures in the administration of a public body'. UN Economic and Social Council Commission on Human Rights 56th Session. 'Civil and Political Rights Including the Question of Freedom of Expression' E/CN.4/2000/63 18 January 2000 [44].

116. Banisar, 'Whistleblowing', 25.
117. South African Protected Disclosures Act 2000, 4, http://www.justice.gov.za/legislation/notices/2011/20110831_gg34572_n702-disclosure-guidelines.pdf.
118. Banisar, 'Whistleblowing', 25.
119. Elletta Sangrey Callahan,Terry Morehead Dworkin and David Lewis, 'Australia, U.K., and U.S. Approaches to Disclosure in the Public Interest', *Virginia Journal of International Law* 44 (2003–2004): 886.
120. 5 U.S.C. § 2302(b)(8)(A)(ii) (2003).
121. Callahan, Dworkin and Lewis , 'Australia, U.K., and U.S. Approaches to Disclosure', 886 and 42 U.S.C. § 300j-9(i) (2002).
122. Banisar, 'Whistleblowing', 25.
123. Transparency International, 'Whistleblower Laws', 10.
124. Tshwane Principles, Principle 37.
125. Resolution 1954 (2013) at [9.5.].
126. Ibid.
127. Chelsea Manning's disclosure of a video of US crew killing Iraqi civilians would fall under the protected category of a violation of international humanitarian law, Snowden's disclosures would fall under mass surveillance, while National Security Agency (NSA) employee Thomas Drake's revelations of waste of funds in the NSA would fall under waste of resources.
128. Tshwane Principles, Principle 10.
129. Ibid., at D1.
130. Ibid.
131. An example of this would be David Kelly, an employee of the Defence Intelligence Staff in the UK, who leaked information to the press that refuted the official government line on the rationale behind the war in Iraq. After the disclosure Kelly committed suicide and an inquiry was established over the circumstances of his death. Lord Hutton, 'Report of the Inquiry into the Circumstances Surrounding the Death of Dr David Kelly C.M.G.', HC 247 2003/4.
132. Tshwane Principles, Principle 37.
133. Benjamin Buckland and Aidan Wills, 'Whistleblowing in the Security Sector', http://whistlenetwork.files.wordpress.com/2014/01/bucklandwills-chapter.pdf.
134. Venice Commission Report, 'Oversight of Security Services', 18.
135. UK Prime Minister Report to Parliament, 'A Strong Britain in an Age of Uncertainty: The National Security Strategy', October 2010 (Cm7953), 24, https://www.gov.uk/government/uploads/system/uploads/attachment_data/file/61936/national-security-strategy.pdf.
136. French Labour Code Article L 1161-1 found in Thad Guyer and Nikolas Peterson, 'The Current State of Whistleblower Law in Europe: A Report by the Government Accountability Project', 2013 American Bar Association Section of Labor & Employment Law International Labor & Employment Law Committee, 15, http://www.whistleblower.org/storage/documents/TheCurrentStateofWhistleblowerLawinEurope.pdf.
137. Mary-Rose Papandrea, 'The Publication of National Security Information in the Digital Age', *Journal of National Security Law and Policy* 5 (2011–2012): 199. See also, Yochai Benkler, 'A Free Irresponsible Press: Wikileaks and the Battle over the Soul of the Networked Fourth Estate', *Harvard Civil Rights – Civil Liberties Law Review* 46 (2011): 311.
138. Brian Martin, *Justice Ignited: The Dynamics of Backfire* (Lanham, MD: Rowman & Littlefield, 2007), 67.

Resisting accountability: transitional justice in the post-9/11 United States

Jonathan Hafetz

Seton Hall University School of Law, New Jersey, USA

The field of transitional justice has traditionally focused on accountability for human rights violations amid regime change, often accompanied by democratisation, rebuilding states and revitalising national communities. But concepts drawn from transitional justice can also shed light on the dynamics of accountability within the ordinary course of political change in a stable and mature democracy. This article utilises transitional justice as a heuristic to frame the post-9/11 United States' effort to confront torture and other grave human rights violations committed in the war on terrorism. The article concludes that not seeking accountability in the face of political opposition and resistance carries significant costs. Terrorism poses particular concerns for adherence to human rights, even in mature democracies, given the multiple pressures to sacrifice liberty for security. A state's failure to pursue accountability may mitigate political controversy and avoid straining the social fabric, particularly where responsibility for torture and other illegal conduct reaches the top echelons of government. But it also propagates a competing security-based narrative that legitimises exceptions to the categorical moral judgements on which a robust and effective human rights regime depends.

Introduction

After the Justice Department declined to pursue disciplinary measures against John Yoo and Jay Bybee, authors of the infamous 'torture memos', United States (US) Senator Richard J. Durbin remarked, 'Mr. Bybee and Mr. Yoo may keep their law licenses, but they will not escape the verdict of history'.[1] History will indeed be the final arbiter, if only because of the privileged place its judgements occupy on the temporal spectrum. But historical judgement is itself contingent, and is influenced by the measures that a state takes – or does not take – following the commission of serious human rights abuses.

How states respond to past abuses is a central focus of transitional justice. Ruti Teitel has defined transitional justice as 'the conception of justice associated with periods of political change, characterised by legal responses to confront the wrongdoing of repressive predecessor regimes'.[2] Others have described transitional justice in similar terms, focusing on the legal, political and moral challenges in addressing past violence.[3] Responses to past violence or repression may include criminal prosecutions or a range of alternatives, from truth commissions to lustration programmes.[4] For this reason, transitional justice has also been described more broadly to encompass a range of 'particularized bargains on the past'.[5]

Transitional justice is generally associated with regime change, typically when accompanied by democratisation, the rebuilding of states and reconstituting of national communities, often after a prolonged period of armed conflict. But it has also been used as a way to help understand accountability processes in stable, mature democracies, particularly where states commit grave human rights abuses in confronting terrorism or other threats to their security.[6] Using transitional justice as a heuristic for assessing the abuses committed by the US during the war on terrorism is particularly appropriate given President Obama's effort to characterise his administration in the language of change. As Obama signalled from his inauguration, his administration would constitute a new regime marked by adherence to the rule of law and human rights, thus breaking from a prior regime that had abandoned them.[7]

Resistance and contestation, moreover, remain an important part of any transitional justice process. Efforts to grapple seriously with past abuses can trigger intense opposition within a state. Even accountability mechanisms that do not involve criminal liability still demand confrontation with the past, apportion blame and stigmatise. Resistance, in turn, can shape the form and direction of transitional justice. Opposition to criminal prosecution, for example, may channel the focus towards other accountability mechanisms, such as truth and reconciliation commissions, national commissions of inquiry or victim compensation schemes. Opposition may also divert the focus from any formal mechanism altogether and instead lead states to confront the past through the political process.

The post-9/11 US provides a window into how resistance and contestation can shape accountability during a period of political transition in a mature democracy. The US experienced fierce opposition to any formal inquiry into abuses committed by the Bush administration during the war on terrorism. This resistance, moreover, long pre-dated the transition to a new administration, when accountability first became possible. Anticipating possible future criminal prosecution, Bush administration officials engaged in *ex ante* resistance by seeking to immunise themselves from liability for torture and other war crimes. This resistance intensified after President Obama's election, and ultimately helped sway the Obama administration against seeking accountability for past crimes, whether through criminal prosecutions, a commission of inquiry, or some other instrument.

This article frames the US response to abuses committed after 9/11 from the perspective of transitional justice. In particular, it examines how a process of resistance and contestation has shaped the US response to abuses committed under a prior administration in the name of national security. It explains how resistance to accountability drove efforts to legitimise torture and other severe mistreatment through Justice Department legal memoranda and to immunise public officials after the fact through enactment of legislation. It also explores how this resistance continued during the Obama administration, manifesting itself in the political process, judicial decisions and public discourse. The absence of criminal prosecutions or other formal processes like a truth and reconciliation commission has driven the accountability debate elsewhere, including over the public release of the Senate Select Committee on Intelligence's 6300-page report into the CIA torture programme[8] and the professional advancement of individuals associated with the programme.[9] The Senate committee's recent release of the 528-page executive summary of that report – the most comprehensive inquiry into the CIA torture programme to date – represents an important step towards confronting the past by detailing the depth, systematic nature and sheer brutality of the abuses committed in connection with the detention and interrogation of terrorism suspects, as well as the efforts to conceal the programme.[10] But the report also highlights the continuing absence of any process to hold individuals responsible – an accounting without accountability.

The article concludes that the failure to pursue accountability in the face of resistance carries significant costs. Allowing past crimes to be dealt with through the regular operation of the democratic process may mitigate political controversy and minimise strain on the social fabric, particularly where responsibility for those crimes reaches the top echelons of a government, as in the post-9/11 US. But the US example also shows how resistance to accountability helps propagate a competing narrative surrounding torture that legitimises utilitarian arguments, undermines categorical moral judgements and perpetuates a national security exceptionalism. This resistance has placed in contention not only the meaning of the past, but also the future protection of human rights.

1. The US post-9/11 torture programme

The US' use of torture after 9/11 has been widely explored and extensively documented.[11] Even before the release of the Senate report, litigation under the Freedom of Information Act (FOIA), leaks by government officials, congressional inquiries and political and public pressure had together helped pry open many of the details surrounding the US mistreatment of terrorism suspects at Guantanamo, Bagram in Afghanistan, Iraq and secret CIA-run 'black sites'. Non-government organisations have compiled detailed reports examining the torture programme,[12] including a comprehensive report by a blue ribbon panel of outside experts.[13] Some information still has not been disclosed, including the remainder of the Senate's report into the CIA torture programme. There is, however, extensive evidence in the public record regarding the government's use of harsh interrogation methods, including waterboarding, stress positions, sleep deprivation, prolonged isolation and acute sensory deprivation. These methods – euphemistically labelled enhanced interrogation techniques (EITs) – violated the US' obligation under domestic and international law not to engage in torture or other cruel, inhuman or degrading treatment, and could have provided the basis for domestic criminal prosecution under the federal anti-torture statute or the War Crimes Act. The lack of prosecutions is thus due not primarily to an informational gap, but rather to a failure to take action in the face of resistance. As Jameel Jaffer has explained in the context of government efforts to suppress information about detainee abuse in judicial proceedings, the facts surrounding the torture programme are well known; the main problem is the failure to hold those responsible accountable.[14]

The resistance to accountability dates to the torture programme's inception. The programme took shape in the months after 9/11 in response to the prospect of future criminal liability under a successor administration and in the shadow of global trends in transitional justice since the 1980s that had exposed even high-level officials to prosecution in their own countries or before international tribunals.[15] Indeed, the US' approach to al-Qaeda after 9/11 may itself be understood as a product of these forces of resistance, as the Bush administration defined both the armed conflict and the enemy in a way that not only facilitated harsh interrogation practices (as the 'gloves came off', in the words of former CIA counter-terrorism chief Cofer Black),[16] but also sought to insulate officials from future liability.

Early on, Bush administration officials took the position that al-Qaeda and Taliban members, as unlawful enemy combatants, were not covered by the Geneva Conventions, including the minimal protections of Common Article 3.[17] International criminal jurisprudence had defined the scope of armed conflict broadly to extend basic humanitarian protections and provide the nexus necessary for war crimes prosecutions of those who denied those protections.[18] The Bush administration sought to define the conflict broadly not to extend, but rather to circumvent, the protections of international humanitarian law to individuals in its custody. It defined both the enemy and the armed conflict in such a way that would allow for the military treatment of terrorism suspects – and thus treatment outside the safeguards of the civilian justice system – while insulating officials from prosecution under the War Crimes Act, which criminalised grave breaches of the Geneva Conventions, including any breach of Common Article 3.[19] Those prohibitions, the administration argued, did not apply since war-on-terrorism detainees fell outside the Geneva Conventions. Additionally, the administration held detainees incommunicado at offshore prisons, from CIA black sites to Guantanamo, to maintain secrecy and avoid court review, thus reducing the risk of inquiries into the legality of its actions.

The Bush administration also acted to preclude future prosecution under the US anti-torture statute. Enacted to implement the US' obligations under the United Nations (UN) Convention against Torture (CAT), the statute prohibits torture committed by any US official outside the US.[20] It thus necessarily covered the treatment of post-9/11 terrorism suspects even if, as the administration argued, they fell outside the scope of the Geneva Conventions and War Crimes Act. The CAT contains no exceptions, barring torture under all circumstances, including war or times of emergency.[21] In August 2002, the Justice Department's Office of Legal Counsel (OLC) drafted a memorandum in response to a request for permission to apply a series of EITs to Abu Zubaydah, an al-Qaeda suspect who was then being held at a secret CIA black site overseas and from whom CIA officials believed they could obtain more information through waterboarding and other EITs. The memo defined torture in absurdly narrow terms (asserting that it must cause pain akin to that accompanying 'death, organ failure, or permanent damage resulting in the loss of significant bodily functions'); asserted that the president could override a congressional prohibition on torture through the exercise of his commander-in-chief authority under Article II of the US Constitution; maintained that officials could be liable only if their specific intent was to cause pain, and not if their intent was to obtain information through techniques that caused pain; and asserted that interrogators could invoke a broadly defined good-faith or necessity defence based on the generalised threat to the nation posed by terrorism.[22] The memo helped create what David Luban has called a 'torture culture' within the executive branch of the US government, and facilitated the use of waterboarding and other unlawful interrogation methods.[23] Its approach to presidential war powers, human rights and national security all demonstrate a resistance to accountability – an effort to preclude future criminal liability through legal rationales that afforded a 'golden shield' to interrogators.[24]

The same pattern of articulating legal positions to thwart future liability continued throughout the Bush administration. Each new revelation about the torture programme and ensuing call for investigation was met with opposition, as the programme was defended to ensure its continued viability and to maintain a bulwark against future liability. After the CIA Inspector General report found that waterboarding had been used in ways not approved by the August 2002 memo, Jack Goldsmith, then the head of the OLC, suspended authorisation for waterboarding. Goldsmith, however, did not suspend approval for any other techniques, and a subsequent 2004 OLC memo, signed by Dan Levin, Goldsmith's successor, secretly authorised the CIA to continue using the same techniques Yoo and Bybee had originally approved.[25]

In response to growing public pressure over revelations of detainee abuse, Congress subsequently enacted the Detainee Treatment Act of 2005 (DTA), prohibiting the use of torture and other cruel, inhuman and degrading treatment against any person in US custody.[26] The DTA was meant to close a perceived gap in US detention policy by clarifying that the prohibition on cruel, inhuman and degrading treatment in the CAT both applied extraterritorially and covered all individuals in US custody, including those held by the CIA. But even before the DTA's passage, the OLC had drafted additional secret memoranda concluding that US war-on-terrorism interrogation methods did not constitute cruel, inhuman or degrading treatment.[27] The memos went so far as to claim that the techniques approved in the August 2002 memo – including when those techniques were used in combination (as they had been) – did not constitute either torture or cruel, inhuman or degrading treatment. The memos sought not only to permit the CIA to continue to engage in interrogation techniques approved after 9/11, but also to shore up protections against liability in a successor administration. Indeed, since the Bush administration had by then ceased using a number of EITs, including waterboarding, these later OLC memos' central purpose may be regarded as preventing against liability for past conduct rather than facilitating future action.

Supreme Court decisions aimed at protecting detainee rights encountered similar resistance. In 2006, the Supreme Court held in *Hamdan* v. *Rumsfeld* that Common Article 3 of the Geneva Conventions applied to all detainees in US custody regardless of how the armed conflict against al-Qaeda was defined.[28] While best known for invalidating the military commissions President Bush had created after 9/11 without congressional authorisation, *Hamdan*'s most significant long-term impact was on detainee treatment. By rejecting the Bush administration's argument that war-on-terrorism detainees fell outside the scope of the Geneva Conventions, the decision opened the door to future prosecutions under the War Crimes Act for violations of Common Article 3, particularly since that provision barred not only torture, but also the type of cruel or degrading treatment prevalent at Guantanamo, Bagram and CIA black sites. But the Bush administration quickly ensured *Hamdan* would not become a launching pad for a future accountability process. Under intense pressure from the Bush administration, Congress agreed in the Military Commissions Act of 2006 (2006 MCA), enacted four months after the *Hamdan* ruling, to immunise those involved in war-on-terrorism interrogations by redefining grave breaches of the Geneva Conventions.[29] The 2006 MCA not only codified the administration's narrow definition of torture, but also excluded degrading and humiliating treatment from the ambit of war crimes subject to prosecution in a US court. The 2006 MCA provided the functional equivalent of amnesty legislation and created an additional barrier to the imposition of criminal responsibility by a future administration.

Arguments by administration lawyers designed to immunise interrogators also laid the groundwork for efforts to sell torture to the public. Aggressive interrogations were characterised as necessary to protect the country from a future terrorist attack. Senior administration officials, meanwhile, continued to resist defining even the most abusive interrogation practices as torture. At his confirmation hearing following his nomination for Attorney General, Michael B. Mukasey, formerly a federal district judge, refused to say definitively whether waterboarding constituted torture.[30] Mary Jo White, the former US Attorney for the Southern District of New York, concurred, stating in an op-ed that the answer to the question posed to Mukasey was 'not so clear and simple'.[31] White's remarks suggest how deeply embedded resistance to criminal liability had become within the legal culture and the strength of corresponding attempts to legitimate torture in the public sphere.

This resistance shaped torture's depiction in popular culture. A notable example is the television show *24*, whose hero, counter-terrorism agent Jack Bauer, prevents one terrorist attack after another by brutalising suspects to gain valuable, time-sensitive information. The show helped popularise and legitimise the 'ticking-time bomb' scenario that served as a primary rationale for the torture programme. It provided a graphic depiction of the torture memos' central thesis: that when it comes to preventing terrorism, government officials cannot be constrained by legality. The show, moreover, reflected a broader shift: not only did depictions of torture on prime-time television increase substantially after 9/11, but the identity of the torturer also changed. Torture increasingly was depicted as something perpetrated by the heroes, and not by the villains.[32] Moral determinations followed inexorably from legal conclusions: once effectively decriminalised, torture became a virtue, or, at minimum, a defensible position within a liberal democratic state threatened by terrorists groups bent on its destruction and demise. Polls reflect this shift, suggesting that the number of Americans who support torturing suspected terrorists increased after the first revelations of the US torture programme.[33]

2. Change without accountability: torture and the Obama administration

President Obama made the elimination of torture a high priority of his first term. On his second day in office, Obama issued an executive order banning torture and ordering the closure of any remaining secret CIA prisons, where the most abusive interrogation practices, including waterboarding, had occurred.[34] Obama required that all interrogations – including those by the CIA – adhere to the US Army Field Manual and Common Article 3. Obama revoked President Bush's prior 2007 executive order narrowly construing US obligations under Common Article 3 and repudiated the Bush administration OLC's torture memos.[35] In a separate order, Obama directed the closure of the US detention centre at Guantanamo – the most prominent site of detainee abuse – promising to return America to the 'moral high ground' in the fight against terrorism.[36]

More broadly, Obama took aim at the rationale of torture advanced after 9/11: that it was necessary to protect the US from the threat posed by al-Qaeda and other terrorist groups. Obama maintained that torture not only was inconsistent with America's values, but also undermined its security.[37] Brutal interrogation methods, he insisted, were ineffective, while serving as a recruitment tool for terrorists and eroding support for the US among its allies. Obama thus placed the power and prestige of the Oval Office behind stopping torture and defining human rights and security as complimentary, not competing, interests. His administration would mark a new beginning in the fight against terrorism.

Obama, meanwhile, studiously avoided pursuing accountability for the abuses committed under his predecessor. Shortly before taking office, Obama famously remarked that the US must 'look forward, as opposed to looking backwards'.[38] Re-litigation of past controversies over interrogation practices, he said, would be both politically divisive and unnecessary. After President Obama released redacted versions of the OLC torture memos to the public, he called for 'reflection, not retribution', saying that 'nothing will be gained by spending our time and energy laying blame for the past'.[39] Obama was always careful to define torture as wrong, even contrary to the rule of law, but not criminal. To the contrary, he coupled any moves towards greater transparency, such as the release of the OLC memos, with assurances that he would not seek to prosecute those who adhered to the torture programme's legal guidelines. In his more recent remarks surrounding the expected release of the Senate report on CIA interrogations, Obama acknowledged that the US had 'crossed a line' and 'done some things that were wrong' when it engaged in torture. But while he said that the US must acknowledge responsibility for its actions, he continued to exclude any form of accountability and underscored the extraordinary pressure US officials were under to protect the country's security after 9/11.[40] And after the report's release, Obama warned not to 'refight old arguments', while praising intelligence agents as 'patriots', even as he acknowledged that the harsh interrogation methods they had used were contrary both to the country's values and security interests.[41]

Attorney General Holder had previously opened a preliminary inquiry into the US interrogation of detainees at several unspecified overseas locations, noting his 'duty to examine the facts and follow the law'.[42] But Holder limited the criminal investigation to cases where interrogation officials failed to act 'in good-faith and within the scope of the legal guidance' provided by the OLC memoranda, thus cordoning off the torture programme – and its architects – from possible liability.[43] Even this limited investigation prompted opposition, with former Vice President Cheney labelling it as 'clearly a political move',[44] and former CIA directors warning, in a letter to President Obama, that the investigation threatened national security and the safety of CIA agents.[45] In June 2011, Holder announced that of the more than 100 prisoners whose treatment had been reviewed in connection with this inquiry, only two cases remained under investigation (one involved a prisoner's death in Afghanistan, the other a prisoner's death in Iraq).[46] The following year, Holder announced the closure of the investigation, stating that no prosecutions would be brought.[47] As a result, the only person prosecuted in connection with the CIA torture programme was former CIA agent John Kiriakou, who had disclosed the identity of other agents who participated in harsh interrogations, including waterboarding, which he labelled torture in an interview on ABC News.[48] These decisions together sent the message that those who revealed information about a secret torture programme would be subject to punishment, while those who planned, authorised and engaged in torture would be exempt from it.

Politicians and members of the intelligence community welcomed the administration's decision not to pursue criminal liability and to focus on a transition without justice. Mike Rogers, the chairman of the House Intelligence Committee, praised Holder's decision not to pursue criminal charges, which he said would allow intelligence officers to focus on protecting the nation's security.[49] Even former CIA director David H. Petraeus, who had publicly spoken out against the past use of harsh interrogation methods, emphasised the need for intelligence officers 'to look ahead to the challenges of the future rather than backwards at those of the past'.[50]

Obama also opposed other forms of accountability besides criminal prosecution. He resisted calls for a national commission of inquiry or any other variant of the truth commissions that have become prominent features of transitional justice.[51] Obama, moreover, sought dismissal of civil suits seeking remedies for CIA rendition and torture, arguing that state secrets and related national security concerns should prevent such suits from going forward in federal court.[52] He likewise sought dismissal of suits challenging the military's mistreatment of enemy combatants.[53]

Obama, to be sure, promised more restrictive use of the state secrets privilege than his predecessor. In issuing new guidelines, Holder announced that the Justice Department would not invoke the privilege to conceal violations of the law or prevent embarrassment.[54] The new guidelines should have allowed for some accountability process to unfold in the courts through civil litigation by victims of torture and other mistreatment. But the Obama administration continued to wield the privilege in the same sweeping manner as the Bush administration. Judges largely agreed, citing the risks civil litigation posed to national security and dismissing suits without ruling on the merits of any claims.[55] Resisting litigation through state secrets and related doctrines did not simply prevent victims from obtaining a remedy, it also helped legitimise torture by deeming the legality of the government's interrogation methods an unfit subject for judicial examination. Torture was not only effectively decriminalised, it was also rendered non-justiciable.

Resistance to accountability also helped limit an internal ethics investigation of Yoo and Bybee in connection with their drafting of the torture memos. In 2010, the Justice Department's Office of Professional Responsibility (OPR) concluded that Yoo had committed 'intentional professional misconduct' by placing his desire to accommodate his client above his duty to provide 'thorough, objective, and candid legal advice', and that Bybee had acted in 'reckless disregard' of the same professional duty.[56] This finding could have served as a basis for referring Yoo and Bybee to their respective state bar associations for disciplinary proceedings. However, a senior Justice Department official, David Margolis, overruled the opinion. Margolis recognised that Yoo and Bybee had exercised 'poor judgment', but he maintained that they did not commit professional misconduct because they did not knowingly provide false advice.[57] Margolis, furthermore, emphasised the difficult circumstances under which Yoo and Bybee operated after 9/11, implicitly validating the torture memos' underlying theory that exigent circumstances warrant exceptional – and otherwise impermissible – measures. Yoo and Bybee thus avoided any sanction. Even the OPR report, which had recommended bar disciplinary proceedings, failed to address the critical question of whether the conduct the memos authorised was illegal.

The *de facto* decriminalisation of torture bolstered various actors and institutions engaged in resisting accountability. Architects and proponents of the torture programme treated each failed opportunity to seek criminal liability, civil sanctions or an official determination of professional misconduct as a vindication of their legal theories. Yoo, for example, publicly applauded an appeals court dismissal of former enemy combatant Jose Padilla's civil suit against him for his role in approving the mistreatment he endured while detained in military custody in South Carolina as an enemy combatant.[58] Yoo invoked the decision to justify Padilla's treatment, which included allegations of threats of death and serious physical abuse, exposure to extreme temperatures and the use of painful stress positions during Padilla's 21 months of incommunicado detention. He further used the ruling to attack advocacy groups for their efforts to pursue accountability, which he said undermined national security by causing officials to become 'risk averse and paralyzed by uncertainty – the very attitudes that allowed the 9/11 attacks to succeed'.[59] These counter-attacks sought not only to legitimise torture in the public eye, but also to delegitimise the premise of accountability.

Yoo even treated the OPR report as a vindication. In an op-ed entitled, 'My Gift to the Obama Presidency', Yoo asserted that the president should show his appreciation for 'winning a drawn-out fight to protect his powers as commander in chief to wage war and keep Americans safe'.[60] In another op-ed, Yoo labelled the OPR's decision not to refer him for bar discipline 'a victory for the people fighting the war on terror'.[61] Yoo's opportunistic characterisation of the OPR report is surely overstated given the report's harsh criticism of his judgement and legal advice. But Yoo was able to spin the report as a victory and vindication only because the Justice Department neither pursued any formal sanctions nor labelled the interrogation methods he had approved illegal. The accountability gap thus helped Yoo characterise his conduct as that of a well-intentioned public official who at worst had acted too zealously to protect his country at a time of great fear and uncertainty, but who had done nothing wrong, let alone illegal.

The resistance continued even after the Senate report laid bare the gross and systemic mistreatment of detainees. The minority report issued by Republican members of the Senate committee supplied an alternative narrative, attacking the findings of the majority report and claiming that the CIA detention and interrogation programme 'saved lives and played a vital role in weakening Al Qaeda'.[62] Former senior Bush administration officials took to the airwaves, publicly defending the programme's effectiveness and criticising the

Senate report as a partisan attack.[63] Former Vice President Dick Cheney boasted on Meet the Press that he would 'do the same thing again in a minute'.[64] Former officials also established a new website to defend the CIA programme.[65] The CIA's current director, John Brennan, also challenged the conclusions of the Senate report, although he acknowledged that it was 'unknowable' whether the information could have been obtained through other, non-coercive methods.[66] Brennan, moreover, provided no assurances that the government would be prevented from authorising the same techniques again, deferring to 'the policy makers in future times'.[67] The Fact Sheet posted to the agencies acknowledged serious mistakes in the implementation of the detention and interrogation programme, but maintained that the programme yielded valuable information and treated its shortcomings largely as a failure of management and internal oversight.[68] Largely lost in the duelling media accounts over the Senate report was the notion of torture's illegality.

The Obama administration's desire to focus exclusively on prospective change can be traced to a process of resistance that began at the outset of the Bush administration, which had created, defined and defended the post-9/11 torture programme precisely to prevent accountability. This resistance not only erected legal barriers to accountability, but also helped lay the groundwork for later opposition. It made it easier, in short, for the Obama administration to pursue a transition without justice even in the face of mounting evidence of past illegality.

3. The dynamics of resistance and accountability in the context of political transition

The post-9/11 US offers several insights into the dynamics surrounding accountability during a political transition in a mature democratic state. It highlights the way in which resistance and contestation can frame the terms of the debate and affect public attitudes over torture and other human rights violations committed in combating terrorism and other security threats. It also demonstrates the potential limitations of relying on electoral shifts and prospective policy reforms without instituting any accountability mechanism for illegal activity under a preceding administration. While a comprehensive factual investigation like the Senate report can serve as an important component of a larger accountability process, it has inherent limitations and, when unaccompanied by any process to hold individuals legally responsible for torture, can undermine the force of legal prohibition itself.

The political and legal tug-of-war over the US torture programme underscores that accountability is not merely contested, but also exerts a powerful impact on how torture is defined, practiced and marketed to the public. Resistance is not simply an *ex post* phenomenon that emerges in response to efforts by a successor government to initiate a criminal investigation, national commission or other accountability mechanism. Resistance instead can take root before the human rights violations occur as well as while they are occurring. This is particularly true in an advanced, stable democracy like the US, with a well-functioning legal system, independent judiciary and professed commitment to the rule of law. The political culture in such countries increases the prospect of a legalistic response to torture and thus creates an incentive for proponents of torture to operationalise resistance *ex ante*, before any accountability mechanism can materialise, through a process of de-legalisation and legitimation. The torture memos served this function after 9/11. They not only sought to decriminalise torture and other abusive interrogation methods by redefining federal law, distorting international law and articulating theories of broad, if not unlimited, executive power. They also provided a good-faith defence to anyone who might be prosecuted in the future by allowing them to rely on the legal advice provided by the Justice Department.

The post-9/11 US highlights how resistance to accountability during political transition can render rights contingent, even where the underlying norms are categorical in nature, such as the prohibition against torture. In the US, resistance effectively created an exemption to this prohibition, as torture was sanctioned through a combination of legal theories that sought to place a broadly defined armed conflict beyond even the most minimal constraints of international humanitarian law and to gut the definition of torture itself.

As many scholars have observed, transitional justice is not an abstract construct but must be understood in its particular political, social and historical context.[69] The society undergoing change must, as Jon Elster observes, weigh the desire for a peaceful transition with the goal of accountability for past crimes.[70] Accountability can facilitate a transition from political repression or internal armed conflict. But it also can risk derailing progress towards peace and reconciliation, even triggering renewed violence. Each society must therefore assess the particular trade-offs of pursuing transitional justice and consider what Paul Horwitz terms the 'costs of settlement'.[71]

Stable democracies with strong legal institutions should be most capable of absorbing the type of resistance that often accompanies transitional justice. In the US, for example, criminal prosecutions might have triggered bitter political fighting and possibly unleashed a cycle of political retaliation that continued into future administrations. They also could have led to 'patriotic acquittals' by juries unwilling to convict intelligence personnel, thereby legitimating torture when done in defence of national security.[72] But there was little risk that criminal prosecutions would have sparked the type of social conflict or unrest that is often cited as a reason not to hold prior officials accountable for human rights violations. Even if the Obama administration had pursued a full criminal investigation of high-ranking Bush administration officials, it would unlikely have triggered violence or otherwise threatened the social fabric, even if it exacted significant political costs. Obama could also have pursued alternatives to criminal prosecution, such as the bipartisan commission Senator Patrick Leahy (D-VT) had proposed modelled on South Africa's Truth and Reconciliation Commission,[73] although it would have been important to couple fact-finding with a mechanism for reaffirming torture's illegality. (South Africa's commission, for example, conditioned amnesty from criminal liability on confessions of wrongdoing and, therefore, depended on the possibility of prosecution.)[74] Reparations, including compensation to victims and rehabilitation, would have supplied another form of accountability for violations of international humanitarian and international human rights law.[75]

Obama, however, ultimately decided against pursuing any such path. Accountability for torture and under human rights violations by the prior regime was sacrificed not for the larger goals of preserving peace after internal armed conflict or shoring up democracy after years of repression, but rather for the more prosaic goal of enabling the president to pursue his larger domestic agenda and to avoid antagonising intelligence agencies and the larger national security apparatus.[76] Resistance had raised the costs of accountability to a sufficient level that it caused the successor administration to, as it put it, look forward not backwards.

Advocacy organisations, to be sure, continue to pressure the Obama administration. Leading human rights organisations have repeatedly pressed for a full criminal investigation.[77] Other groups have demanded a national commission of inquiry, which could not only verify facts, but also assess individual complicity in the torture programme and allocate responsibility.[78]

But despite aggressive public campaigns, these groups have yet to gain significant traction for accountability among the broader public. While this failure is due partly to the strength of forces resisting accountability, it also reflects the marginalisation and otherness of the victims themselves. US interrogation techniques were carried out on a relatively small number of individuals; nearly all were foreign nationals and many were accused of engaging in or supporting terrorism, even if, in a significant number of instances, those suspicions were unfounded.[79] The US post-9/11 torture programme thus did not directly affect a substantial segment of the US population – in contrast, for example, to the abuses committed during the dirty wars in Latin America during the 1970s and 1980s.

In Latin America, human rights violations were directed primarily against an individual state's own population and, consequently, created political and social pressure to confront the past as a means of moving beyond a continuing cycle of conflict and repression.[80] To be sure, the main victims of state repression in some Latin American countries, such as Peru and Guatemala, were the historically excluded segments of society (the poor, rural and indigenous) whom the more educated middle and upper classes did not necessarily see as endowed with rights or worthy of redress.[81] But even in those countries, the scale of the abuses helped sow the seeds for grass-roots pressure for accountability.

A number of Latin American countries also underwent significant regime change, from brutal dictatorship to democracy, and not, as in the US, a democratic transition between administrations. Regime change created a rupture with the past that provided space and momentum for accountability. Countries with pacted transitions negotiated between an outgoing nondemocratic regime and opposition groups forming the incoming democratic government that left the military largely intact, such as Brazil and Uruguay, were less likely to have human rights prosecutions in the immediate aftermath of a transition than countries that experienced rupture, such as Argentina, where the military suffered defeat.[82] Regime change necessarily carried risks of renewed violence and unrest in all countries. Those risks – and the perceived need to prioritise a peaceful transition – prompted a number of countries in Latin America to initially favour truth commissions over prosecutions[83] and to adopt a pragmatic approach that, in the words of Chilean truth commissioner José Zalaquett, sought justice 'within the realm of the possible'.[84] Over time, the increased stability of democratic institutions, external pressure from the inter-American human rights system, and global shifts in norms favouring accountability has helped lead to human rights prosecutions in some, but not all, of the countries in the region.[85] Despite the weakness of Latin American judiciaries, the general lack of political will to hold individuals accountable for their crimes, and a perception among many that trials would undermine the opportunity for reconciliation, Latin America has helped pioneer the use of domestic courts to prosecute past human rights violations.[86]

This comparison highlights a central paradox of the US' approach to accountability: if the stability of the US political system made it more capable of pursuing criminal charges against former officials who committed torture and other grave human rights violations, the vast gulf between the domestic population and the victims of the US torture programme and the absence of regime change lessened the pressure to do so.

4. The consequences of the failure to seek accountability

The failure of the US to pursue accountability has several consequences. It has helped transform torture into a competing policy choice about which reasonable people may differ and made the rule of law itself 'just another policy preference', as Elaine Scarry has observed.[87] Torture's effective decriminalisation has also created a space in the public domain for utilitarian arguments that tie torture's legitimacy to its purported efficacy in enhancing security. It has, for example, made it possible to defend the CIA's torture programme by claiming that it produced valuable intelligence that helped prevent a future terrorist attack, as the programme's defenders have continued to do even in the face of contrary evidence in the Senate report. While those assertions could still have been made, if prosecutions had been brought, they would have been defences to charges of illegality, and not competing policy options. Evidence of torture's ineffectiveness can help bolster public support for the legal prohibition against torture. But the public will remain vulnerable to pro-torture arguments as long as they can be supported by contrary claims about torture's efficacy – claims, moreover, that can be difficult to debunk given the state's proclivity towards over-classification and secrecy.

The absence of any criminal prosecution or other accountability mechanism has emboldened proponents of the torture programme. After Bush left office, for example, he admitted personally authorising the waterboarding of terrorism suspects, which he justified as necessary to protect the nation's security.[88] Bush, moreover, denied waterboarding was illegal, citing the advice provided by his lawyers.[89] Dick Cheney, the former vice-president, publicly declared that EITs produced 'phenomenal' results, claiming that the US would not have been able to track down Osama bin Laden without them.[90] Cheney also labelled the Obama administration's limited investigations into the use of those techniques as 'objectionable' and a 'terrible precedent'[91] – a point he made from the beginning of Obama's presidency to underscore the high political costs that accountability would entail[92] and one he maintained after release of the Senate's torture report.[93] Marc Thiessen, a former Bush speechwriter, similarly asserted that waterboarding was not only useful but also morally sound.[94] These defences helped erode a sense of moral and legal clarity surrounding torture in the US.

The absence of accountability has also facilitated what Marita Sturken has described as the 'mediation of torture' – the process by which torture is made acceptable in American culture.[95] It allows the public to remain agnostic about, if not accepting of, torture, while also permitting the ideal of American exceptionalism to persist. If criminal prosecutions had been pursued, it would have made it more difficult for the US to maintain these conflicting notions. Torture's de-legalisation has helped sustain the idea that democratic states may engage in human rights violations – even of peremptory norms – when necessary to protect themselves against terrorism or other threats to their security.

Some would nevertheless argue that for nations such as the US, with mature, functioning political systems, elections and stable transitions can provide for accountability.[96] Torture, extraordinary rendition and Guantanamo, all played an important role in the 2008 presidential election, which served partly as a referendum on President Bush's war-on-terrorism policies. Obama's victory may thus be seen as a repudiation of those policies and an illustration of how the democratic process itself can provide a form of accountability. Moreover, the policies instituted following Obama's election – particularly the withdrawal of the Bush administration OLC torture memos and the issuance of new executive orders closing secret CIA prisons and banning torture – provide further evidence of how the democratic process can respond to torture in the absence of criminal prosecutions. If torture has been publicly disavowed and halted through the ordinary political process, some have asked, might that not diminish the need for prosecutions or other formal accountability mechanisms?[97]

One problem with this argument is that the changes to interrogation policy made by President Obama remain vulnerable. Pursuing criminal prosecutions or establishing a national commission will not necessarily prevent a future reversal. But a formal judgement or determination – detailing how officials engaged in torture *and*, in doing so, violated the law –

would have made it more difficult for an administration to change course in the future. The absence of any such determination makes it easier for proponents of the torture programme to reinstitute past interrogation practices, which have never been formally declared illegal and which they can continue to characterise as legitimate policy options. Even after release of the Senate report, polling suggested that a majority of Americans believe the harsh interrogation tactics used on terrorism suspects after 9/11 were justified, even though approximately half the population acknowledges that the treatment amounted to torture.[98]

Another problem is that public disavowal of past torture fails to satisfy the US' international obligations. The CAT requires states to conduct a meaningful and effective investigation into allegations of torture and, where appropriate, to prosecute the perpetrators.[99] The CAT has also been interpreted to prohibit amnesties for torture.[100] The US recently went to great lengths to demonstrate its commitment to the CAT to the Committee against Torture, the body that oversees compliance with the treaty, by acknowledging that the prohibition against torture and other cruel, inhuman or degrading treatment applies extraterritorially and at all times, including during armed conflict.[101] The US' continued refusal to open a full criminal investigation in light of the Senate report not only undermines its professed commitment to the treaty, but also weakens the force of the CAT's prohibition against torture.

The US position similarly undermines the protection of rights guaranteed under the International Covenant on Civil and Political Rights (ICCPR) and regional human rights treaties. While these treaties do not include an express obligation to prosecute, they do include language regarding the right to a remedy or duty of states to ensure the protection of the rights they guarantee.[102] This language has been interpreted to include an obligation to investigate and, where appropriate, prosecute acts of torture.[103]

The potential frailty of an electoral-process-based accountability model was displayed during the 2012 election, when Republican candidate Mitt Romney offered a preview of what interrogation policy might look like under his administration. According to an internal Romney campaign memorandum, Romney's advisers privately urged him to 'rescind and replace' President Obama's executive order on interrogations and permit secret 'enhanced interrogation techniques against high-value detainees that are safe, legal and effective in generating intelligence to save American lives'.[104] Whether Romney would have acted on this advice will never be known. But the fact that his advisers were able to advocate so freely for a return to the torture programme underscores the potential vulnerability of changes unaccompanied by an accountability process designed to constrain future decision-making.

It is possible, of course, that political winds and public sentiment may shift. The Senate report has generated renewed pressure for criminal prosecutions. It is also possible that the present approach – which combines reinforcing the barriers to torture's future use (e.g., Obama's executive orders) with evidence of its use in the past (e.g., the Senate report) will be sufficient to prevent its reoccurrence. But merely making more information available, without also pursuing accountability, risks making torture into a competing policy option. And a future president could revise those executive orders. More broadly, failing to pursue accountability underscores the politically contingent nature of human rights obligations, which may be sacrificed in the name of national security and transgressed without legal consequence.

Conclusion

The post-9/11 US provides important insights into the obstacles to accountability for past human rights violations committed in the name of national security. It illustrates how resistance to accountability can take root and spread in a stable, advanced democratic society. It demonstrates, for example, how proponents of torture will anticipate the possibility of a transitional justice paradigm and reshape the legal framework *ex ante* to minimise the risk of liability down the road. It also suggests how a nascent opposition to any future accountability process can effectively decriminalise categorical norms and reframe the terms and direction of the public debate, even in a society with a long rule-of-law tradition and stable and sophisticated legal system. The experience of the US following 9/11 further highlights the problems associated with the decision by a new administration to engage in prospective change without instituting any effective measures to address the crimes of the past.

Disclosure statement
No potential conflict of interest was reported by the author.

Notes on contributor
Jonathan Hafetz is Associate Professor of Law, Seton Hall University School of Law and Visiting Associate Research Scholar, Princeton University Law & Public Affairs Program, 2014–2015.

Notes

1. Eric Lichtblau and Scott Shane, 'Report Faults 2 Authors of Bush Terror Memos', *New York Times*, 19 February 2010.
2. Ruti Teitel, 'Transitional Justice Genealogy', *Harvard Human Rights Journal* 16 (2003): 69.
3. Dustin N. Sharp, 'Addressing Economic Violence in Times of Transition: Toward a Positive-Peace Paradigm for Transitional Justice', *Fordham International Law Journal* 35 (2012): 786.
4. Martha Minow, *Between Vengeance and Forgiveness: Facing History after Genocide and Mass Violence* (Boston, MA: Beacon Press, 1998).
5. Christine Bell, 'Transitional Justice, Interdisciplinarity, and the State of the "Field" or "Non-Field"', *International Journal of Transitional Justice* 3 (2009): 15.
6. Nasser Hussain and Austin Sarat, 'Responding to Lawlessness: What Does the Rule of Law Require', in *When Governments Break the Law: The Rule of Law and the Prosecution of the Bush Administration* (New York: New York University Press, 2010), 20.
7. Linton Weeks, 'Obama Orders Guantanamo Bay Prison Closure', *NPR*, 22 January 2009, http://www.npr.org/templates/story/story.php?storyId=99728679.
8. Mark Mazzetti, 'Behind Clash Between C.I.A. and Congress, a Secret Report on Interrogations', *New York Times*, 7 March 2014; Mark Mazzetti and Scott Shane, 'Senate and C.I.A. Spar Over Secret Report on Interrogation Program', *New York Times*, 19 July 2013.
9. Mark Mazzetti, 'New Head of C.I.A.'s Clandestine Service Is Picked, as Acting Chief Is Passed Over', *New York Times*, 7 May 2013; Scott Shane, 'C.I.A.'s History Poses Hurdle for an Obama Nominee', *New York Times*, 6 March 2013.
10. Senate Select Committee on Intelligence, *Committee Study of the Central Intelligence Agency's Detention and Interrogation Program* (Executive Summary) (3 December 2014), http://www.washingtonpost.com/wp-srv/special/national/cia-interrogation-report/document/.
11. David Cole, ed., *Torture Memos: Rationalizing the Unthinkable* (New York: New Press, 2009); Jonathan Hafetz, *Habeas Corpus after 9/11: Confronting America's New Global Detention System* (New York: New York University Press, 2011); Joseph Margulies, *Guantanamo and the Abuse of Presidential Power* (New York: Simon & Schuster, 2006).
12. Larry Siems, *The Torture Report: What the Documents Say about America's Post-9/11 Torture Program* (New York: OR Books, 2012); Human Rights Watch, *Getting Away with Torture: The Bush Administration and the Mistreatment of Detainees* (New York: Human Rights Watch, 2011).

13. The Constitution Project, *The Report of the Constitution Project's Task Force on Detainee Treatment* (Washington, DC: The Constitution Project, 2013), http://detaineetaskforce.org/pdf/Full-Report.pdf.
14. Jameel Jaffer, 'Known Unknowns', *Harvard Civil Rights-Civil Liberties Law Review* 48 (2013): 457.
15. Kathryn Sikkink, *The Justice Cascade: How Human Rights Prosecutions are Changing World Politics* (New York: W.H. Norton & Co., 2011); Naomi Roht-Arriaza, *The Pinochet Effect: Transitional Justice in the Age of Human Rights* (Philadelphia: University of Pennsylvania Press, 2006).
16. Testimony of Cofer Black to Joint House and Senate Select Intelligence Committee, 26 September 2002, http://www.fas.org/irp/congress/2002_hr/092602black.html.
17. John Yoo and Robert J. Delahunty to William J. Haynes II, Memorandum: 'Application of Treaties and Laws to al Qaeda and Taliban Detainees', 9 January 2002, in Karen J. Greenberg and Joshua L. Dratel, eds, *The Torture Papers: The Road to Abu Ghraib* (New York: Cambridge University Press, 2005), 38–79; Jay S. Bybee to Alberto R. Gonzales and William J. Haynes, Memorandum: 'Application of Treaties and Laws to al Qaeda and Taliban Detainees', in Greenberg and Dratel, eds, *The Torture Papers*, 81–117.
18. *Tadic Appeal on Jurisdiction*, Case No. IT-94-1-AR72, 2 October 1995, 70.
19. War Crimes Act of 1996, Pub. L. No. 104-192, 110 Stat. 2104 (1996) (codified at 18 U.S.C. § 2441).
20. 18 U.S.C. §§ 2340, 2340A.
21. Convention against Torture and other Cruel, Inhuman and Degrading Treatment, art. 2, 10 December 1984, S. Treaty Doc. No. 100-20, 1465 U.N.T.S. 85.
22. Memorandum from Jay S. Bybee, Assistant Attorney General, Office of Legal Counsel to Alberto R. Gonzales, Counsel to the President, 1 August 2002, in Greenberg and Dratel, eds, *The Torture Papers*, 172–222.
23. David Luban, 'Liberalism, Torture, and the Ticking Time Bomb', in *The Torture Debate in America*, ed. J. Karen Greenberg (Cambridge: Cambridge University Press, 2006), 35–83.
24. Jack Goldsmith, *The Terror Presidency: Law and Judgment inside the Bush Administration* (New York: W.W. Norton, 2007), 144.
25. David Cole, 'The Taint of Torture: The Roles of Law and Policy in Our Descent to the Dark Side', *Houston Law Review* 49 (2012): 59.
26. Detainee Treatment Act of 2005, Pub. L. No. 109-148, § 1003, 119 Stat. 2739.
27. Scott Shane, David Johnston, and James Risen, 'Secret U.S. Endorsement of Severe Interrogations', *New York Times*, 4 October 2004.
28. *Hamdan* v. *Rumsfeld*, 548 U.S. 557 (2006).
29. Military Commissions Act of 2006, Pub. No. 109-366, § 6, 120 Stat. 2600, 2632–35 (2006).
30. Scott Shane and David Stout, 'White House Moves to Save Mukasey Nomination', *New York Times*, 1 November 2007.
31. Mary Jo White, 'No Easy Answers to al-Qaeda Threat', *USA Today*, 14 November 2007.
32. Jane Mayer, 'Whatever It Takes; The Politics of the Man Behind "24"', *New Yorker*, 19 February 2007.
33. Elisa Massimino, 'Leading by Example?: Torture Ten Years after 9/11', *Human Rights* 38 (Winter 2011): 21; Amy Zegart, 'Controversy Dims as Public Opinion Shifts', *New York Times*, 7 January 2013.
34. Executive Order No. 13,491, 74 Fed. Reg. 4893 (27 January 2009).
35. Ibid.
36. Executive Order No. 13,492, 74 Fed. Reg. 4897 (27 January 2009); 'Obama Signs Order to Close Guantanamo Bay Facility', *CNN.com*, 22 January 2009, http://www.cnn.com/2009/POLITICS/01/22/guantanamo.order/index.html?eref=rss_us.
37. President Barack Obama, 'Remarks by the President on National Security at the National Archives, Washington, D.C.' (21 May 2009), http://www.whitehouse.gov/the_press_office/Remarks-by-the-President-On-National-Security-5-21-09/.
38. George Stephanopoulos, 'Obama Leaves Door Open (a Bit) on Prosecuting Bush Officials', *ABC News*, 11 January 2009, http://abcnews.go.com/blogs/politics/2009/01/obama-leaves-do/.
39. Statement by President Obama on Release of OLC Memos, 16 April 2009.
40. The White House, Press Conference by the President, 1 August 2014, http://www.whitehouse.gov/the-press-office/2014/08/01/press-conference-president.

41. Statement by the President on the Report of the Senate Select Committee on Intelligence, 9 December 2014, http://www.whitehouse.gov/the-press-office/2014/12/09/statement-president-report-senate-select-committee-intelligence.
42. Press Release, US Department of Justice, 'Attorney General Eric Holder Regarding a Preliminary Review into Interrogation of Certain Detainees', 24 August 2009, http://www.justice.gov/ag/speeches/2009/ag-speech-0908241.html.
43. Ibid.
44. Rachel L. Swarns, 'Cheney Offers Sharp Defense of C.I.A. Tactics', *New York Times*, 31 August 2009.
45. Former CIA Directors' Letter to Obama, 18 September 2009, http://www.keepamericasafe.com/?page_id=221.
46. Scott Shane, 'No Charges Filed on Harsh Tactics Used by the C.I.A.', *New York Times*, 30 August 2012.
47. Press Release, Department of Justice, 'Statement of Attorney General Holder on Closure of Investigation into the Interrogation of Certain Detainees', 30 August 2012, http://www.justice.gov/opa/pr/2012/August/12-ag-1067.html.
48. Michael S. Schmidt, 'Ex-C.I.A. Officer Sentenced to 30 Months in Leak', *New York Times*, 25 January 2013.
49. Shane, 'No Charges Filed'.
50. Ibid.
51. Mark A. Drumbl, *Atrocity, Punishment, and International Law* (Cambridge: Cambridge University Press, 2007); Alex Boraine, *A Country Unmasked: Inside South Africa's Truth and Reconciliation Commission* (New York: Oxford University Press, 2000).
52. *Mohamed* v. *Jeppesen Dataplan, Inc.*, 614 F.3d 1070 (9th Cir. 2010) (en banc).
53. *Lebron* v. *Rumsfeld*, 670 F.3d 540, 550 (4th Cir. 2012); *Ali* v. *Rumsfeld*, 649 F.3d 762 (D.C. Cir. 2011).
54. Memorandum from Attorney General, 'Policies and Procedures Governing Invocation of the State Secrets Privilege', 23 September 2009, http://legaltimes.typepad.com/files/ag-memo-re-state-secrets-dated-09-22-09.pdf.
55. Jonathan Hafetz, 'Reconceptualizing Federal Courts in the War on Terror', *Saint Louis University Law Review* 56 (2012): 1055.
56. US Department of Justice, Office of Professional Responsibility, 'Investigation into the Office of Legal Counsel's Memoranda Concerning Issues Relating to the Central Intelligence Agency's Use of "Enhanced Interrogation Techniques" on Suspected Terrorists', 29 July 2009, https://www.aclu.org/files/pdfs/natsec/opr20100219/20090729_OPR_Final_Report_with_20100719_declassifications.pdf.
57. David Margolis, Associate Deputy Attorney General, 'Memorandum of Decision Regarding the Objections to the Findings of Professional Misconduct in the Office of Personal Responsibility's Report of Investigation into the Office of Legal Counsel's Memoranda Concerning Issues Relating to the Central Intelligence Agency's Use of "Enhanced Interrogation Techniques" on Suspected Terrorists', 5 January 2010, http://www.aclu.org/files/pdfs/natsec/opr20100219/20100105_DAG_Margolis_Memo.pdf.
58. John Yoo, 'Litigating for Terrorists', *Wall Street Journal*, 3 May 2012.
59. Ibid.
60. John Yoo, 'My Gift to the Obama Presidency', *Wall Street Journal*, 24 February 2010.
61. John Yoo, 'Closing Arguments: Finally, an End to Justice Dept. Investigations', *Philadelphia Inquirer*, 28 February 2010.
62. Senate Select Committee on Intelligence, Committee Study of the Central Intelligence Agency's Detention and Interrogation Program; Minority Views, 5 December 2014, http://www.intelligence.senate.gov/study2014/sscistudy3.pdf.
63. Cheryl Gay Stolberg and Eric Lichtblau, 'Ex-Chief Leads Vocal Defense of C.I.A.', *New York Times*, 12 December 2014.
64. Amy Davidson, 'Torture in a Dick Cheney Minute', *New Yorker*, 14 December 2014, http://www.newyorker.com/news/amy-davidson/torture-dick-cheney-minute.
65. The website is entitled 'CIA Saved Lives'.
66. Mark Mazzetti and Matt Apuzzo, 'C.I.A. Director Defends Use of Interrogation Tactics, Avoiding Issue of Torture', *New York Times*, 11 December 2014.
67. Ibid.

68. Central Intelligence Agency, 'CIA Fact Sheet Regarding the SSCI Study on the Former Detention and Interrogation Program', https://www.cia.gov/news-information/press-releases-statements/2014-press-releases-statements/cia-fact-sheet-ssci-study-on-detention-interrogation-program.html.
69. Ruti G. Teitel, *Transitional Justice* (Oxford: Oxford University Press, 2000).
70. Jon Elster, *Closing the Books: Transitional Justice in Historical Perspective* (Cambridge: Cambridge University Press, 2004).
71. Paul Horwitz, 'Democracy as the Rule of Law', in Hussain and Sarat, eds, *When Governments Break the Law.*
72. David Luban, *Torture, Power, and Law* (Cambridge: Cambridge University Press 2014), 283.
73. Philip Rucker, 'Leady Proposed Panel To Investigate Bush Era', *Washington Post*, 10 February 2009.
74. Michael Scharf and Valerie Epps, 'The International Trial of the Century?: A "Cross-Fire" Exchange on the First Case Before the Yugoslavia War Crimes Tribunal', *Cornell Journal International Law* 29 (1996): 638, n.8.
75. Basic Principles and Guidelines on the Right to a Remedy and Reparation for Victims of Gross Violations of International Human Rights Law and Serious Violations of International Humanitarian Law, para. 18 G.A. Res. 60/147, annex, UN Doc. A/RES/60/147 (2006).
76. Jane Mayer, 'Eric Holder and the Battle over Khalid Sheikh Mohammed', *New Yorker*, 15 February 2010.
77. ACLU, *The U.S. Torture Program: A Blueprint for Accountability*, https://www.aclu.org/sites/default/files/assets/torture_accountability_blueprint.pdf; Kenneth Roth, 'The CIA Torturers Should be Prosecuted', *Washington Post*, 12 December 2014; Amnesty International, 'USA: "We Torture Some Folks"; The Wait for Truth, Remedy, and Accountability Continues as Redaction Delays Release of Senate Report on CIA Detentions' (2014), http://www.amnesty.org/en/library/asset/AMR51/046/2014/en/8d0c7580-56f8-4b33-b8c9-78994c4e2c55/amr510462014en.pdf.
78. National Religious Campaign against Torture, 'Torture is a Moral Issue', http://www.nrcat.org/post-911-detainees/commission-of-inquiry.
79. Scott Shane, 'Amid Details on Torture, Data on 26 Who Were Held in Error', *New York Times*, 12 December 2014.
80. Bell, 'Transitional Justice'.
81. I am grateful to Jo-Marie Burt for this observation. For example, during the early 1980s, the most violent period of the Guatemalan civil war, government forces systematically raped, tortured and murdered thousands of members of indigenous Mayan communities as part of a 'scorched earth' campaign. See Center for Justice and Accountability, *Guatemala, 'Silent Holocaust': The Mayan Genocide*, http://www.cja.org/article.php?list=type&type=294. In Peru, the poor, rural and indigenous were often the targets of grave human rights violations committed during that country's internal armed conflict. See Jo-Marie Burt, 'Guilty as Charged: The Trial of Former Peruvian President Alberto Fujimori for Human Rights Violations', *International Journal Transitional Justice* 3, no. 3 (2009): 384.
82. Jo-Marie Burt, 'The New Accountability Agenda in Latin America: The Promise and Perils of Human Rights Prosecutions', in *Challenges of the Past and Challenges for the Future*, ed. Katherine Hite and Mark Ungar (Washington, DC: Woodrow Wilson Center for International Scholars Press, 2013), 105.
83. Lisa J. Laplante, 'Outlawing Amnesty: The Return of Criminal Justice in Transitional Justice Schemes', *Virginia Journal International Law* 49 (2009): 915.
84. José Zalaquett, 'Balancing Ethical Imperatives and Political Constraints: The Dilemma of New Democracies Confronting Human Rights Violations', in *Transitional Justice: How Emerging Democracies Reckon with the Past*, ed. Neil Kritz (Washington, DC: United States Institute of Peace, 1992).
85. Burt, 'The New Accountability Agenda in Latin America'; Sikkink, *The Justice Cascade.*
86. Burt, 'The New Accountability Agenda in Latin America'.
87. Elaine Scarry, 'Presidential Crimes: Moving On Is Not an Option', *Boston Review*, September–October 2008.
88. George W. Bush, *Decision Points* (New York: Crown, 2010), 169–70.
89. Anne E. Kornblut, 'In Interview, Bush Defends Iraq War and Waterboarding', *Washington Post*, 9 November 2010.

90. Chris McGreal, 'Dick Cheney Defends Use of Torture on al-Qaida Leaders', *The Guardian*, 9 September 2011.
91. Ibid.
92. Dick Cheney, 'Speech to American Enterprise Institute', 21 May 2009, http://www.politico.com/news/stories/0509/22823_Page2.html.
93. Davidson, 'Torture in a Dick Cheney Minute'.
94. Marc A. Thiessen, *Courting Disaster: How the CIA Kept America Safe* (Washington, DC: Regnery Publishing, 2010).
95. Marita Sturken, 'Comfort, Irony, and Trivialization: The Mediation of Torture', *International Journal of Cultural Studies* 14 (2011): 423.
96. Hussain and Sarat, 'Responding to Lawlessness', 20.
97. Horwitz, 'Democracy as the Rule of Law'.
98. Adam Goldman and Peyton Craighill, 'New Poll Finds Majority of Americans Think Torture was Justified after 9/11 Attacks', *Washington Post*, 16 December 2014.
99. Convention against Torture, arts 7, 12.
100. King, 'Amnesties in a Time of Transition', 603; Naomi Roht-Arriaza, 'Combating Impunity: Some Thoughts on the Way Forward', *Law & Contemporary Problems* 59 (1996): 93, 94.
101. Mary E. McCleod, Acting US Legal Advisor, US Department of State, Opening Statement before the UN Committee against Torture, 12–13 November 2014, https://geneva.usmission.gov/2014/11/12/acting-legal-adviser-mcleod-u-s-affirms-torture-is-prohibited-at-all-times-in-all-places/.
102. See Elizabeth B. Ludwin King, 'Amnesties in a Time of Transition', *George Washington International Law Review* 41 (2010): 577, 604.
103. See *Velásquez-Rodríguez* v. *Honduras*, Merits, Judgment, Inter-Am.Ct.H.R. (ser. C) No. 4, P 166 (29 July 1988) (ruling that implicit in a state's duty to ensure the rights recognised in the American Convention on Human Rights is the duty to 'prevent, investigate, and punish' violations of those rights); *Barrios Altos* v. *Peru*, Merits, Judgment, Inter-Am. Ct. H.R. (ser. C) No. 75, P 41 (14 March 2001) (ruling that an amnesty law enacted by Peru after a government death squad massacred 15 people violated the American Convention on Human Rights and that the perpetrators could be held accountable).
104. Charlie Savage, 'Election to Decide Future Interrogation Methods in Terrorism Cases', *New York Times*, 27 September 2012.

From the barrier to refugee law: national security's transformation from a balancing right to a background element in the realms of Israeli constitutionalism

Solon Solomon

Dickson Poon School of Law, Kings College London, UK

Mapping cardinal cases of the Israeli Supreme Court, the article will demonstrate how, in the Israeli constitutional experience, the concept of national security came to be transformed from a balancing right to a background element. Along these lines, the article will argue that while Israeli constitutionalism indeed awarded national security parameters a decisive role in the realms of the human rights balance judicial discourse, it equally embarked on a procedure of delineating the existence of national security as an autonomous consideration, in cases where national security exigencies ceased to be obvious in the Israeli reality. Compelling the examination of a national security debate under the human rights lens, the Israeli Supreme Court aligned its jurisprudence with that of other supreme courts as well as with the international thematic constitutionalism model, aspiring to interpret the different fields of laws and various provisions under the concept of the right to dignity.

Introduction

One of the cardinal questions surrounding the place of national security in the legal discourse is whether it should be perceived as a situation, similar to the declaration of a public emergency,[1] and justifying derogation of other human rights provisions[2] or whether it should be deemed a separate parameter, in the form of a state concern or interest to be taken into account by the international and domestic adjudicator in a balancing process vis-à-vis civil liberties.[3]

The current article will focus on how this equation has been treated in the concept of Israeli constitutionalism. The notion of constitutionalism has been defined as a 'three-faceted concept', involving the imposition of limits on governmental powers, adherence to the rule of law and the protection of human rights,[4] but for the purpose of this article, it will be examined in the functions that it demonstrates and as 'the judicial habit of enforcing broad constitutional norms through rules that make intrusions politically harder without ever deeming them "unconstitutional"'.[5]

Israel does not have a written constitution; as such, it does not have a Bill of Rights. Yet, it has Basic Laws which entrench various human rights, most famously the right to dignity.[6]

Therefore, in the realms of the Israeli domestic order, the role of the country's Supreme Court in setting this balance between national security and other rights is cardinal. Moreover, it is in societies at war that national security dilemmas usually appear.[7] Israeli constitutionalism on the matter, as shaped by the Supreme Court decisions, is thus of extreme importance.

The article will follow the evolution of national security in the background of Israeli constitutionalism. It will focus on the wider context of the war on terror and its aftermath, spanning the first two decades of the twenty-first century, which viewed frequent suicide attacks in Israel and the 9/11 attacks on a global level. The reference to terrorism and to armed conflict therefore became more acute in these cases[8] and questions of human rights thereby emerged, leading courts to ask whether the latter can be curtailed on national security grounds.[9]

The present article will examine how this national security versus human rights and liberties discourse took place in the context of Israeli constitutionalism and in the specific war on terror background. While the cases discussed here are being adjudicated within different normative frameworks, ranging from the application of international humanitarian law in Israel, to citizenship and immigration law, they all share the following common characteristic: they all address the question of how national security parameters should interplay with other human rights values and interests. It is this specific aspect of cases that the current article will focus on, without, for lack of space, analysing in detail all the legal aspects of each case.

In this respect, it will be demonstrated that in Israeli constitutionalism, as exemplified in the Supreme Court jurisprudence, national security gradually came to be cited, not only as a mere balancing parameter – as has been the case in other foreign jurisdictions – but as a major element of the factual background surrounding the case and thus acquiring an augmented, and even metaphysical importance.[10] With national threats subsiding in the country, the court consequently came to distance itself from such general national security rhetoric, instead focusing on other issues facing the state.[11]

It is this shift in the court's stance towards national security that the present article would like to record and welcome. Indeed, national security should not be used in a broad sense and as a general concept in order to deter certain policies, especially in issues that are not directly connected with the physical or mental survival of the individual or a social group.[12] Vagueness in the use of the 'national security' concept can only lead to the limitation of judicial review over government measures, at the expense of certain cardinal rights and liberties. Limited judicial review, in turn, undermines the idea that courts are the keepers of the rule of law, a consistent element of modern democracies.[13]

At the same time, this article will further demonstrate how in the context of Israeli constitutionalism, Israel's Supreme Court not only incorporated national security back into the human rights discourse, but, similar to how human rights are interpreted in other major domestic constitutions, the court subjected any interpretation of national security needs to a discussion on the right to human dignity.[14] In that sense, the court aligned Israeli constitutionalism with international thematic constitutionalism. In this article, international thematic constitutionalism is understood as the framework that interprets international legal order as a cohesive legal scheme, which can be likened to a domestic constitution, by harmonising conflicting interests and values under the lens of the right to human dignity and by using various fields of international law, such as human rights law, international humanitarian law, international economic law, as relevant provisions instead of isolated rights and freedoms, which is often the case with domestic constitutions.[15]

Israeli constitutionalism: national security as a balancing right

For years, in the so-called 'first generation jurisprudence',[16] of the Israeli Supreme Court, national security was perceived as part of the military needs of the army and of the military necessity concept and was therefore not awarded an autonomous role as a balancing factor in case law.[17] This changed in the first decade of the twenty-first century on account of the acute terrorist attacks the Israeli society witnessed, obliging the Supreme Court judges to award a balancing value to national security in the human rights law discourse, similar to their peers in other domestic jurisdictions. In a number of cases, the Supreme Court underlined that 'we do everything possible to balance between human rights and national security'.[18] What differentiated Israeli constitutionalism from other states' jurisprudence however, was that national security was also considered as a background element of the factual and normative analysis. This would allow both the state and the court to resort to it, with more or less success, also in cases where threats to life were not in question.

The present article will therefore analyse such cases and will sketch how national security was treated by Israeli constitutionalism both as a balancing factor and as a background element. It will examine what the implications of this were for the use of national security arguments in cases where national security did not seem to be directly implicated. At the same time, the article will show how the emphasis on human dignity put Israeli constitutionalism on a par with international developments as far as the national security discourse is concerned.

The cases of Israel's barrier

Following an unprecedented wave of terrorist attacks, Israel, stating that the measure was adopted on security and not political grounds,[19] decided to erect a barrier in the West Bank, comprised mostly of a fence, and of a wall in parts where the distance from habited areas did not permit otherwise.[20] In this context, the UN General Assembly asked the International Court of Justice (ICJ) to give its advisory opinion on whether the particular construction violated international law.[21] The Israeli Supreme Court had also become seized of the matter, following a petition from the Beit Sourik village council whose inhabitants were directly affected by the barrier's route. In summer 2004, and within a few days, both judicial bodies gave their decisions. Yet, the position they awarded to national security parameters is strikingly different.

The ICJ, lacking the ability to militarily assess the viability of the barrier's route due to its reliance on second-hand sources only,[22] could only restrict itself to positioning national security in the background. The court interpreted the evocation by Israel of national security elements as 'concerns' rather than as autonomous factors that have to be separately taken into account in each judgment.[23]

The court concluded that the general information on Israel's dire security situation, also contained in the folder provided by the United Nations (UN) Secretariat, was enough for the legal evaluation of Israel's national security arguments.[24] It further acknowledged that Israel had to face numerous indiscriminate and deadly acts of violence against its civilians. Yet, any reference to these national security challenges was limited to one paragraph of the opinion and was done in a rather formalistic way.[25] Emphasis was put on the project's political aspects. Military exigencies or the requirements of national security were not considered to be enough to justify the project's erection.[26] Accordingly, for the court, the barrier constituted an implicit and de facto annexation of the West Bank.[27]

Not surprisingly, criticism was raised by some members of the court regarding the place accorded to national security as a surrounding and marginal parameter only. Thus, Judge Buergenthal noted in his declaration that the court completely invalidating the project without taking into account Israel's security needs could not be justified as a matter of law.[28] On the contrary, for him, the court should place Israel's national security argumentation in the foreground and grapple with it, trying to attest whether it should or not be asserted in light of the harm inflicted on the Palestinian residents' human rights. Failure to conduct such a national security-human rights dialogue leaves, according to the judge, the entire opinion unconvincing.[29] Judge Owada deplored in his separate opinion the lack of an in-depth analysis of Israel's national security argumentation.[30]

For the Israeli Supreme Court, national security serves both as a background landscape as well as a separate legal basis for the proportionate restraint of Palestinian residents' rights.[31] From the first paragraphs of its judgment, the court paints the dire picture created by Palestinian attacks, making more urgent the enactment of measures on national security grounds. In the court's words

> Terror attacks take place both in the area and in Israel. They are directed against citizens and soldiers, men and women, elderly and infants, regular citizens and public figures. Terror attacks are carried out everywhere: in public transportation, in shopping centers and markets, in coffee houses and in restaurants ... The armed conflict has left many dead and wounded on the Palestinian side as well. Bereavement and pain wash over us.[32]

Just how important national security is as a background factor was demonstrated by the fact that, once again, in the closing paragraphs of the judgment, the court returned to regret the situation:

> We are aware of the killing and destruction wrought by the terror against the state and its citizens. As any other Israelis, we too recognize the need to defend the country and its citizens against the wounds inflicted by terror ... Regarding the state's struggle against the terror that rises up against it, we are convinced that at the end of the day, a struggle according to the law will strengthen her power and her spirit. There is no security without law.[33]

Yet the court did not restrict itself to the mere depiction of national security as a background factor justifying certain measures, but through the expansion of the notion of 'military necessity',[34] it also proceeded to award it a normative value in the balance between security and liberty, a balance which according to the court 'is a general problem in the law, both domestic and international'.[35] The court, viewing the barrier as a defensive structure meant to thwart Palestinian attacks, conceded in essence that national security grounds oblige its erection.[36]

Relying on its own previous jurisprudence allowing military needs to justify the erection of a military fence,[37] the Israeli Supreme Court interpreted such needs to also encompass the human rights of the Israeli victims of the attacks, even if the latter reside in the West Bank.[38]

This is more evidently depicted in the *Mara'abe* case.[39] There, the court was asked to adjudicate on the legality of the barrier's route at a point where the project encircled the Israeli settlement of Alfei Menashe as well as five Palestinian villages, which as a result were disconnected from the major urban centre of the area, the Palestinian town of Kalkilya.[40]

The case holds many similarities with the *Beit Sourik* case, more notably the fact that national security is once again portrayed first as the background to the normative picture in order to consequently, and through the proportionality principle, form one of its interpretive tools.[41] Yet, the *Mara'abe* case goes one step further and national security measures, such as the barrier, were held to also legitimately protect the right to life of Israelis residing in the West Bank.[42] Israelis living in settlements are viewed as human beings entitled to the right to life and their protection becomes disconnected from the question of the settlements' illegality.[43]

As such, national security undergoes a linear evolution. From a parameter lurking in the background, national security becomes a balancing parameter. It is taken into account both when human rights of the state's nationals are infringed as well as when these rights' infringement concerns the rights of non-nationals.

The Targeted Killings *case*

In 2005, the court rendered its judgment on Israel's policy of targeted killings. In a much anticipated decision due – in parts – to the public outcry following the targeted killing of a major Hamas member with a two-ton bomb, which also led to the death of a number of civilians, the court unfolded its rationale by posing, once again, national security as the background of its legal thinking.

> A massive assault of terrorism was directed against the State of Israel, and against Israelis, merely because they are Israelis. This assault of terrorism differentiates neither between combatants and civilians, nor between women, men, and children. The terrorist attacks take place both in the territory of Judea, Samaria, and the Gaza Strip, and within the borders of the State of Israel. They are directed against civilian centers, shopping centers and markets, coffee houses and restaurants. Over the last five years, thousands of acts of terrorism have been committed against Israel ... In its war against terrorism, the State of Israel employs various means. As part of the security activity intended to confront the terrorist attacks, the State employs what it calls 'the policy of targeted frustration' of terrorism. Under this policy, the security forces act in order to kill members of terrorist organizations involved in the planning, launching, or execution of terrorist attacks against Israel.[44]

Yet, in subsequent paragraphs, the court proceeded to inaugurate national security as a separate balancing parameter.[45] Similarly to the *Beit Sourik* case, it did not do so directly, but through the embodiment of national security in the general notion of military needs.[46] Moreover, once again, these military needs were interpreted by the court to encompass the duty of the state to also protect the lives of its soldiers and civilians.[47] While the court noted that 'state security' is not a magic word, it still granted special weight to the opinion of the military commander who was bound to express himself in a national security language.[48] Thus, this rhetoric became part of the court's discourse and ultimately led to the court examining the question of the legality of the targeted killings practice not only from a human rights law point of view, but also through international humanitarian law (IHL).

In this context, national security signals the interrelation of the situation with war and the application of IHL thereby becomes an issue that both characterises the particular judgment as well as limits its scope. Coming to interpret the 'direct participation in hostilities' criterion embedded in article 51 of the first Additional Protocol to the Geneva Conventions, the court held that participation can be deemed 'direct' even when individuals were not actually engaged in war activities but in supportive acts, including distribution of propaganda material or the providing of food, medicine and monetary aid, but excluding mere sympathy for the causes of a terrorist group.[49]

By defining the direct participation criterion, the court in essence also limited it and enclosed the national security discourse in certain parameters. As Chief Judge Barak noted that a balancing act is being undertaken by the court between human rights and military needs and its result is the recognition by the court of the fact that as human rights enforcement is subject to limitations, the same is true also for national security concerns.[50] This acknowledgement will prove cardinal in subsequent cases analysed below, concerning citizenship and immigration, where the court will refuse to expand the national security argumentation.

On a circular mode, the *Targeted Killings* judgment closed with the plight terrorism caused to the wider society and the challenges posed for the preservation of human rights.[51]

While the particular decision was criticised,[52] the court's stance was also viewed as a paradigm for the United States (US) Supreme Court.[53] In that sense, the particular judgment showed how national security can be balanced with human rights and it provided a legal platform for the response to the national security challenges the US also faces in its war on terror.[54]

The Gaza blockade

In September 2007 the Israeli government declared Gaza a 'hostile territory' and limited the electricity and gas supplies to the Strip.[55] National security appeared in the background of this policy, in the Israeli aspirations that such policies would exert pressure on the Palestinians to halt the rocket attacks, ultimately reassuring Israel's security.[56]

In October 2007, Palestinians and Israeli humanitarian organisations petitioned Israel's Supreme Court. The court, in its decision in January 2008 ultimately ruled that in the particular case, security was served in the frame of law and that the measures should be perceived as non-forcible defensive measures, taken on account of the rocket attacks.[57] In the particular judgment, indeed, national security parameters sit in the background. As the court's president, Judge Beinisch, writes

> The background to the petition is the belligerent actions that have taken place in the Gaza Strip for a long period, and the ongoing campaign of terrorism directed against the citizens of Israel. The terrorist attacks have intensified and worsened since the Hamas organization took control of the Gaza Strip. These attacks include the continuous firing of rockets and mortar shells at civilian targets in the territory of the State of Israel, as well as terrorist attacks and attempted attacks targeting civilians and IDF soldiers at the border crossings between the Gaza Strip and the State of Israel, along the border fence and in the territory of the State of Israel. The respondents' decision to limit the supply of fuel and electricity to the Gaza Strip was made in the framework of the State of Israel's operations against the ongoing terrorism.[58]

Similar to the barrier cases, national security is also put into the background in the closing statement of the court

> In conclusion, we reiterate that the Gaza Strip is controlled by a murderous terrorist organization, which acts relentlessly to inflict harm on the State of Israel and its inhabitants, violating every possible rule of international law in its violent acts, which are directed indiscriminately at civilians – men, women and children. Despite this, as we said above, the State of Israel is committed to fighting the terrorist organizations within the framework of the law and in accordance with the provisions of international law, and to refrain from intentional harm to the civilian population in the Gaza Strip.[59]

Yet, the court does not only retain the reference to the dire security situation as simply a factor setting the tone of a particular policy. Similar to its ruling in the cases of Israel's barrier, the court uses the national security parameter as a balancing concept that has to be taken into account once the question of whether human rights violations occurred has been asked. As such, the court gives some weight to the state's national security arguments, ultimately holding that

> some of the fuel that enters the Gaza Strip is in fact used for the various purposes of the terrorist organizations; in such circumstances the reduction of the fuel supply, in the controlled manner in which it is implemented, is likely to damage the terrorist infrastructures and affect their ability to operate against the citizens of the State of Israel, since the amount of fuel that enters the Gaza Strip is supposed to suffice only for the humanitarian purposes that require the use of fuel ... the State of Israel is under no obligation to allow an unlimited amount of electricity and fuel to enter the Gaza Strip in circumstances in which some of these commodities are in practice being used by the terrorist organizations in order to attack Israeli civilians. The duty of the State of Israel derives from the essential humanitarian needs of the inhabitants of the Gaza Strip.[60]

The Gaza blockade also offered another opportunity for the national security discourse to develop in the realms of Israeli constitutionalism, this time through the channels of quasi-judicial bodies,[61] such as the Turkel Committee,[62] instituted to examine the Flotilla incident in May 2010, when an attempt by activists to break Gaza's naval blockade led to clashes with Israeli marines and the subsequent death of nine Turks.[63]

When it came to discuss the legality of the blockade, the Turkel Committee Report viewed it as a *jus in bello* measure,[64] integrating also security elements in its rationale. The committee also took into consideration the testimonies of major actors of the Israeli security echelon who testified of Israel's need to impose a blockade on security grounds.[65] Accordingly, the committee reached the conclusion that the blockade's aim was 'to restrict the military resources available to the Hamas for carrying out hostilities against Israel'[66] and that it was imposed 'for military-security reasons, which focused on preventing weapons, ammunition, military supplies, terrorists and money from entering the Gaza Strip, and the need to prevent the departure of terrorists, vessels filled with explosives and other maritime borne threats from Gaza'.[67]

Until now, Israeli constitutionalism demonstrated its treatment of national security issues in cases where this aspect was more easily discernable, due to their connection with policies engaged with the war on terror. The following sections will examine how the national security parameters found themselves adjudicated by the Supreme Court in cases where their relevance was not obvious at the onset.

Israeli constitutionalism: national security as a background element

The cases around the Citizenship Law Amendment

In 2003, the Israeli parliament adopted an amendment to the Citizenship Law.[68] The amendment was adopted as a temporary measure for five years, forbidding the entrance to the country and naturalisation of Palestinians, even in cases of family unification with Israeli Arabs. The amendment had a sweeping character, not taking into account other instances worth being noted, as is traditionally the case with humanitarian reasons.[69]

Although dealing with a demographic issue, the influence of the harsh security conditions prevalent at the time of its enactment merit examination here.[70] The Israeli state authorities argued that the law was a security measure, designed to prevent Palestinian terrorists from coming into Israel through family unification.[71] Coming into force in a period when Israel faced almost daily terrorist attacks, the amendment raised the issue of the broadness of measures necessary in order to attain security. Yet, and in contrast to the previous cases concerning security measures, the amendment also posed for the first time the question whether national security can be used as an excuse for the imposition of measures linked to a certain ideology and approach in government circles.[72] In that sense, the particular case stands in the twilight zone between previous cases where national security was a legitimate parameter to be balanced with human rights considerations and a new emerging era, where national security would fall to the background. This happens because national security is, in these cases, a background argument, which the court correctly did not deem prudent to bring to the forefront. It is in this context that the Israeli Supreme Court treated the cases that were brought before it on account of the specific amendment.

The first case was adjudicated in 2006.[73] Presumably, there was an attempt to present the case in the mode chosen by previous cases where national security measures fell in the scope of judicial review. Thus for example, the court's president, Judge Barak, cites, in the beginning of his opinion, the paragraph inserted in the *Beit Sourik* case and describing the climate of terror created in Israel.[74] At the same time, and similar again to his tactic in the *Beit Sourik* case, Barak proceeds to balance national security parameters and the harm inflicted on specific human rights.[75] Yet, because of its ideological extensions and because of its numerous legal questions, the *Citizenship Law Amendment* case is more complex. The court's decision ultimately mirrors this in the slight majority – six to five – with which it upheld the provision. While the petitioners argued that the amendment should only be seen on demographic terms, the court accepted that the amendment was about promoting national security.[76] Yet, lurking in the judges' thought, the demographic contour can be traced.[77]

Following the court's decision and the debate that erupted over it,[78] the Israeli lawmaker intervened regarding the specific provision. Apparently trying to address the problems created by the law's sweeping character, a provision was added stipulating the creation of a committee bound to examine humanitarian cases, as long as the applicant did not reside in areas where activities detrimental to Israel's security took place.[79]

A second petition to the court followed. Once again, the judges upheld the amendment.[80] Yet, while the national security argumentation was repeated and ultimately prevailed, for some of the judges, national security's hegemony over other human rights considerations should not be seen as absolute. The opinion of Judge Levy is indicative. Upholding the amendment the first time, he subsequently ruled in the second petition against it, holding that despite the fact that the national security perils still exist, the harm inflicted to human rights was too serious to be able to sustain it.[81]

In that sense, the *Citizenship Amendment* cases herald the court to a new jurisprudential era where national security ceases to be an automatic trump in the human rights discourse. What is important to note is that this new era is not attached to how national security concerns are treated specifically in citizenship law cases or in another group of cases. Moreover, the *Citizenship Amendment* cases also signal the emergence of human dignity as the ultimate arbitrator. With Israel lacking a Bill of Rights, the court engaged in rhetoric in which the right to human dignity, deemed a constitutional right, was broadened to include also the right to equality and the right to family.[82] This cardinal role of the right to human dignity would acquire an additional role in the positioning of Israeli constitutionalism in the realm of the international legal context.

The case of the Sudanese and Eritrean refugees

In refugee law, national security does not appear as a right to be balanced together with other rights, but as the background in which the protection of human rights has to be examined. As such, article 31(2) of the Refugees' Convention allows host states to limit freedom of movement for the time needed to ensure that a person claiming a refugee status does not pose a threat to national security.[83] Yet, in this framework, emphasis is clearly on the refugees' human rights. Apart from the fact that judicial review must be provided for every decision ordering detention on national security grounds,[84] the whole discourse becomes obsolete once an individual applies for a residence permit. Accordingly, it is replaced by a human rights rhetoric that focuses on the refugees' fundamental rights and freedoms. Thus, all restrictions to the right of free movement have to be applied in tandem with article 26 of the convention.[85]

In refugee law, national security acts in the same way as emergency clauses function in human rights law, in an exceptional and catalytic way. Indeed, it changes the prism through which the refugees' rights have to be examined, yet it can only be asserted in some cases.[86] The existence of national security grounds for the detainment or not of a particular refugee is assessed on a case-by-case basis, and not on the basis of a general atmosphere or feelings created in society when individuals illegally cross the country's borders. Contrary to emergency clauses which refer to a general climate that is prevalent and can justify derogation of human rights clauses, national security in refugee law has to relate to certain fears that emanate from a specific person and not from the situation in general.[87] In *A* v. *United Kingdom*, the general fear of the state regarding the occurrence of a terrorist attack was not enough to justify the detention of individuals who despite not having engaged in acts endangering national security were still perceived as terrorist threats.[88]

Yet, before the Israeli Supreme Court, refugee/immigrant issues acquired a war-like polemic and a national security tone. In the rounds of litigation concerning the policy of these refugees' placement in detention centres,[89] national security threats were tied to the fact that these refugees came from countries, like Sudan and Eritrea, with which Israel does not have formal diplomatic relations [90] and thus posed a considerable national security threat to Israel's sovereignty as well as social and economic prosperity.[91]

The petitioners correctly noted in their petition to the court that such detachment of the national security argumentation from any actual danger to a focus on the individuals' country of origin introduced a dangerous novelty to the extent that it allowed the indefinite detention of individuals against whom there is no evidence of personal involvement in hostile acts against the state's security.[92]

The legislation's intent in the case of the Sudanese and Eritrean refugees is to portray national security on emotional grounds, recalling traumatic memories to the Israeli society. These refugees are presented as threatening Israel's social fabric.[93] In legislation they are branded as 'infiltrators', a term used for the Arab *fedayeen*, crossing Israel's borders and performing terrorist attacks in the 1950s.[94] The court felt uneasy with this term and rejected this rationale. In the first case reviewing the constitutionality of the legislation introducing the detention of these people, Judge Arbel noted 'we do not have before us terrorists but people who live in hardship'.[95]

While national security is not a parameter on the balancing scales, it does exist in the background. The judges do not disregard the fact that the issue can have national security implications and the reason this is not currently the case is because of the fact that the numbers of the Sudanese/Eritrean refugees in Israel are not massive.[96]

Thus, Judge Arbel, writing the court's judgment, indirectly referred to national security considerations when she expressed her empathy with the local population suffering from the social and security problems caused by the influx of illegal immigrants and when she noted that the issue merits a 'fitting comprehensive political solution'.[97] Similarly, in his concurring opinion, Judge Fogelman underlined that 'the challenge which the State of

Israel must confront and has had to confront in light of the unarranged immigration of tens of thousands of people from Africa into its borders is a difficult one'.[98]

Nevertheless, these national security parameters did not acquire an autonomous existence able to render relative the absolute entrenchment of the right to human dignity in the court's legal thought. As the various judges proclaim 'a person's liberty and right to dignity constitute the foundation norms for common living in the realms of a state, and they apply to citizens and foreigners alike'[99]; 'we cannot deny basic rights and thus blatantly violate people's dignity and their right to freedom as solution of a problem that requires an adequate political response'[100] and 'incarcerating a person is like treating him as a "means" to the achievement of state purposes.'[101]

Therefore, in September 2013, the court ruled[102] that the holding of these people in detention centres prior to their expulsion from the country was unconstitutional, since it violated the right to human dignity embedded in Israel's Basic Law: Human Dignity and Liberty.[103] Accordingly, the court struck the relevant piece of legislation and set a 90-day-period during which the government had to release the refugees already held.[104]

Following the court's judgment, the law was amended. Yet, detention of the refugees still remained an option. What differed was its duration. While the law's previous version envisioned detainment up to three years, the amended version reduced this period to one year. Moreover, a refugee centre was established, deemed 'open' because refugees could exit it through their own volition throughout the day. Yet, the fact that the centre was isolated from inhabited areas made such exit in essence futile. Deciding on a second relevant petition brought after the law's amendment,[105] the court in September 2014, almost one year after its first judgment, annulled again the amendment to the law.[106]

In that sense the Israeli Supreme Court's judgments in the particular refugee cases follow in the discourse between refugee law and national security, the lines sketched by international theory, as analysed above, and pose the court as a gatekeeper of international legality in the Israeli constitutional landscape.

As was the case with its analysis of national security arguments in its judgment on the Citizenship Law, in the case of the Sudanese and Eritrean refugees, the court also successfully managed to reject any attempt by the government or legislature to give national security arguments a value in the legal debate. In that sense, and by not succumbing to any opportunistic interpretations and uses of national security discourse, the court managed to engage with national security in a constructive way.

The Israeli national security debate in the realms of international constitutionalism

In Israeli constitutionalism, there is an effort for harmonisation to be achieved between national security and human rights.[107] The Israeli court's position is unique to the extent that contrary to other constitutional orders, in states which have experienced terrorism, such as India[108] or the US,[109] national security grounds are not viewed under the prism of human rights, but as an explicit parameter in jurisprudence. Such treatment of national security issues by the Israeli Supreme Court[110] can be partially explained by the country's decade-long exposure to incidents of terror and war[111] as well as the fact that relevant past decisions had already undergone criticism, which were ultimately absorbed by the judges.[112] At the same time, this *sui generis* postulation of national security in the constitutional discourse was bound to change once security perils ceased to be evident. While governments continued to frame their argumentation on national security grounds, this rhetoric started sounding obsolete.[113] Human rights started to be stressed in a pyramid mode with the right to human dignity at the top. The Israeli Supreme Court judgments on family unifications and on the Sudanese refugees simply express this trend. Obviously this does not mean that if acts of terror and evident national security grounds appear again in the foreground in such an acute way, as was the case in the 2000s, the court would not resort to its 'pure' national security argumentation. This examination of the court's jurisprudence only stresses the fact that the court is unwilling to do so once these national security grounds are not as genuine and manifested.

Israeli constitutionalism thus embraces international constitutionalism both on trans-national as well as international grounds.[114] On a trans-national level, a number of superior courts in various countries have consistently refused to acknowledge that national security considerations can trump individual rights and liberties. Adjudicating on issues of detention of terrorist suspects, the Canadian Supreme Court held that the use of secret evidence as a basis for the imposition of this detainment was unconstitutional.[115] In the case of Khadr, a Canadian national, the court ruled that the Canadian government had to disclose to him evidence obtained throughout his interrogation in Guantanamo.[116] Similarly, in Spain, criminal proceedings have been launched against lawyers of the Bush administration who authorised the interrogation techniques of suspected terrorists.[117] In Germany, the country's highest court has ruled that computer 'data mining' measures designed to identify terrorists violate privacy rights.[118] The German Federal Court went one step further, assigning a superior function to the right of dignity when it held that the human dignity of the passengers aboard did not permit the shooting down of a plane on account of suspicions that it was hijacked for terrorist purposes, even if this shooting down meant that lives would be saved on the ground.[119]

At the same time, the emphasis Israel's Supreme Court puts on human dignity as a guiding torch in its legal conclusions resembles the emphasis that international thematic constitutionalism puts on human dignity as the notion under which all legal notions and fields should be interpreted.[120] In that sense, Israeli constitutionalism, like a pendulum, recoils from its proactive first decade stance in counter-terrorism issues as the terrorist threats subside and aligns itself with the universal treatment of the subject by applying human dignity in tandem with national security considerations in other cases.

Conclusion

Israeli constitutionalism has passed various phases in its treatment of national security arguments. From a more conservative approach to the realisation that security sometimes needs to be used as a legal argument; and from the preponderance of the security-related discourse to its move to the background in safer times, the Israeli Supreme Court has aptly applied the national security-human rights nexus according to the exigencies of the times and the situations it faced. In that sense, Israeli constitutionalism managed to survive even in times of deep security crisis and perils. Once these perils subsided, the court showed a relative capacity to adequately respond by stepping down from the national security wagon. The greatest challenge lying before Israeli constitutionalism is ultimately whether, apart from the judiciary, the other two powers in a democracy, the legislative and the executive branches, will be equally persuaded to abandon the easy – yet many times unjustified – recourse to the national security discourse.

Disclosure statement

No potential conflict of interest was reported by the author.

Notes on contributor

Solon Solomon is a researcher at the King's College London Dickson Poon School of Law.

Notes

1. Diane Desierto, *Necessity and National Emergency Clauses: Sovereignty in Modern Treaty Interpretation* (The Netherlands: Brill, 2012), 187, 271. For the fact that in a number of jurisdictions including Israel, Canada, New Zealand and the United Kingdom as well as in international jurisprudence a state of emergency is linked inter alia with national security issues see Emanuel Gross, 'How to Justify an Emergency Regime and Preserve Civil Liberties in Times of Terrorism', *South Carolina Journal of International Law & Business* 5 (2008): 1; Ben Golder and George Williams, 'Balancing National Security and Human Rights: Assessing the Legal Response of Common Law Nations to the Threat of Terrorism', *Journal of Comparative Policy Analysis* 8 (2006): 43, 45; Janet Hiebert, 'The Evolution of the Limitation Clause', *Osgoode Hall Journal* 28 (1990): 103, 113. For the fact that this state of emergency can draw from the drastic change of the economic landscape in a country see 'The Protection of National Security in IIAs', UNCTAD Series on International Investment Policies for Development, United Nations (2009), 8 (on file with the author). But see also Hannes Schloemann and Stefan Ohlhoff, '"Constitutionalization" and Dispute Settlement in the WTO: National Security as an Issue of Competence', *American Journal of International Law* 93 (1999): 424, 426 (referring to national security as the Achilles' heel of international law).
2. Thus for example article 4 of the International Covenant on Civil and Political Rights stipulates that 'in time of public emergency which threatens the life of the nation and the existence of which is officially proclaimed, the States Parties to the present Covenant may take measures derogating from their obligations under the present Covenant to the extent strictly required by the exigencies of the situation, provided that such measures are not inconsistent with their other obligations under international law and do not involve discrimination solely on the ground of race, colour, sex, language, religion or social origin'. See also article 15 of the Guidelines of the Committee of Ministers of the Council of Europe on Human Rights and the Fight Against Terrorism, 11 July 2002, http://www1.umn.edu/humanrts/instree/HR%20and%20the%20fight%20against%20terrorism.pdf.
3. Stephan Schill and Robyn Briese, '"If the State Considers": Self-Judging Clauses in International Dispute Settlement', *Max Planck United Nations Yearbook* 13 (2009): 61, 63; Laura Conn, 'The Enumeration of Vital Civil Liberties within a Constitutional State of Emergency Clause: Lessons from the United States, the New Democracy of South Africa and International Treaties and Scholarship', *University of Pennsylvania Journal of Constitutional Law* 10 (2008): 791, 794 (noting that during times of emergency, civil liberties have been pushed back to allow for the concerns of national security and after the threat has ceased, civil liberties have bounced back). Richard Posner, *Not a Suicide Pact: The Constitution in a Time of National Emergency* (Oxford: Oxford University Press, 2006), 5; Richard Falk, 'Encroaching on the Rule of Law: Post-9/11 Policies within the United States', in *National Insecurity and Human Rights: Democracies Debate Counterterrorism*, ed. Alison Brysk and Gershon Shafir (Berkeley and Los Angeles: University of California Press, 2007), 15. See also Robert Jennings, 'Recent Cases on Automatic Reservations to the Optional Clause', *International and Comparative Law Quarterly* 7 (1958): 349, 362 (noting that in national security issues, domestic governments should be the sole trustees and international courts cannot have a useful opinion). For the fact that national security concerns can be taken into account also outside the realms of a balancing between rights and interests see article 72 of the ICC Statute stipulating that document production requests can be refused in cases where the display of information would, in the opinion of a state, prejudice its national security interests. For the balancing process and the problems it may entail see Moshe Cohen-Eliya and Gila Stopler, 'Probability Thresholds as Deontological Constraints in Global Constitutionalism', *Columbia Journal of Transnational Law* 49 (2010): 75, 82–9.
4. Michel Rosenfeld, 'Modern Constitutionalism as Interplay between Identity and Diversity', in *Constitutionalism, Identity, Difference and Legitimacy: Theoretical Perspectives*, ed. Michel Rosenfeld (Durham and London: Duke University Press, 1994), 27–8.

5. Abigail Moncrieff, 'Common-Law Constitutionalism, the Constitutional Common Law, and the Validity of the Individual Mandate', *Boston University Law Review* 92 (2012): 1245, 1248.
6. Menachem Mautner, *Law and the Culture of Israel* (New York: Oxford University Press, 2011), 178.
7. See for example Yoram Dinstein, noting that 'the law of war usually creates a delicate balance between two poles: military necessity on one hand, and humanitarian considerations on the other', in Yoram Dinstein, 'Legislative Authority in the Administered Territories' [in Hebrew], *Iyunei Mishpat* 2 (1973): 505, 509.
8. On this see Derek Jinks, Jackson Maogoto and Solon Solomon, 'Introducing International Humanitarian Law to Judicial and Quasi Judicial Bodies', in *Appling International Humanitarian Law in Judicial and Quasi Judicial Bodies: International and Domestic Aspects*, ed. Derek Jinks, Jackson Maogoto and Solon Solomon (The Hague: TMC Asser Press, 2014), 4–5.
9. C. William Michaels, *No Greater Threat: America After September 11 and the Rise of a National Security State* (New York: Algora Publishing, 2005), 506; S. Neil MacFarlane and Yuen Foong Khong, *Human Security and the UN: A Critical History* (Bloomington: Indiana University Press, 2006), 254.
10. Guy Harpaz and Yuval Shany, 'The Israeli Supreme Court and the Incremental Expansion of the Scope of Discretion under Belligerent Occupation Law', *Israel Law Review* 43 (2010): 544–5. See also infra the case of *A. and Others* v. *United Kingdom*, where both the House of Lords as well as the European Court of Justice held that erroneously national security perils had been cited for the derogation of the European Convention on Human Rights and the restriction of the right to liberty of certain individuals.
11. David Kretzmer, *The Occupation of Justice: The Supreme Court of Israel and the Occupied Territories* (Albany: State University of New York Press, 2002), 115.
12. For the fact that migrants have been portrayed as a national security peril see Ioannis Kolovos, 'Illegal Immigration, A Multifaceted National Security Threat: The Case of Greece', Research Paper No.145, September 2010, Research Institute for European and American Studies, 15–16; HCJ 7385/13, para. 29; Natalie Klein, *Maritime Security and the Law of the Sea* (Oxford: Oxford University Press, 2011), 6; Columba Peoples and Nick Vaughan-Williams, *Critical Security Studies* (London: Routledge Press, 2010), 91, 134; Reinhard Lohrmann, 'Migrants, Refugees and Insecurity: Current Threats to Peace?', *International Migration* 38, no. 4 (2000): 3, 6; Reinhard Lohrmann, 'Migrants, Refugees and Insecurity: Current Threats to Peace?', *International Migration* 38, no. 4 (2000): 3, 4; Jef Huysmans, *The Politics of Insecurity: Fear, Migration and Asylum in the EU* (London: Routledge, 2006), 18, 20; David Harris, 'Immigration and National Security: The Illusion of Safety through Local Law Enforcement Action', *Arizona Journal of International and Comparative Law* 28 (2011): 383, 384.
13. National Security and Secret Evidence in Legislation and before the Courts: Exploring the Challenges: Study for the LIBE Committee, European Parliament, Directorate-General for Internal Policies 2014, 7–8, http://www.europarl.europa.eu/RegData/etudes/STUD/2014/509991/IPOL_STU%282014%29509991_EN.pdf; for the idea that courts should have a cardinal role in the keeping of the rule of law and human rights even through engaging in what is to be perceived as 'judicial lawmaking' see Aharon Barak, 'The Role of a Supreme Court in a Democracy', *Hastings Law Journal* 53 (2002): 1205, 1206–7. See also Eyal Benvenisti and George Downs, 'National Courts, Domestic Democracy, and the Evolution of International Law', *European Journal of International Law* 20 (2009): 59, 63.
14. For the fact that constitutionally entrenched human rights and liberties are seen in domestic constitutions under the lens of the right to human dignity see Solon Solomon, 'The Dynamic Law of Occupation: Inaugurating International Thematic Constitutionalism', *Harvard International Law Journal Online* 54 (2012): 59, 70–3.
15. Ibid., 59.
16. Harpaz and Shany, 'The Israeli Supreme Court and the Incremental Expansion of the Scope of Discretion under Belligerent Occupation Law', 514, 526.
17. On this see characteristically the Supreme Court position that military needs are the needs of the military commander and not national security needs in a broad sense. (HCJ 393/82 *Jamayit Iscan Almalmun Althaunia Almahduda Almesaulia* v. *The Commander of IDF in the Judea and Samaria Area* 37(4) PD 738, para. 13 [1983]. See also HCJ 2977/91, *Thaj* v. *Minister of Defence*, para. 474).

18. HCJ 7015/02 *Ajouri* v. *IDF Commander*, PD 56 (6) 352, 383 (2002). See also HCJ 7052/03, *Adallah* v. *Minister of Interior*, PD 61 (2) 202 (2006), 468.
19. Written Statement of the Government of Israel, Advisory Opinion, 2004 ICJ 131, at 7 (30 January 2004), http://www.icj-cij.org/docket/files/131/1579.pdf; Israeli Ministry of Foreign Affairs, Saving Lives: Israel's Anti-Terrorist Fence – Answers to Questions (1 January 2004), http://www.mfa.gov.il/MFA/Terrorism+Obstacle+to+Peace/Palestinian+terror+since+2000/Saving+Lives-+Israel-s+anti-terrorist+fence+-+Answ.htm; HCJ 2056/04 *Beit Sourik Village Council* v. *Israel* PD 58(5) 807, paras 28–9 [2004].
20. Legal Consequences of the Construction of a Wall in the Occupied Palestinian Territory, ICJ Rep. 2004 131, para. 82; Sarah Williams, 'Has International Law Hit the Wall? An Analysis of International Law in Relation to Israel's Separation Barrier', *Berkeley Journal of International Law* 24 (2006): 192, 197; Emanuel Gross, 'Perspective: Combating Terrorism: Does Self-Defense Include the Security Barrier? The Answer Depends on Who You Ask', *Cornell International Law Journal* 38 (2005): 569; Mimi Trenk, 'An Unfair Advantage: Comparing the International Court of Justice to a Form of ADR and why it was Inappropriate for the Court to Issue an Advisory Opinion in the case of Israel's Separation Fence', *Cardozo Journal of Conflict Resolution* 8 (2006): 371, 377.
21. Illegal Israeli actions in Occupied East Jerusalem and the Rest of the Occupied Palestinian Territory, G.A. Res. ES-10/14, at 3, U.N. GAOR, 10th Emergency Special Sess., 23d plen. mtg., U.N. Doc. A/Res/ES-10/14 (12 December 2003).
22. Yuval Shany, 'Capacities and Inadequacies: A Look at the Two Separation Barrier Cases', *Israel Law Review* 38 (2005): 230, 234.
23. Legal Consequences of the Construction of a Wall in the Occupied Palestinian Territory, ICJ Rep. 2004 131, para. 57.
24. Ibid., para. 58.
25. Ibid., para. 141. See also Shany, 'Capacities and Inadequacies', 235, 239–40 (deploring the sweeping manner with which the court rejected Israel's assertions for the military necessity of the barrier's erection as well as noting the limited empathy of the ICJ towards the victims of terrorism as well as the Palestinian villagers).
26. Legal Consequences of the Construction of a Wall, para. 137.
27. Ibid., para. 121.
28. Declaration of Judge Buergenthal, ICJ Rep. 131, 240, para. 3 [2004].
29. Ibid., 243–4, para. 7 [2004].
30. Separate Opinion of Judge Owada, ICJ Rep. 131, 271, para. 30 [2004].
31. HCJ 2056/04 *Beit Sourik Village Council* v. *Israel* PD 58(5) 807, paras 35, 39 [2004].
32. Ibid., para. 1.
33. Ibid., para. 86.
34. For arguments against such an expansion see Ardi Imseis, 'Agora: Advisory Opinion on Construction of a Wall in the Palestinian Occupied Territory: Critical Reflections on the International Humanitarian Law Aspects of the ICJ Wall Advisory Opinion', *American Journal of International Law* 99 (2005): 102.
35. *Beit Sourik*, para. 36.
36. Ibid., para. 32.
37. HCJ 24/91, *Timraz et al.* v. *IDF Commander of the Gaza Strip*, 45(2) PD 325.
38. HCJ 2056/04, *Beit Sourik* v. *Israel*, para. 32.
39. HCJ 7957/04, *Mara'abe* v. *Prime Minister of Israel* PD 38 (2) 393 [2005].
40. Solon Solomon, *The Justiciability of International Disputes: The Advisory Opinion on Israel's Security Fence as a Case Study* (Nijmegen: Wolf Legal Publishers, 2009), 176.
41. On this see *Mara'abe*, paras 1, 24.
42. Ibid., paras 18, 21.
43. Solomon, *The Justiciability of International Disputes*, 140; David Kretzmer, 'The Light Treatment of International Humanitarian Law', *Am. J. Int'l. L.* 99 (2005): 88, 93; Shany, 'Capacities and Inadequacies', 243.
44. HCJ 769/02, *Public Committee Against Torture* v. *Israel*, Judgment of 11 December 2005, paras 1–2, http://elyon1.court.gov.il/files_eng/02/690/007/A34/02007690.a34.htm.
45. Ibid., para. 63.
46. Ibid., para. 22.

47. Ibid., para. 46. On the right to protect the life of the soldiers see also Solon Solomon, 'Targeted Killings and the Soldiers' Right to Life', *ILSA Journal of International Law* 14 (2007): 99.
48. Public Committee Against Torture, para. 57.
49. Ibid., para. 35. See also Inter-American Commission on Human Rights, Third Report on Human Rights in Colombia, paras 53, 56 (1999).
50. Ibid., para. 22.
51. Ibid., paras 61–4.
52. Kristen Eichensehr, 'On Target? The Israeli Supreme Court and the Expansion of Targeted Killings', *Yale Law Journal* 116 (2007): 1873.
53. Feisal Mohamed, 'The Targeted Killing Memo: What the U.S. could Learn from Israel', *The Huffington Post*, 2 June 2013; Lesley Wexler, 'The Role of the U.S. Judicial Branch during the Long War: Drone Courts, Damage Suits, and Freedom of Information Act (FOIA) Requests in Applying International Humanitarian Law', in *Judicial and Quasi-Judicial Bodies: International and Domestic Aspects*, ed. Derek Jinks, Jackson Nyamuya Maogoto, and Solon Solomon (The Hague: TMC Asser Press, 2014), 61.
54. For a critical stance on the influence of the particular decision on the International Committee of the Red Cross Interpretative Guidance see W. Hays Parks, 'Direct Participation in Hostilities: Perspectives on the ICRC Interpretive Guidance: Part IX of the ICRC "Direct Participation in Hostilities" Study: No Mandate, No Expertise, and Legally Incorrect', *New York University Journal of International Law & Policy* 42 (2010): 769, 793.
55. Israeli Ministry of Foreign Affairs, 'Security Cabinet Declares Gaza Hostile Territory', 19 September 2007, http://www.mfa.gov.il/MFA/Government/Communiques/2007/Security+Cabinet+declares+Gaza+hostile+territory+19-Sep-2007.htm.
56. Ibid. See also the relevant statements of senior Israeli defence officials that 'we need to show the residents of Gaza that life does not carry on freely when Kassam rockets fall in Israel. If rockets are fired, then the Palestinians will pay a price'.Quoted by Yaakov Katz, 'Barak Set to Approve List of Sanctions against Gaza', *Jerusalem Post*, 23 October 2007, http://www.jpost.com/servlet/Satellite?cid=1192380628338&pagename=JPost%2FJPArticle%2FPrinter. See also this statement made in the plaintiff's writ to the Supreme Court, *Al-Bassiouni et al.* v. *Prime Minister of Israel*, Plaintiff's Writ (28 October 2007), 14, 46, http://www.gisha.org/UserFiles/File/Legal%20Documents%20/fuel%20and%20electricity_oct_07/petition-fuel%20and%20electricity%20-%20final-no%20details.pdf.
57. Solon Solomon, 'The Great Oxymoron: Jus in Bello Violations as Legitimate non-forcible Measures, of Self-Defence: The Post-Disengagement Israeli Measures towards Gaza as a Case Study', *Chinese Journal of International Law* 9 (2010): 501, 522.
58. HCJ 9132/07, *Al-Bassiouni et al.* v. *Prime Minister of Israel*, Judgment of 30 January 2008, para. 2, http://elyon1.court.gov.il/files/07/320/091/N25/07091320.n25.pdf.
59. Ibid., para. 22.
60. Ibid., paras 4, 11.
61. For the augmenting role of quasi-judicial bodies in the application of international humanitarian law see Russell Buchan, 'The Mavi Marmara Incident and the Application of International Humanitarian Law by Quasi-Judicial Bodies', in *Applying International Humanitarian Law in Judicial and Quasi-Judicial Bodies*, 479, 496.
62. Turkel Committee Report: Public Commission to Examine the Maritime Incident (2011), http://www.turkel-committee.gov.il/files/wordocs/8808report-eng.pdf.
63. 'Turkey FM: We Can't Stop Upcoming Aid Flotilla to Gaza, Haaretz', 30 May 2011, http://www.haaretz.com/news/diplomacy-defense/turkey-fm-we-can-t-stop-upcoming-aid-flotilla-to-gaza-1.364980.
64. Turkel Committee Report, 51.
65. Ibid., 50.
66. Ibid., 48.
67. Ibid.
68. Citizenship and Entry into Israel Law (Temporary Order), 2003, S.H. 544.
69. Daphne Barak-Erez, 'Israel: Citizenship and Immigration Law in the Vise of Security, Nationality, and Human Rights', *International Journal of Constitutional Law* 6 (2008): 184, 185.
70. Guy Davidof and others, 'State or Family? Citizenship Law and Law of Entry to Israel (Provisional Measure)-2003′ [in Hebrew] *Law & Governance* 8 (2005): 643, 646.

71. Yoav Peled, *The Challenge of Ethnic Democracy: The State and Minority Groups in Israel, Poland and Northern Ireland* (Oxford: Routledge, 2014), 134; Ruth Lapidoth and Ofra Friesel, 'Some Reflections on Israel's Temporary Legislation on Unification of Families', *Isr. L. Rev.* 43 (2010): 457, 459; HCJ 7052/03, *Adalah et al.* v. *Minister of Interior*, Judgment of 14 May 2006 (Rivlin), para. 17.
72. On this see Barak-Erez, 'Israel', 185 (noting that the amendment was enacted is based on an assumption that all Palestinians residing in Israel would uniformly place loyalty to their people above loyalty to the state).
73. HCJ 7052/03, *Adalah et al.* v. *Minister of Interior*, Judgment of 14 May 2006.
74. Ibid. (Barak), para. 1.
75. Ibid. (Barak), para. 84.
76. Ibid. (Barak), paras 79–81.
77. Ibid. (Barak), para. 81.
78. Daphne Barak-Erez, 'Preserving Civil Liberties in an Age of Global Terror: International Perspectives: Terrorism and Profiling: Shifting the Focus from Criteria to Effects', *Cardozo Law Review* 29 (2007): 1, 6–9.
79. Peled, *The Challenge of Ethnic Democracy*, 138.
80. HCJ 466/07, *Galon and als.* v. *Minister of Interior*, Judgment 11 January 2012, http://elyon1.court.gov.il/files/07/660/004/o30/07004660.o30.htm.
81. Ibid. (Levy), paras 32, 46.
82. HCJ 7052/03 (Chesin), para. 47; ibid. (Barak), paras 38–9; ibid. (Levy), para. 7.
83. See also Guidelines on the Applicable Criteria and Standards relating to the Detention of Asylum-Seekers and Alternatives to Detention, UN Refugee Agency, 2012 Guideline No. 30, http://www.unhcr.org/505b10ee9.html.
84. Guideline No. 30.
85. Article 26 of the Refugees Convention prohibits posing restrictions to individuals that have presented themselves before state authorities. On this see also James Hathaway, *The Rights of Refugees under International Law* (Cambridge: Cambridge University Press, 2005), 706–8. For the fact that this is the position adopted also by the European Union see Directive 2008/115/EC of 16 December 2008 on Common Standards and Procedures in Member States for Returning Illegally Staying Third-Country Nationals, O.J. L 348/98, Preamble, Recital 9.
86. Donald Kerwin, 'The Use and Misuse of "National Security" Rationale in Crafting U.S. Refugee and Immigration Policies', *International Journal of Refugee Law* 17 (2005): 749, 763.
87. Ibid., 758–9. See also Reuven Ziegler, noting that the lengthy detention period of up to three years is meant to deter future asylum-seekers from crossing Israel's border and as such is not in tandem with the Geneva Convention on the Status of Refugees. Reuven Ziegler, 'The New Amendment to the "Prevention of Infiltration" Act: Defining Asylum-Seekers as Criminals', 16 January 2012, http://en.idi.org.il/analysis/articles/the-new-amendment-to-the-prevention-of-infiltration-act-defining-asylum-seekers-as-criminals. Ibid., 758–9.
88. *A. and Others* v. *United Kingdom*, Grand Chamber, Application No. 3455/05, Judgment, 19 February 2009.
89. Ruvi Ziegler, 'Detention of African Asylum Seekers: Welcome to Round Three', Interest Group on Migration and Refugee Law, 19 December 2014, https://migreflaw.wordpress.com/2014/12/19/detention-of-african-asylum-seekers-welcome-to-round-three/.
90. *N.* v. *Knesset*, Petition for Provisional Decree and Emergency Hearings, 4 October 2012, paras 208–9 (on file with the author) (in Hebrew).
91. HCJ 7385/13, para. 29.
92. *N.* v. *Knesset*, Petition for Provisional Decree and Emergency Hearings, 4 October 2012, para. 195 (on file with the author) (in Hebrew).
93. Reuven Ziegler, 'A Matter of Definition: On Infiltrators and Asylum Seekers in Israel', The Israel Democracy Institute, 26 January 2011, http://en.idi.org.il/analysis/articles/a-matter-of-definition-on-infiltrators-and-asylum-seekers-in-israel. For a similar tendency in the Canadian legal order see Sharryn Aiken, 'Manufacturing "Terrorists": Refugees, National Security and Canadian Law, part 2, 19 *Refuge*, 116 (2001).
94. HCJ 7146/12, para. 50; ibid. (Folgeman), paras 10–11.
95. Ibid. (Arbel), para. 120.

96. HCJ 7385/13, para. 37.
97. Ibid.
98. Ibid. (Folgeman), para. 45.
99. Ibid. (Arbel), paras 112–13.
100. Ibid. (Arbel), para. 120.
101. Ibid. (Jubran), para. 3.
102. HCJ 7146/12, *Adam* v. *The Knesset*, Judgment 16 September 2013 [in Hebrew], http://elyon1.court.gov.il/files/12/460/071/b24/12071460.b24.htm.
103. Reuven Ziegler, 'On the Israeli Supreme Court Judgment', Blogpost, Interest Group on Migration and Refugee Law, 22 September 2013, http://migreflaw.wordpress.com/2013/09/22/blogpost-on-the-israeli-supreme-court-judgment/.
104. *Adam* v. *The Knesset*, 120.
105. *Anonymous et al.* v. *The Knesset*, Petition, 15 December 2013 [in Hebrew], http://www.acri.org.il/he/wp-content/uploads/2013/12/hit8425.pdf.
106. HCJ 7385/13 *Eitan* v. *Israel*, Judgment 22 September 2014.
107. For the need of such a balance see Golder and Williams, 'Balancing National Security and Human Rights', 49; contra Simon Bronitt, 'Constitutional Rhetoric v. Criminal Justice Realities: Unbalanced Responses to Terrorism?' *Public Law Review*, 14 (2003): 70, 80; Mark Neocleous, 'Security, Liberty and the Myth of Balance: Towards a Critic of Security Politics', *Contemporary Political Theory*, 6 (2007): 131.
108. Thus in the realms of Indian constitutionalism see the opinion of former Chief Justice Venkatachaliah that national security and human rights are not antithetical, in: 'Editorial, National Security and Human Rights Not Antithetical', *Times of India*, 20 April 1998, at 11. Moreover, in Indian constitutionalism such balancing between national security and human rights is not taking place explicitly but in a more discreet way through the restrictive reading of national security measures such as that of preventive detention. On this see C. Raj Kumar, 'Human Rights Implications of National Security Laws in India: Combating Terrorism while Preserving Civil Liberties', *Denver Journal of International Law & Policy* 33 (2005): 195, 213–14. For the fact that in Indian Supreme Court jurisprudence invocation of the 'public interest' sometimes has national security grounds lying behind it, see Sudha Setty, 'Litigating Secrets: Comparative Perspectives on the State Secrets Privilege', *Brooklyn Law Review* 75 (2009): 201, 251–4 .
109. Lorenzo Zucca, 'A Transantlantic Divide on the Balance Between Fundamental Rights and Security', *Boston College International and Comparative Law Review* 32 (2009): 231, 232. On the US position see also William W. Burke-White, 'Human Rights and National Security: The Strategic Correlation', *Harvard Human Rights Journal* 17 (2004): 249; Eillen Kaufman, 'Deference or Abdication: A Comparison of the Supreme Courts of Israel and the United States in cases involving Real or Perceived Threats to National Security', *Washington University Global Studies Law Review* 12 (2013): 95, 96.
110. Nicolo Nourafchan, 'Judging Torture: Lessons from Israel', *Georgetown Journal of International Law* 43 (2012): 1259, 1314–15.
111. See also the view of Professor Shlomo Shlonim in Malvina Halberstam, 'Judicial Review: A Comparative Perspective: Israel, Canada and the United States', *Cardozo Law Review* 31 (2010): 2393, 2434.
112. See Alison Brysk, 'Human Rights and National Insecurity in National Insecurity and Human Rights: Democracies Debate Counterterrorism', in *National Insecurity and Human Rights*, 4 (noting that whereas the US faced 9/11 with a relative dearth of recent security doctrine, Germany had absorbed a systematic reconstitution of its identity following defeat in World War II, previous democratic response to a more manageable terrorist threat during the 1970s and a strong normative and institutional commitment to European regional security). See also Lorenzo Zucca's observation that 'decades of conflict, which brought condemnation by the European Court of Human Rights, taught the United Kingdom that terrorism should be addressed within the established criminal justice system'. Zucca, 'A Transantlantic Divide on the Balance Between Fundamental Rights and Security', 236. For the fact that the Israeli Supreme Court has been criticised in the way it treated national security matters in the 1990s see Ardi Imseis, '"Moderate" Torture on Trial: Critical Reflections on the Israeli Supreme Court judgment concerning the legality of General Security Service Interrogation Methods', *Berkeley J. Int'l. L.* 19 (2001): 328.

113. See for example the issue of the drones and the Al-Aulaqi lawsuits in the US. On this see Lesley Wexler, 'The Role of the U.S. Judicial Branch during the Long War', in *Applying International Humanitarian Law in Judicial and Quasi-Judicial Bodies*, 61.
114. David Cole, 'International Law and the War on Terror: Rights over Borders: Transnational Constitutionalism and Guantanamo Bay', *Cato Supreme Court Review* 47 (2007–2008).
115. *Charkaoui* v. *Canada* (Citizenship and Immigration) [2007] 1 S.C.R. 350, 2007 SCC 9.
116. *Canada (Prime Minister)* v. *Khadr* [2010] 1 S.C.R. 44, 2010 SCC 3.
117. Manuel Altozano, Garzon Investigara Guantanamo al no Constar Causas Abiertas en EE UU, El Pais, 30 January 2010, http://elpais.com/diario/2010/01/30/espana/1264806007_850215.html.
118. Bundesverfassungsgericht [BVerfG] [Federal Constitutional Court] 4 April 2006, 1 BvR 518/02 (F.R.G.); Bundesgerichtshof [BFG] [Federal Court of Justice] 26 October 2006, III ZR 40/06 (F.R.G.).
119. Olivier Lepsius, 'Human Dignity and the Downing of Aircraft', *German Law Journal* 7 (2006): 761.
120. Solomon, 'The Dynamic Law of Occupation', 59.

The use of incapacitating chemical agent weapons in law enforcement

Michael Crowley and Malcolm Dando

University of Bradford, UK

This article explores the implications for human rights and human security arising from the development and use of weapons employing certain toxic chemicals, termed incapacitating chemical agents (ICAs), ostensibly intended for law enforcement operations. Publicly accessible information clearly indicates that China, Israel and the Russian Federation have acquired or developed ICA weapons, and that such weapons are either in the possession, or have been used by law enforcement or security services, of those countries since the coming into force of the Chemical Weapons Convention (CWC) in 1997. Although there is evidence of potentially applicable dual-use research in additional states, the full nature and purpose of such research, in certain states, is unclear as are the intended applications to which it will be put. Following a survey of state practice, existing obligations upon states derived from relevant international law are examined, specifically the CWC and applicable human rights instruments. Whilst existing international law certainly severely constrains and arguably prohibits the development, acquisition and use of such weapons for law enforcement, there are areas of contested interpretation, which need to be urgently addressed by the international community.

1. Introduction

The use of the toxic properties of any chemical as a weapon in armed conflict is absolutely prohibited under international law, specifically customary international humanitarian law and also under the Chemical Weapons Convention (CWC).[1] However, there has been long-standing interest by certain states in exploring the development and potential utility of weapons employing certain toxic chemicals, termed incapacitating chemical agents (ICAs), ostensibly intended for law enforcement operations; and there has been one large-scale use of such an ICA weapon by the Russian Federation in a counter-terrorist operation in 2002. This article explores the potential implications for human rights and human security arising from the further development and use of such weapons.

The article surveys contemporary chemical and life science research potentially applicable to the study or development of ICA weapons, and highlights reported possession or use of such weapons by states. It also explores contemporary advances in relevant science and technologies and the potential implications for ICA weapons development.

The article subsequently analyses existing obligations upon states in this area derived from relevant international law, specifically the CWC as well as applicable regional and international human rights instruments. The article argues that whilst existing international law certainly severely constrains and arguably prohibits the development, acquisition and use of such weapons for law enforcement purposes, there are areas of contested interpretation. The article consequently recommends that the international community, through relevant mechanisms and forums, address these disputed issue areas; if it does not do so in the near future, a growing number of states may seek to harness advances in relevant scientific disciplines in ICA weapons development programmes with the consequent threat of the proliferation and misuse of such weapons.

2. ICA weapons – difficulties with definitions

Although certain states and pluri-lateral organisations[2] have sought to characterise incapacitating chemical agents (ICAs), there is currently no internationally accepted definition for these substances. Indeed certain leading scientific experts and international organisations believe that such a technical definition is not possible.[3] Whilst recognising the contested nature of this discourse, a provisional working description of ICAs based upon that developed by the United Kingdom's (UK) Royal Society[4] will be employed in this article. Consequently, ICAs will be considered as: substances whose purported intended use is to cause prolonged but non-permanent disability; they include centrally acting agents producing loss of consciousness, sedation, hallucination, incoherence, paralysis, disorientation or other such effects. Potential candidate ICAs for weaponisation could include a broad range of pharmaceutical chemicals many of which are legitimately used in medicine, as well as bio-regulators and toxins.

For the purposes of this article, an 'ICA weapon' will be considered to comprise an ICA and/or associated means of delivery, developed with the purported intention of temporarily incapacitating but not killing a target.[5] Candidate agents for ICA weapons typically possess a very low safety margin (the difference between desirable and undesirable effects), so the effects of ICA weapons are in fact variable and can include death.[6] ICA weapons are distinct from riot control agents (RCAs), which act on the peripheral nervous system to produce rapid sensory irritation of the eyes, mucus membranes and skin, and whose effects disappear shortly after termination of exposure.[7]

3. ICA weapons – potential dangers and purported utility

Proponents of ICA weapons have promoted their development and use in certain law enforcement scenarios where there is a need to rapidly and completely incapacitate a single individual or a group without causing death or permanent disability, for example in armed sieges where hostages have been taken. They have also been raised as a possible tool in a variety of military operations, especially in situations where fighters and civilians are in close proximity with each other.[8] Such perceptions of utility were noted in the 2011 report of a high-level expert panel convened by the Director General of the Organisation for the Prohibition of Chemical Weapons (OPCW), which stated:

> ... distinctions between law enforcement, counter-terrorism, counter-insurgency and low-intensity warfare may get blurred, and certain types of chemical weapons such as ICAs [incapacitating chemical agents] may appear to offer tactical solutions to operational scenarios where civilians and combatants cannot easily be separated or distinguished.[9]

In contrast, a broad range of observers, including scientific and medical professionals, arms control organisations, international legal experts, human rights and humanitarian organisations, as well as a number of states, are critical of the development and utility of ICA weapons, highlighting that the use of such weapons presents potentially grave dangers to health and well-being. The British Medical Association, for example, has concluded that:

> The agent whereby people could be incapacitated without risk of death in a tactical situation does not exist and is unlikely to in the foreseeable future. In such a situation, it is and will continue to be, almost impossible to deliver the right agent to the right people in the right dose without exposing the wrong people, or delivering the wrong dose.[10]

Further concerns that have been raised are the risk of 'creeping legitimisation' of ICA weapons with the erosion of the norm against the weaponisation of toxicity[11]; the dangers of ICA weapons proliferation to both state and non-state actors[12]; their potential use as a lethal 'force multiplier'; their employment to facilitate torture and other human rights violations[13]; the further misuse and militarisation of the life sciences[14]; the potential for states to use law enforcement ICA weapons development as a cover for covert offensive chemical weapons programmes[15]; and the danger of creating a 'slippery slope' that could lead to chemical warfare.[16]

4. Survey of state practice

Past research and implications of contemporary advances in science and technology

From the late 1940s onwards, military, security or police bodies and policymakers of certain countries have explored the potential utility of ICA weapons. States that reportedly conducted research and attempted development of ICA weapons or acquired such weapons at some stage prior to the signing of the CWC in 1993 included: Albania, China, Iraq, Israel, (Apartheid) South Africa, the Soviet Union, the United Kingdom, the United States of America and Yugoslavia.[17]

Given the previous concerted attempts by a number of states to develop ICA weapons, concerns have grown that the revolutionary changes occurring in a range of relevant chemical and life science disciplines and technologies including neuroscience, medicinal pharmacology and synthetic biology may be exploited in the weaponisation of ICAs and the development of other chemical weapons. Dr Ralf Trapp voiced such concerns during a 2010 expert meeting on ICAs convened by the International Committee of the Red Cross (ICRC):

> The explosion of knowledge in neuroscience, bioregulators, receptor research, systems biology and related disciplines is likely to lead to the discovery, amongst others, of new physiologically-active compounds that can selectively interfere with certain regulatory functions in the brain or other organs, and presumably even modulate human behavior in a predictable manner. Some of these new compounds (or selective delivery methods) may well have a profile that could make them attractive as novel candidate chemical warfare agents.[18]

Advances in the discovery or synthetic production of potential ICAs are just part of the story and have occurred in parallel with developments in particle engineering and nanotechnology that could allow the delivery of biologically active chemicals to specific target organs or receptors. The implications of this were highlighted in the 2008 report by the National Research Council (NRC) on Emerging Cognitive Neuroscience and Related Technologies, which warned that nanotechnologies could be used to overcome the blood-brain barrier and thereby 'enable unparalleled access to the brain. Nanotechnologies can also exploit existing transport mechanisms to transmit substances into the brain in analogy with the Trojan horse.'[19]

The 2008 NRC report also highlighted the potential threats resulting from developments in nanotechnologies or gas-phase techniques that allow dispersal of highly potent chemicals over wide areas. It noted that at the present time 'pharmacological agents are not used as weapons of mass effect, because their large-scale deployment is impractical' as it is 'currently impossible to get an effective dose to a combatant'. However, the report stated that 'technologies that could be available in the next 20 years would allow dispersal of agents in delivery vehicles that would be analogous to a pharmacological cluster bomb or a land mine'.[20]

Analysis of contemporary dual-use research potentially applicable to ICA weapons; and/or reported development or use of ICA weapons

In the light of such ongoing concerns, a survey of contemporary dual-use[21] chemical and life science research of potential relevance to the study or development of ICAs and associated means of delivery was conducted by the authors of this article, in two stages.[22] In stage one, an initial survey of relevant open source literature was undertaken including: scientific and medical databases and publications detailing research activities in relevant disciplines; government documents pertaining to past state ICA weapons development programmes; technology monitoring or evaluation reports from relevant bodies such as the Scientific Advisory Board of the OPCW and the International Union of Pure and Applied Chemistry. The information obtained was reviewed against a range of indicators of potential concern so as to narrow the focus of subsequent in-depth research conducted in stage two to a discrete number of illustrative country case studies. In addition to documenting a range of potentially applicable research, the survey also collected and analysed information concerning reported development, possession or use of such weapons in certain states. Prior to publication, repeated attempts were made to contact the relevant government authorities of those states identified in the survey to provide them with an opportunity for clarification; substantive responses were cited in the study report, as appropriate.

China

From at least the mid-1990s there appears to have been development, production and promotion of a weapon incorporating an unidentified ICA for use in law enforcement operations against individuals. In 1995, marketing materials distributed internationally by the state-owned China North Industries Corporation (NORINCO) promoted the 'BBQ-901 anaesthetic gun system'. This weapon discharges a projectile, with an effective range of 40 metres, which on impact injects a liquid incapacitating chemical agent into the target.[23] According to NORINCO:

> The Model BBQ-901 Anaesthetic system is a fine unlethal [sic] special weapon system for SWAT units and other special usage ... It can be used for reconnaissance and capture of criminals in a concealed place. It is also used as a riot control weapon to subdue the ruffians and maintain public order.[24]

In 2004 and 2006, the essentially similar if not identical 'BBQ-901 narcosis gun' was promoted by a second Chinese state-owned company, State 9616 Plant, at the Asia Pacific

China Police Expo held in Beijing.[25] In 2012 such weapons were reportedly held by the Chinese Peoples' Liberation Army.[26] China has provided no public information regarding its stockpiles of these weapons nor the specific purposes of their intended employment. To date, China has made no statement clarifying whether any Chinese entity has conducted or is conducting research activities related to the development of ICA weapons targeting groups of individuals.

Czech Republic

From 2005 to 2007, Czech scientists published papers describing their investigations over several years relating to a range of pharmaceutical chemicals including various opioids, ketamine, medetomidine and midazolam, specifically highlighting their potential utility as, in their own words, 'pharmacological non-lethal weapons'.[27] Research into such chemicals continued after 2007, but additional papers contained no explicit reference to their potential application as so-called 'pharmacological non-lethal weapons'.[28] The Czech Republic CWC National Authority subsequently investigated Czech research activities and in 2014 correspondence with the authors stated that 'There was no connection [between] the research [and] creation of any sort of weapons or devices which could be used for military or police purposes.'[29] With regard to the Czech 'pharmacological non-lethal weapons' papers, the National Authority stated that 'research programmes had justifiable medical goals, but their reporting in public media exceeded actual results of the research thus creating a false impression of possible development of some sort of chemical weapons'.[30]

India

Scientists at the Defence Research and Development Organisation (DRDO) have conducted work related to the synthesis, aersolisation and bio-efficacy of fentanyl and its analogues, as described in papers from 2005 till 2013.[31] In 2014 correspondence with the authors, the Indian CWC National Authority, gave 'categorical and unambiguous clarifications' that India has no stockpile of ICAs and is not involved in the weaponisation of ICAs.[32] In its response, the Indian CWC National Authority did confirm that 'DRDE/DRDO undertakes research into fentanyl and its analogues' but that this was 'only for purposes of characterization including its detection and protection aspects'.[33] It is not known whether such activities have been reported to the OPCW as part of India's annual declaration of national programmes related to 'protective purposes'.[34]

Iran

Research scientists at Imam Hossein University (IHU) have explored the structural-activity relationships of fentanyl and its analogues and have attempted to generate stable long-lasting aerosols of medetomidine and other potential ICAs; their work has been detailed in papers from 2007 till 2013.[35] IHU is an academic institution run along military lines and controlled by the Iranian Revolutionary Guard.[36] In 2014 correspondence with the authors, the Iranian CWC National Authority stated this 'academic research is financed by [the] ministry of science and technology' and is 'solely [for] scientific purposes'.[37]

Israel

In its 2005 analysis of Israel's biological and chemical programmes, the Swedish Defence Research Institute concluded that: 'The state previously developed offensive biological and chemical warfare capabilities. It has not been possible to conclude if these offensive programs still remain active today.'[38] In addition, the authors contended that Israel had the 'scientific know-how and the industrial infrastructure to de novo produce and deploy militarily significant CBW rapidly if so desired' and that the 'focus of the Israeli chemical and biological capacity today is to develop agents for small-scale covert use, i.e. a so-called "dirty tricks" program'.[39]

There has, to date, been one widely reported use of an incapacitating chemical agent (thought to be fentanyl) by the Israeli security services (Mossad) in October 1997, in either a failed assassination attempt or a kidnapping operation that subsequently went awry.[40] The target was Mr Khalid Mishal, a then mid-ranking Hamas leader living in Jordan. Israeli officials subsequently interviewed by *Janes Intelligence Review* and *Time* magazine claimed that Mossad had employed such techniques in previous operations.[41] The Israeli government is reported to have publicly admitted responsibility for the attack on 5 October 1997, and on 7 October initiated an inquiry into the incident.[42] There have been no subsequent reports of use by the Israeli security or military forces of weapons employing fentanyl or other ICAs.

There is insufficient publicly available information to determine whether any Israeli entity is currently undertaking research into, or attempting to develop weapons employing, ICAs, or whether Israel holds stockpiles of such weapons. There is limited information available indicating that the Israel Institute for Biological Research may be conducting work in potentially relevant dual-use fields, although the details of the specific research projects are not available.[43]

Russian Federation

There are indications of long-standing research into ICA weapons by the Russian Federation prior to and following the coming into force of the CWC. Disquiet about such activities grew following the large-scale employment by Russian security forces of an ICA weapon, believed to affect the central nervous system, in an attempt to save 900 hostages held in the Dubrovka theatre in Moscow by armed Chechen fighters.[44] Although the majority of the hostages were rescued, at least 125 were killed by the chemical agent and an undetermined, but large, additional number suffered long-term damage, or died prematurely in the years after the siege.[45]

Treatment of the hostages who had been poisoned was delayed and compromised by the refusal of the Russian authorities to state publicly what type of ICA had been used in the theatre.[46] Although the Russian Health Minister, Yuri Shevchenko, finally identified the incapacitating agent as 'a mixture of derivative substances of the fast action opiate Fentanyl' on 30 October 2002,[47] the Russian Federation has, to date, provided no further public information on the chemical(s) employed. However, trace analysis undertaken by researchers from the UK's Defence Science and Technology Laboratory of clothing and urine from survivors of the siege indicated that the ICA weapon comprised a mixture of two anaesthetics: carfentanil and remifentanil.[48]

Russian researchers have subsequently continued work of potential application to the development of ICA weapons including computer modelling of so-called 'calmative gas flows' in enclosed spaces, as detailed in a 2005 paper,[49] and a 2009 presentation of a then ongoing research project called *Project 'Gas Flow'*.[50] Research has also been undertaken relating to opiate receptors (OR) and their interaction with OR ligands, detailed in papers from 2005 till 2012.[51] To date, the Russian Federation has provided no public information as to whether stockpiles of weaponised ICAs are currently held in the Russian

Federation, nor whether research into the development and employment of weaponised ICAs is taking place, and if so, for what purposes.

Syria

Since the 1970s, Syria has reportedly acquired and/or developed and stockpiled a range of chemical weapons and agent precursors[52] – this stockpile has now been declared and is being destroyed under OPCW supervision.[53] From early 2012, there have been repeated but, to date, unconfirmed allegations that the Syrian government armed forces employed ICA weapons during the ongoing conflict with armed opposition forces.[54]

United Kingdom (UK)

The UK government has released documents detailing the country's previous attempts to develop ICA weapons for military purposes from 1959 to 1972.[55] There is no evidence of a subsequent military ICA weapons development programme. There are indications of ICA research continuing into the 1980s, although the nature and purpose of such activities are not known.[56] In the early-to-mid-2000s, the UK government assessed the feasibility of introducing ICA weapons for certain law enforcement purposes,[57] but subsequently rejected this option.[58] In 2013, the UK 'unequivocally' declared that it 'neither holds nor is developing any ICAs for law enforcement'.[59] UK researchers based at Porton Down have conducted research into ICAs for 'protective purposes', and the UK has provided some information on these activities to the OPCW in its annual Article X declarations, and also to the UK parliament.[60]

United States of America (US)

The US has a long history of research into ICA weapons dating back to the 1950s. Approximately 60,000 kilograms of BZ (3-quinuclidinyl benzilate) were manufactured and the agent was weaponised in two munition types that entered the US arsenal in 1964.[61] There are no confirmed reports that ICA weapons were ever employed in armed conflict by the US, and all stockpiles were subsequently destroyed in the late 1980s and 1990s.[62] Research into ICA weapons continued for both military and law enforcement purposes, even after the coming into force of the CWC, although there is no evidence of completed development or production of ICA weapons.[63] In 2013 and then again in 2014, the US formally declared that it 'is not developing, producing, stockpiling, or using incapacitating chemical agents'.[64] It is not currently known whether the US undertakes dual-use research related to ICAs for 'protective purposes', and if so how and whether this is reported to the OPCW.

5. Application of the Chemical Weapons Convention

The Chemical Weapons Convention, under Article I, prohibits the development, production, stockpiling, transfer and use of chemical weapons 'under any circumstances'.[65] The CWC does not explicitly prohibit research relating to chemical weapons (for example for 'protective purposes').[66] However, where research is an intrinsic part of a weapons development programme it clearly will fall within the scope of the Article I prohibition. The convention also requires that all existing stocks of chemical weapons[67] and chemical weapons production facilities be destroyed.[68] Although the convention prohibits chemical weapons, it allows for the controlled peaceful use of toxic chemicals.[69]

The convention defines chemical weapons, under Article II(1), as including: 'toxic chemicals and their precursors, except where intended for purposes not prohibited, as long as the types and quantities are consistent with such purposes'.[70] Article II(2) defines a toxic chemical as: ' ... any chemical, regardless of its origin or method of production, which, through chemical action on life processes, can cause death, temporary incapacitation or permanent harm to humans or animals'.[71]

Although the convention includes three Annexes of scheduled toxic chemicals specifically 'identified for the application of verification measures',[72] the scope of the convention is not constrained to these schedules but is determined by Article II(1), otherwise known as the general purpose criterion (GPC). Because the GPC establishes a prohibition based on intent rather than on a limited list of toxic chemical agents, it allows the convention to accommodate and reflect developments in science; consequently, as Meselson and Perry Robinson have highlighted, 'even toxic chemicals whose existence is not yet known are covered' by its provisions.[73]

Since those chemicals promoted for use as ICA weapons can 'through chemical action on life processes ... cause death, temporary incapacitation or permanent harm' to their targets, they are toxic chemicals and are covered under the scope of the convention.[74] Such toxic chemicals would be deemed to be chemical weapons (and therefore prohibited) if they were used for purposes other than those exemptions stipulated under Article II(9) of the convention,[75] or if their use was inconsistent with the types and quantities restriction of Article II.

Use of ICA weapons in armed conflict

The use in armed conflict of the toxic properties of chemical agents as weapons is absolutely prohibited,[76] as is their development, production, acquisition, stockpiling, retention or transfer when intended for such purposes, under Articles I and II. If states have undertaken programmes to develop ICAs and/or associated means of delivery for such purposes, they are required to halt such activities, declare any chemical weapons and chemical weapons production facilities they possess (under Article III[77]) and ensure they are verifiably destroyed (under Article I, and in accordance with Articles IV and V respectively[78]).

Use of ICA weapons in law enforcement

Among the 'purposes not prohibited' listed in Article II(9) of the convention is: '(d) Law enforcement including domestic riot control purposes'.[79] However, toxic chemicals can only be employed for such purposes provided their use is consistent with the 'types and quantities' restriction of Article II. Differing interpretations regarding the application of II(1) and Article II (9) d, have led to alternative views from arms control and legal scholars as to whether toxic chemicals promoted as ICAs can ever be used for law enforcement purposes.

One line of interpretation supported by Chayes and Meselson,[80] Krutzsch,[81] Krutzsch and Trapp,[82] and Von Wagner[83] holds that only riot control agents can be used for law enforcement activities under the CWC,[84] and consequently that the use of ICA weapons for law enforcement would be prohibited. Chayes and Meselson, argue that:

> [a] toxic chemical used by virtue of its toxic properties is only of a type consistent with the purpose of law enforcement, in the sense of Article 2.1.a, if it meets the Convention definition of a riot control agent in Article 2.7. Thus such chemicals must be 'not listed in a Schedule' and

> must 'produce rapidly in humans sensory irritation or disabling physical effects which disappear within a short period of time following termination of exposure'.[85]

Whilst Krutzsch and Trapp argue that:

> Article II, subparagraph 9(d) does not permit the use of toxic chemicals other than RCAs for law enforcement purposes. Accepting, in principle, the use of certain toxic chemicals such as ICAs for law enforcement in exceptional situations, for instance during an anti-terrorist operation, would undermine the prohibition on Article I of the Convention and wrongly imply that there was a 'choice' between applying binding rules of treaty interpretation and replacing them by explanations constructed as required by military interest.[86]

A second line of interpretation, as advanced by Fidler,[87] and supported by Neil,[88] contends that international law on treaty interpretation indicates that the CWC does not limit the range of toxic chemicals that can be used for law enforcement purposes to riot control agents. This line of interpretation may allow the use of ICA weapons for law enforcement in certain circumstances. However, Fidler notes that the 'use of a toxic chemical for law enforcement purposes is still subject to the CWC requirements that the types and quantities of chemicals developed, produced, acquired, stockpiled, retained, transferred, or used must be consistent with such permitted purposes (Article II.1 [a.]).'[89] According to Fidler, this restriction therefore 'requires scrutiny of the relationship between the chemical or biochemical agent and the law enforcement objective in question. The more difficult it is to control the effects of the use of a chemical or biochemical in a law enforcement operation, the more suspect such use becomes in terms of the agent being of a type or quantity consistent with a law enforcement purpose.'[90] Consequently, Fidler believes that: 'For domestic law enforcement, use of incapacitating agents in contexts in which the government could control neither dosage nor the exposure environment would only be legitimate in extreme law enforcement situations … For extraterritorial law enforcement activities undertaken by military forces and sanctioned by international law, States can at present only legitimately use riot control agents, not incapacitating agents.'[91] This situation is further complicated by there being no definition of 'law enforcement' in the convention. In addition, the demarcation between potentially permissible 'law enforcement' activities and prohibited 'methods of warfare' under the convention remains unresolved.

The potential threats arising from the development and use of ICAs have led a growing number of CWC state parties to call for this issue to be addressed by the OPCW. Switzerland in particular has repeatedly championed this issue,[92] and at the CWC Third Review Conference in 2013, highlighted its 'fear that the silence and uncertainty surrounding the use of toxic chemicals for law enforcement purposes other than riot control agents risks eroding the Convention … a debate on this issue in the framework of the OPCW should no longer be delay[ed] … '[93] Concerns regarding ICAs were also raised at the Review Conference by Germany which submitted a working paper on this issue, as did Ireland, Norway, Romania, Slovakia, the UK, the US, and the International Committee of the Red Cross.[94] However, despite widespread support, the Third Review Conference failed to agree a process for the organisation to initiate consultations on this issue.

At the 19th Conference of States Parties, in December 2014, renewed calls for action were raised, most notably by Australia, which: confirm[ed] that it was not 'developing, producing, stockpiling or intending to weaponise or use any CNS [central nervous system] acting chemicals such as anaesthetics, sedatives or analgesics for law enforcement purposes',[95] and called on other states parties which have not already done so[96] 'to make their positions known on the weaponisation of CNS acting chemicals … for law enforcement purposes'.[97] Australia also called for 'consultations, in particular among members of the Executive Council of the OPCW, with a view to commencing discussions as to whether weaponisation of CNS acting chemicals should be permitted for law enforcement purposes'.[98]

However, to date, no OPCW policy-making organ (PMO) has made any interpretative statements regarding application of the CWC in this area or issued guidance as to whether toxic chemicals intended for use as ICA weapons can be employed for law enforcement purposes and, if so, under what circumstances. It is therefore left to individual states parties to interpret the scope and nature of their obligations in this area. When interpreting and implementing their obligations in this area, states parties must also consider their obligations under all relevant international law, with particular attention given to international human rights law.

6. Application of international human rights law

Although human rights law does not specifically address the use of ICA weapons it is certainly applicable to the employment of such weapons, as it regulates the use of force by law enforcement officials and other agents of the state. Human rights law is particularly important to the discussion of ICA weapons as it potentially covers the full 'use of force' spectrum from law enforcement activities through to armed conflict, including 'grey areas' such as counter-terrorist, counter-insurgency and military operations outside armed conflict where use of these weapons has been proposed. While several human rights norms may be applicable, the rights to life, and to freedom from torture and cruel, inhuman or degrading treatment, together with attendant obligations on the restraint of force, are the most relevant.[99]

Protection of the right to life and restrictions on the use of force

Although the issue is contested, certain legal experts believe that the use of ICA weapons may be permissible in extreme law enforcement emergencies (such as hijacking or hostage taking situations) where the authorities need to resort to potentially lethal force to resolve urgent, life-threatening situations because less violent and dangerous methods have failed, are impractical or have low chance of success. However, even in such extreme conditions, the obligations upon states under international[100] and regional[101] human rights instruments to protect the right to life still apply with contingent constraints upon employment of an ICA weapon as well as the requirement to take appropriate remedial measures. Aceves, for example, states that:

> [T]he right to life norm places strict limits on the use of force, which includes the use of incapacitating biochemical weapons ... States must, therefore, act with due diligence in all cases involving these weapons. The use of these weapons must be carefully regulated and cannot cause indiscriminate harm. Their use must be proportionate to the perceived threat and must be justified under the circumstances.[102]

Similarly, Fidler believes that:

> The inability to control dosage or exposure environment in extreme law enforcement emergencies heightens government responsibility to ensure all precautions are taken to minimize harm to innocent people and to provide immediate and adequate medical attention to those exposed and perhaps adversely affected.[103]

Case law in this area is limited. To date, there has been only one well-documented instance of an ICA weapon being used in such a situation, by the Russian Federation in 2002. Two UN human rights authorities issued statements on this case.[104] In a January 2003 report, the UN Special Rapporteur on Extra-Judicial, Summary or Arbitrary Executions expressed concern 'about the actions by Russian police/security forces' and stated that he 'has been collecting information from various sources about the incident and plans to take the issue up in 2003 with the Government of the Russian Federation'.[105] To date, however, the results of the rapporteur's actions on this issue have not been made public. Subsequently, in June 2003, the UN Human Rights Committee declared that: 'While acknowledging the serious nature of the hostage-taking situation, the Committee cannot but be concerned at the outcome of the rescue operation in the Dubrovka theatre in Moscow on 26 October 2002.'[106] The committee further expressed 'its concern that there has been no independent and impartial assessment of the circumstances, regarding medical care of the hostages after their liberation and the killing of the hostage-takers'.[107] It called upon the Russian Federation to 'ensure that the circumstances of the rescue operation in the Dubrovka theatre are subject to an independent, in depth investigation, the results of which are made public, and, if appropriate, prosecutions are initiated and compensation paid to the victims and their families'.[108] No further reference appears to this incident in subsequent reports of the UN Human Rights Committee.

A highly significant development has been a judgment in December 2011 by the European Court of Human Rights on this case. In August 2003, a group of 64 former hostages and relatives filed a complaint before the court claiming that their right to life (protected under Article 2 of the European Convention on Human Rights, ECHR) had been violated by the actions of the Russian authorities.[109] The case was accepted by the court in December 2007 and on 20 December 2011 it announced its ruling.[110]

The court rejected the Russian Federation authorities' assertions that the ICA weapon had been harmless, and that according to the official medical examinations of the bodies, no direct causal link had existed between the use of the ICA weapon and the death of the hostages.[111] The court found that even if the ICA weapon had not been a 'lethal force' but rather a 'non-lethal incapacitating weapon', the ICA was, 'at best, potentially dangerous for an ordinary person, and potentially fatal for a weakened person',[112] so the case clearly fell within the ambit of Article 2 of the ECHR.[113] The court declared that: 'it is safe to conclude that the gas remained a primary cause of the death of a large number of the victims'.[114]

Nonetheless, with regard to the decision to storm the theatre and use an ICA weapon, the court stressed that in situations of such a scale and complexity, it was prepared to grant the domestic authorities 'a margin of appreciation,[115] even if now, with hindsight, some of the decisions taken by the authorities may appear open to doubt'.[116] In this particular case, the court believed there had been a real, serious and immediate risk of mass human losses and the authorities had every reason to believe that a forced intervention had been 'the lesser evil'. Although the solution, using a 'dangerous and even potentially lethal' gas, had put at risk the lives of hostages and hostage-takers alike, the court considered 'it was not used "indiscriminately" as it had left the hostages a high chance of survival, which depended on the efficiency of the authorities' rescue effort'.[117] Indeed, the court believed that the use of the ICA weapon facilitated the liberation of the hostages and reduced the likelihood of an explosion. The court therefore concluded that, in the circumstances, the authorities' decision to end the negotiations and resolve the hostage crisis by force by using an ICA weapon and storming the theatre had not been disproportionate and had not, as such, breached Article 2 of the ECHR.[118]

However, the court found that, as a whole, the Russian authorities had not taken all feasible precautions to minimise the loss of civilian life as the rescue operation had been inadequately prepared and carried out, in violation of Article 2.[119] In addition, the court concluded that the investigation into the authorities' alleged negligence during the rescue operation had been neither thorough nor independent and had not therefore been effective, in further violation of Article 2.[120]

The ICRC[121] as well as certain academics[122] have raised concerns about the court's judgment, and there are certainly aspects of this ruling that would benefit from further legal analysis, including: the inexplicable failure of the court to assess the legality of the use of the ICA weapon under the Chemical Weapons Convention[123]; the court's willingness to make a judgment without knowledge of the identity, nature and consequently (predicted) effects of the ICA weapon employed; and the court's claims that it was impossible for it 'to establish whether or not the gas was a "conventional weapon" or to identify the rules for its use'.[124]

However, such concerns notwithstanding, the initial decision, though subject to an appeal, was subsequently made final.[125] Consequently, this ruling is important given the bearing it may have on future judgments on the use of ICA weapons, as well as the interpretations which both proponents and opponents of such weapons may take from its decision. It is notable that the court considered the use of the ICA weapon as definitely falling under the ambit of the ECHR and that such use could potentially be a violation of Article 2 of the convention. It appears that the use of such ICA weapons would only be considered consistent with the convention in very limited, extreme situations (i.e. where there was an immediate and direct threat to life and where there was no recourse to other measures to resolve the situation with less risk of injury or death), and only when such use occurred in conjunction with proper planning and the provision of adequate medical care and remedial support. Although the court gave the Russian Federation some 'margin of appreciation' regarding its decision to use an ICA weapon with then-unknown effects, the consequences of such action have subsequently been shown to include the deaths of a large proportion of the hostages and serious long-term injury for many of the survivors. Given such empirical data on the deleterious effects of the ICA weapon, it is unclear and debatable whether a court would give such a 'margin of appreciation' or range of discretion to a state for the use of an ICA weapon in similar situations in the future.

Finally, and with more general application, this case has highlighted the potential utility of regional human rights mechanisms as a means that victims of human rights violations (including those inappropriately targeted with ICA weapons) can employ to hold the relevant authorities to account (and also in the case of the ECHR to obtain financial compensation for the wrongs done to them).[126] Although the relevant courts[127] have a number of limitations and only have jurisdiction over those states that have ratified the relevant conventions and protocols, they deliver legally binding judgments.[128] Furthermore, as Hampson notes:

> An important feature of these enforcement mechanisms is that, almost uniquely in international law, they can be directly or indirectly triggered by individuals ... who are far more likely to bring such complaints than are foreign States, particularly where the claim concerns something that the State has done on its own territory.[129]

The prohibition against torture and cruel, inhuman or degrading treatment or punishment

Important additional constraints upon the use of ICA weapons arise from the prohibition against torture and cruel, inhuman or degrading treatment or punishment, which is recognised in a wide range of international[130] and regional[131] human rights agreements, and is a customary norm, applicable at all times and in all circumstances, including armed conflict. It is one of the few human rights for which no derogation is permitted.[132] Torture is defined under Article 1 of the United Nations Convention against Torture as:

> any act by which severe pain or suffering, whether physical or mental, is intentionally inflicted on a person for such purposes as obtaining from him or a third person information or a confession, punishing him for an act he or a third person has committed or is suspected of having committed, or intimidating or coercing him or a third person, or for any reason based on discrimination of any kind, when such pain or suffering is inflicted by or at the instigation of or with the consent or acquiescence of a public official or other person acting in an official capacity. It does not include pain or suffering arising only from, inherent in or incidental to lawful sanctions.[133]

Elements of cruel, inhuman or degrading treatment or punishment have been defined in other relevant legal texts. For example, 'inhuman treatment', in the context of war crimes, has been defined in the Elements of Crimes for the International Criminal Court as the infliction of 'severe physical or mental pain or suffering'.[134] The notion of 'degrading treatment' has been defined by the European Commission of Human Rights as treatment or punishment that 'grossly humiliates the victim before others or drives the detainee to act against his/her will or conscience'.[135] The commentary to Principle 6 of the UN Body of Principles for the Protection of All Persons under Any Form of Detention or Imprisonment (which prohibits torture and other forms of cruel, inhuman or degrading treatment or punishment) states that:

> The term 'cruel, inhuman or degrading treatment or punishment' should be interpreted so as to extend the widest possible protection against abuses, whether physical or mental, including the holding of a detained or imprisoned person in conditions which deprive him, temporarily or permanently, of the use of any of his natural senses, such as sight or hearing, or of his awareness of place and the passing of time.[136]

The UN Special Rapporteur on Torture has indicated that the prohibition on cruel, inhuman or degrading treatment or punishment places limits on the lawful use of force. The UN Special Rapporteur has emphasised that the use of force must be regulated by the principles of proportionality and that the disproportionate exercise of police powers might constitute cruel, inhuman or degrading treatment or punishment in certain circumstances.[137]

The consequent obligations upon states are of particular relevance where ICA weapons are being considered for use against prisoners or detainees. After a review of the relevant law, Aceves concludes that:

> [T]he prohibition against cruel, inhuman or degrading treatment places significant restrictions on the use of incapacitating biochemical weapons. These weapons are designed to impair the physical and mental integrity of the individual. Depending on the nature, duration and long-term effects of this impairment, the use of incapacitating biochemical weapons can give rise to a claim of cruel, inhuman, or degrading treatment.[138]

In its report exploring the potential use and misuse of neuroscience, the Royal Society highlights the European Commission of Human Rights' definition of degrading treatment[139] and considers it of 'particular importance in considering the potential applications of neuroscience that could, for example, manipulate behaviour or thought processes'.[140] A supporting note in the Royal Society report observes that: 'the use of potential militarised agents including noradrenaline antagonists such as propranolol to cause selective memory loss, cholecystokinin B agonists to cause panic attacks, and substance P agonists to induce depression could all be considered violations of the prohibition against degrading treatment'.[141]

Fidler states that: 'Non-consensual, non-therapeutic use of any chemical or biochemical against detained individuals would constitute degrading treatment and could, constitute cruel or inhumane treatment and perhaps even torture.'[142] He does, however, believe that there may be situations where use of ICAs might be compatible with international human rights law: where the detained person poses an immediate, violent threat to himself (e.g. attempting suicide) or to safety and order in the detention facility (e.g. attacking guards or participating in riots).[143] Although legal scholars believe that obligations upon states to prevent torture and ill-treatment, under international human rights law, clearly restrict the potential employment of ICA weapons; to date, these issues have not been addressed in relation to such weapons by relevant international and regional treaty bodies or judicial mechanisms.[144]

7. Conclusions

Analysis of open source information conducted by the authors concerning both historical ICA weapons development programmes and contemporary research potentially applicable to the study or development of ICA weapons, indicates that such activities have been undertaken either by scientists operating within state research establishments principally linked to defence, security or law enforcement bodies, or by scientists working in civilian research institutions who are funded or controlled by such bodies. Currently there is no evidence of concerted attempts by non-state actors, such as terrorist groups, to conduct research and development of ICAs as weapons.

Publicly accessible information analysed by the authors clearly indicates that China, Israel and the Russian Federation have acquired or developed ICA weapons, and that such weapons are either in the possession, or have been used by, law enforcement or security services of those countries since the coming into force of the CWC in 1997. Although there is evidence of potentially applicable dual-use research in additional states, the full nature and purpose of such research in certain states is unclear as are the intended applications to which it will be put.

It is clear that incapacitating chemical agents come under the scope of the Chemical Weapons Convention with their use being absolutely prohibited for armed conflict. There are differing interpretations as to whether, and in what circumstances, ICA weapons could be employed for law enforcement purposes. To date no OPCW PMO has made any interpretative statements clarifying whether ICA weapons can legitimately be employed for law enforcement purposes and if so in what circumstances and under what constraints. Consequently states must interpret obligations in this area for themselves, with the potential danger that a 'permissive interpretation' may emerge. States parties should address this regulatory lacuna without delay by initiating a mechanism within the OPCW such as an open-ended working group allowing all states parties to collectively discuss these issues. In addition, individual states parties should affirm that current national practice is to restrict use of toxic chemicals for law enforcement to RCAs. Where such restriction is not existing policy, states should introduce national moratoria on the development, acquisition, stockpiling, transfer and use of ICA weapons intended for law enforcement purposes.

In addition to the CWC, there are a number of international agreements that either prohibit or constrain the employment of ICA weapons.[145] In the context of the potential use of such weapons for law enforcement purposes, the most relevant is human rights law. Consequently, states should explore the constraints on ICA weapons use arising from international and regional human rights instruments and customary international human rights law. States should also bring cases of reported ICA weapons misuse to the attention of the appropriate human rights mechanisms, including: UN Special Procedures and the UN Human Rights Council; relevant international and regional treaty bodies; regional judicial mechanisms capable of delivering binding legal judgments regarding violations of regional treaties. Since a number of such regional mechanisms are potentially open to individual petition, victims and their families can also directly seek redress in cases of agent misuse, and civil society organisations can attempt to employ such mechanisms to develop human rights case law on these issues.

The international community's response to advances in weapons-related science and technology has often been inadequate and late, introducing partial and ineffective controls (if any are introduced at all) long after a new weapons technology has spread to and been employed by state and non-state actors. With the issue of ICA weapons – because proliferation has been relatively limited – there is still time to act. There is now an opportunity for the international community to take a precautionary and preventative approach. If action is not taken in the near future there is a danger that advances in relevant scientific disciplines together with current and potential future state research and development of ICA weapons may well lead to their widespread proliferation and misuse.

Disclosure statement

No potential conflict of interest was reported by the authors.

Notes on contributors

Michael Crowley is Project Coordinator of the Bradford Non-Lethal Weapons Research Project, and is also a Senior Research Associate with the Omega Research Foundation. He has worked for nearly 20 years on arms control, security and human rights issues, including as Executive Director of the Verification Research, Training and Information Centre (VERTIC).

Malcolm Dando is Professor of International Security at the Department of Peace Studies, University of Bradford, and co-director of its project on strengthening the Biological and Toxin Weapons Convention. He has published widely on biological warfare, bio-terrorism, non-lethal weapons and related international security issues. He is a fellow of the Society of Biology.

Notes

1. Organisation for the Prohibition of Chemical Weapons (OPCW), Convention on the Prohibition of the Development, Production, Stockpiling and Use of Chemical Weapons and on their Destruction (Chemical Weapons Convention or CWC), 1993.
2. See for example: NATO Glossary of Terms and Definitions (English and French), NATO Document AAP-6(2012), 2012, 2-I-2.
3. See for example: Spiez Laboratory, Technical Workshop on Incapacitating Chemical Agents, Spiez, Switzerland, 8–9 September 2011, 2012; International Committee of the Red Cross (ICRC), 'Toxic Chemicals as Weapons for Law Enforcement: A Threat to Life and International Law?', ICRC Synthesis Paper, September 2012; ICRC, Expert Meeting, '"Incapacitating Chemical Agents": Law Enforcement, Human Rights and Policy Perspectives', Switzerland, 24–26 April 2012, January 2013; OPCW, Conference of the States Parties, 'Scientific Advisory Board Report on Developments in Science and Technology for the Third Review Conference', RC-3/DG.1, 29 October 2012.

4. Royal Society, 'Brain Waves Module 3: Neuroscience, Conflict and Security', RS Policy Document 06/11, February 2012, 44–5. See also: Royal Society, 'The Chemical Weapons Convention and Convergent Trends in Science and Technology', RS Seminar held at the Organisation for the Prohibition of Chemical Weapons (OPCW), 18 February 2013, 2.
5. ICA weapons have also been called advanced riot control agents, biochemical weapons, calmatives, immobilising agents, knock-out gas and pharmacological weapons.
6. See for example, OPCW, 'Scientific Advisory Board Report on Developments in Science and Technology for the Third Review Conference'; Royal Society, 'Brain Waves Module 3', 44; Royal Society, 'The Chemical Weapons Convention and Convergent Trends in Science and Technology', 2.
7. Riot control agents are specifically defined under the Chemical Weapons Convention as 'Any chemical not listed in a Schedule, which can produce rapidly in humans sensory irritation or disabling physical effects which disappear within a short time following termination of exposure (see OPCW, Chemical Weapons Convention, Article II.7).
8. See, for example, G. Fenton, 'Current and Prospective Military and Law Enforcement Use of Chemical Agents for Incapacitation', in *Incapacitating Biochemical Weapons*, ed. A. Pearson, M. Chevrier, and M. Wheelis (Lanham, MD: Lexington Books, 2007), 103–23; G. Whitbred, 'Offensive Use of Chemical Technologies by US Special Operations Forces in the Global War on Terrorism', Maxwell Paper Number 37, Maxwell Air Force Base, Air University Press, Alabama, July 2006.
9. OPCW, Director General, 'Report of the [Ekeus] Advisory Panel on Future Priorities of the Organisation for the Prohibition of Chemical Weapons', S/951/2011, 25 July 2011, para. 13.
10. British Medical Association, *The Use of Drugs as Weapons: The Concerns and Responsibilities of Healthcare Professionals* (London: BMA, 2007), 1.
11. J. Perry Robinson, 'Categories of Challenge Now Facing the Chemical Weapons Convention', 52nd Pugwash CBW Workshop, '10 Years of the OPCW: Taking Stock and Looking Forward', Noordwijk, The Netherlands, 17–18 March 2007.
12. A. Pearson, 'Incapacitating Biochemical Weapons: Science, Technology, and Policy for the 21st Century', *Nonproliferation Review* 13, no. 2 (2006): 172; M. Wheelis and M. Dando, 'Neurobiology: A Case Study of the Imminent Militarization of Biology', *International Review of the Red Cross* 87, no. 859 (2005): 564.
13. M. Crowley, *Dangerous Ambiguities: Regulation of Riot Control Agents and Incapacitants under the Chemical Weapons Convention* (Bradford: Bradford University, 2009), 61–2.
14. British Medical Association, *The Use of Drugs as Weapons*, 1; Wheelis and Dando, 'Neurobiology'.
15. Perry Robinson, 'Categories of Challenge Now Facing the Chemical Weapons Convention', 19.
16. ICRC, 'Toxic Chemicals as Weapons for Law Enforcement', 5.
17. Further information concerning historical ICA weapons research and development activities conducted by a number of these states is included in the country case studies detailed in this report. See also: J. Perry Robinson, 'Incapacitating Chemical Agents in Context: An Historical Overview of States' Policy', in ICRC, 'Incapacitating Chemical Agents', 89–96; Royal Society, 'Brain Waves Module 3', 10–13; Crowley, *Dangerous Ambiguities*; M. Dando and M. Furmanski, 'Midspectrum Incapacitant Programs', in *Deadly Cultures: Biological Weapons Since 1945*, ed. M. Wheelis, L. Rózsa, and M. Dando (Cambridge, MA: Harvard University Press, 2006), 236–251.
18. R. Trapp, '"Incapacitating Chemical Agents": Some Thoughts on Possible Strategies and Recommendations', in *Expert Meeting: Incapacitating Chemical Agents: Implications for International Law*, ed. ICRC (Switzerland, 24–26 March 2010, October 2010), 65.
19. National Research Council, 'Emerging Cognitive Neuroscience and Related Technologies', 2008, http://www.nap.edu/openbook.php?record_id=12177 (accessed 18 January 2015).
20. Ibid.
21. Dual use is a concept that can be applied to the tangible and intangible features of a technology that enable it to be utilised for both hostile and peaceful ends with no, or only minor, modifications. The hostile use of a specific technology does not arise automatically from the inherent properties of that technology, but requires the active intervention of relevant actors. (For further discussion see: J. Molas-Gallart and J. Perry Robinson, 'Assessment of Dual-use Technologies in the Context of European Security and Defence' (Report for the Scientific and

Technological Options Assessment (STOA), European Parliament, 1997); C. McLeash, 'Reflecting On the Dual-Use Problem', in *A Web of Prevention: Biological Weapons, Life Sciences, and the Governance of Research*, ed. B. Rappert and C. McLeish (London: Routledge, 2007), 189–208.

22. For further information about the survey methodology and the survey findings incorporating detailed country case studies see: M. Crowley and M. Dando, *Down the Slippery Slope? A Study of Contemporary Dual-Use Research Potentially Applicable to Incapacitating Agent Weapons*, Biochemical Security 2030 Project/Bradford Non-Lethal Weapons Research Project, October 2014.
23. Security, Anti-Riot Weapons and Ammunition brochure, China North Industries Corporation (NORINCO), undated, brochure distributed at MILIPOL security exhibition, Paris, France, 1995, 11.
24. Ibid., 11.
25. State 9619 Plant company brochures, undated, distributed during Asia Pacific China Police Expo 2004 (23–26 June 2004), and Asia Pacific China Police Expo 2006 (24–27 May 2006) held at Beijing Exhibition Centre, Beijing, China.
26. G. Arthur, 'New Equipment in Hong Kong', *Defence Review Asia*, 19 March 2012, 35, http://www.defencereviewasia.com/articles/153/NEW-EQUIPMENT-IN-HONG-KONG (accessed 18 January 2015).
27. See for example: L. Hess, J. Schreiberova, and J. Fusek, 'Pharmacological Non-Lethal Weapons' (Proceedings of the 3rd European Symposium on Non-Lethal Weapons, 10–12 May 2005, Ettlingen, Germany, European Working Group on Non-Lethal Weapons, Pfinztal: Fraunhofer ICT, V23); L. Hess, J. Schreiberova, and J. Fusek, 'Ultrapotent Opioids as Non-Lethal Weapons' (paper given at meeting of NATO RTO TG-004, 23–26 May 2005, University of Defence, Faculty of Military Health Sciences, Hradec Kralove, Czech Republic); L. Hess, J. Schreiberová, J. Málek, M. Votava, and J. Fusek, 'Drug-Induced Loss of Aggressiveness in the Macaque Rhesus' (Proceedings of 4th European Symposium on Non-Lethal Weapons, 21–23 May 2007, Ettlingen, Germany, European Working Group on Non-Lethal Weapons, Pfinztal: Fraunhofer ICT, V15).
28. See for example: L. Hess, M. Votava, J. Schreiberová, J. Málek, M. Horáček, 'Experience with a Naphthylmedetomidine-Ketamine-Hyaluronidase Combination in Inducing Immobilization in Anthropoid Apes', *Journal of Medical Primatology* 39, no. 3 (2010): 151–9; M. Votava, L. Hess, J. Schreiberová, J. Málek, K. Štein, 'Short Term Pharmacological Immobilization in Macaque Monkeys', *Veterinary Anaesthesia and Analgesia* 38, no. 5 (2011): 490–3.
29. Czech Republic, National Authority of the CWC, Reply to the University of Bradford, Re: Request for Information Concerning Research Potentially Related to Incapacitating Chemical Agents, 14 July 2014, 4.
30. Ibid., 5.
31. See for example: P.K. Gupta, K. Ganesan, A. Pande, and R.C. Malhotra, 'A Convenient One-Pot Synthesis of Fentanyl', *Journal of Chemical Research* (July 2005): 452–3; P.K. Gupta, K. Ganesan, P.K. Gutch, L. Manral, and D.K. Dubey, 'Vapor Pressure and Enthalpy of Vaporization of Fentanyl', *Journal of Chemical & Engineering Data* 53, no. 3 (2008): 841–5; L. Manral, P.K. Gupta, M.V.S. Suryanarayana, K. Ganesan, and R.C. Malhotra, 'Thermal Behaviour of Fentanyl and its Analogues during Flash Pyrolysis', *Journal of Thermal Analysis and Calorimetry* 96, no. 2 (2009): 531–4; L. Manral, N. Muniappan, P.K. Gupta, K. Ganesan, R.C. Malhotra, and R. Vijayaraghavan, 'Effect of Exposure to Fentanyl Aerosol in Mice on Breathing Pattern and Respiratory Variables', *Drug and Chemical Toxicology* 32, no. 2 (2009): 108–13; P.K. Gupta, S.K. Yadav, Y.D. Bhutia, P. Singh, P. Rao, N.L. Gujar, K. Ganesan, and R. Bhattacharya, 'Synthesis and Comparative Bioefficacy of N-(1-Phenethyl-4-Piperidinyl) Propionanilide (Fentanyl) and its 1-Substituted Analogs in Swiss Albino Mice', *Medicinal Chemistry Research* 22, no. 8 (2013): 3888–96.
32. Correspondence to Dr M. Crowley, BNLWRP, from R.K. Singh, Deputy Chief of Mission, Embassy of India, The Hague, Netherlands, forwarding the response of the Indian CWC National Authority, 22 July 2014.
33. Ibid.
34. See: OPCW, Chemical Weapons Convention, Article X(4), for relevant state reporting requirements.

35. See for example: T. Nezamoleslam, B. Javahery, N. Shakiba, and H. Fakhraian, 'Structure-Activity Relationship, Atomic Electron Density and Conformational Investigation of Fentanyl Analogues', *Journal of Passive Defence Science &Technology* 1 (2010): 23–32; H. Kamranpey, 'Aerosolisation of Medetomidine Hydrochloride as an Incapacitating Agent', *Journal of Passive Defence Science & Technology* 3 (2011): 51–6; M.S. Abazari, 'Investigating the Phase Behavior of Medetomidine Hydrochloride, Ketamine Hydrochloride and Sevoflurane in the Presence of Ethanol and Propellant', *Journal of Passive Defence Science & Technology* 1 (2013): 65–70.
36. See for example: Nuclear Threat Initiative, Imam Hossein University (IHU), http://www.nti.org/facilities/251/ (accessed 9 May 2014). For more information see the university website http://www.ihu.ac.ir/?q=fa/node/1 (accessed 9 May 2014).
37. Correspondence to Dr M. Crowley, BNLWRP, from Dr H. Farajvand, Secretary of the National Authority for the CWC, Ministry of Foreign Affairs of the Islamic Republic of Iran, 15 July 2014.
38. M. Normack, A. Lindblad, A. Norqvist, B. Sandstrom, and L. Waldenstrom, *Israel and WMD: Incentives and Capabilities* (Swedish Defence Research Agency (FOI), December 2005), 41.
39. Ibid., 41.
40. *Harvard Sussex Programme, News Chronology, CBW Conventions Bulletin*, 38, December 1997, 29; 'Physician Member of Hit Team, Paper Says', *Canadian Medical Association Journal* 157, no. 11 (1997): 1504; L. Beyer, 'Don't Try This at Home – Or in Aman', *Time* 150, no. 17 (27 October 1997); L. Beyer, J. Hamad, and A. Klein, 'What Went Wrong?; The Botched Hit on a Hamas Leader in Jordan is the Latest Big Problem for Israel's Benjamin Netanyahu', *Time* (27 October 1997); M. Ginsburg, '"Should There Be a need": The Inside Story of Israel's Chemical and Biological Arsenal', *Times of Israel*, 17 September 2013; A. Cowell, 'The Daring Attack That Blew Up in Israel's Face', *New York Times*, 15 October 1997; 'Israeli Intelligence Agencies Come Under Fire', *Janes Intelligence Review*, 1 January 1998.
41. 'Israeli Intelligence Agencies Come Under Fire'; Beyer, Hamad, and Klein, 'What Went Wrong?'
42. Amnesty International, 'Attempt to Kill Hamas Leader Follows a Pattern of Extrajudicial Killings', News Service 168/97, 8 October 1997, AI Index: MDE 15/89/97; *Harvard Sussex Programme CBW Conventions Bulletin*, 29.
43. For information about IIBR and its research activities see: Israel Institute for Biological Research, http://iibr.gov.il/Default.aspx (accessed 8 January 2015).
44. For descriptions of the incident see, for example, Amnesty International, *Amnesty International 2003 Annual Report* (London: Amnesty International, 2003), entry for the Russian Federation, p. 208; Amnesty International, *Rough Justice: The Law and Human Rights in the Russian Federation*, October 2003 (AI Index EUR 46/054/2003); D. Koplow, 'The Russians and the Chechens in Moscow in 2002', in *Non-Lethal Weapons: The Law and Policy of Revolutionary Technologies for the Military and Law Enforcement* (Cambridge: Cambridge University Press, 10 April 2006); see also BBC news coverage, in particular: 'How Special Forces Ended Siege', 29 October 2002; and BBC 2, 'Horizon: The Moscow Theatre Siege' (broadcast 15 January 2004), transcript on: http://www.bbc.co.uk/science/horizon/2004/moscowtheatretrans.shtml (accessed 6 October 2014).
45. M. Wheelis, 'Human Impact of Incapacitating Chemical Agents', in ICRC, *Expert Meeting*.
46. Amnesty International, *Amnesty International 2003 Annual Report*; and Human Rights Watch, 'Independent Commission of Inquiry Must Investigate Raid on Moscow Theater: Inadequate Protection for Consequences of Gas Violates Obligation to Protect Life' (Press Release, 30 October 2002).
47. ITAR-TASS, from Moscow in English, 21.12 GMT 30 October 2002, as in FBIS-SOV-2002-1030, 'Russian Experts Discuss Use of Fentanyl in Hostage Crisis', as cited by Perry Robinson, 'Categories of Challenge'.
48. J. Riches, R. Read, R. Black, N. Cooper, and C. Timperley, 'Analysis of Clothing and Urine from Moscow Theatre Siege Casualties Reveals Carfentanil and Remifentanil Use', *Journal of Analytical Toxicology* 36, no. 9 (2012): 647–656.
49. V. Klochikhin, A. Lushnikov, V. Zagaynov, A. Putilov, V. Selivanov, and M. Zatekvakhin, 'Principles of Modelling of the Scenario of Calmative Application in a Building with Deterred

Hostages' (Proceedings of the 3rd European Symposium on Non-Lethal Weapons, Ettlingen, Germany, 10–12 May 2005, V17, Pfinztal: Fraunhofer ICT).

50. V. Klochikhin and V. Selivanov, 'Report on the 1st Phase of the Project "Gas Flow"' (Presentation in MBDA, 24–27 November 2009, London).
51. See for example: N. Kuzmina and V. Kuzmin, 'Development of Concepts on the Interaction of Drugs with Opioid Receptors', *Russian Chemistry Reviews* 80 (2011): 145–69; F. Dukhovich, M. Darkhovskii, E. Gorbatova, and V. Polyakov, 'The Agonist Paradox: Agonists and Antagonists of Acetylcholine Receptors and Opioid Receptors', *Chemistry & Biodiversity* 2 (2005): 354–66; N. Kuzmina, V. Yashkir, V. Merkulov, and E. Osipova, 'Method for Estimating a Compound's Opiate Activity Based on a Versatile Three-Dimensional Model of Nonselective Opiate Pharmacophore', *Russian Journal of Bioorganic Chemistry* 38, no. 5 (2012): 507–19. For further papers see: Crowley and Dando, *Down the Slippery Slope?*, 49.
52. See for example: Country Profiles, Syria, Chemical, Nuclear Threat Initiative, http://www.nti.org/countryprofiles/syria/chemical/ (accessed 11 August 2014).
53. On 14 October 2013, Syria formally acceded to the CWC. As required under the convention, Syria declared its existing stockpile of chemical weapons and agreed to facilitate their verification and subsequent destruction under the supervision of the OPCW.
54. See for example: Ipek Yezdani, 'Chemical Weapons Used Against Syrians, Says Defected Soldier', *Hürriyet Daily News*, 21 February 2012; J. Rogin, 'Exclusive: Secret State Department Cable: Chemical Weapons Used in Syria', 15 January 2013, http://thecable.foreignpolicy.com/posts/2013/01/15/secret_state_department_cable_chemical_weapons_used_in_syria (accessed 18 January 2015); D. Friedman, 'Chemical Weapons in Syria: Has a Red Line Been Crossed?', *INSS Insight No. 421*, 29 April 2013; Zaher Al-Saket, interview broadcast on Al-Arabiya TV on 27 April 2013, transcript as excerpted and translated in 'Defecting Syrian Officer Brigadier-General Zaher Al-Saket: I Was Ordered to Use Chemical Weapons' (The Middle East Media Research Institute (MEMRI) clip no. 3822, 27 April 2013); 'Israeli Official Says Syria Has Used Chemical Incapacitant against Insurgents', *Janes Defence Weekly*, 10 April 2014.
55. For further information see: J. Walker, '"Inappropriately Hilarious": An Historical Overview of the Interest In and Use of Incapacitating Chemical Agents', March 2010; A. Maclean, *Historical Survey of the Porton Down Volunteer Programme* (Ministry of Defence, June 2006); Dando and Furmanski, 'Midspectrum Incapacitant Programs'.
56. Three UK research papers on fentanyl and related analgesic chemicals produced by the Chemical Defence Establishment were cited in: Agent Research Studies: 1966–1990, US Army Armament Munitions Command, Chemical Research, Development & Engineering Center, Aberdeen Proving Ground MD, Report CRDEC-TR-345, April 1992, declassified with redactions from CONFIDENTIAL.
57. T. Donnelly, *Less Lethal Technologies: Initial Prioritization and Evaluation* (UK Home Office, Policing and Crime Reduction Group, Police Scientific Development Branch, Publication No. 12/01).
58. Northern Ireland Office, *Patten Report Recommendations 69 and 70 Relating To Public Order Equipment. A Research Programme Into Alternative Policing Approaches Towards The Management of Conflict* (Fourth Report prepared by the Steering Group led by the Northern Ireland Office, in consultation with the Association of Chief Police Officers. Belfast: Northern Ireland Office, January 2004).
59. OPCW, Conference of States Parties, United Kingdom: Statement by Mr Alistair Burt, Parliamentary Under Secretary of State for Foreign and Commonwealth Affairs, Third Review Conference, RC-3/NAT.22, 8–19 April 2013, 9 April 2013.
60. Biomedical Sciences Department, CBD Sector [of Defence Evaluation and Research Agency] Porton Down, An Overview of Research carried out on Glycollates and Related Compounds at CBD Porton Down, DERA/CBD/CR990418, September 1999; Riches, 'Analysis of Clothing and Urine from Moscow Theatre Siege Casualties Reveals Carfentanil and Remifentanil Use'; United Kingdom, 'Format for the Annual Reporting of Information on National Programmes for Protection Against Chemical Weapons, Under Article X of the Chemical Weapons Convention', Annex A, 29 February 2012, 5.
61. For discussion of historical US ICA weapons research, see for example: Dando and Furmanski, 'Midspectrum Incapacitant Programs'; N. Davison, *Bradford Science and Technology Report*

No. 8 'Off the Rocker' and 'On the Floor': The Continued Development of Biochemical Incapacitating Weapons, August 2007; M. Furmanski, 'Historical Military Interest in Low-Lethality Biochemical Agents', in *Incapacitating Biochemical Weapons*, ed. Pearson, Chevrier, and Wheelis, 35–66; A. Pearson, 'Late and Post-Cold War Research and Development of Incapacitating Biochemical Weapons', in *Incapacitating Biochemical Weapons*, ed. Pearson, Chevrier, and Wheelis, 67–102; J. Perry Robinson, 'Disabling Chemical Weapons: A Documented Chronology of Events, 1945–2011' (copy provided by author), 20 November 2012.

62. Dando and Furmanski, 'Midspectrum Incapacitant Programs', 250.
63. For detailed discussion of US ICA weapons research see: Crowley and Dando, *Down the Slippery Slope?*, 63–73.
64. OPCW, Executive Council, Seventy-Second Session, United States of America: Statement by Ambassador Robert P. Mikulak, United States Delegation to the OPCW, at the Seventy-Second Session of the Executive Council, EC-72/NAT.8 6 and 7 May 2013, 6 May 2013; OPCW, United States of America: Statement by Rose E. Gottemoeller, Under Secretary for Arms Control and International Security, to the 19th Session of the Conference of States Parties, 3 December 2014.
65. OPCW, Chemical Weapons Convention, Article I.
66. Under Article X, states are permitted to 'conduct research into, develop, produce, acquire, transfer or use means of protection against chemical weapons, for purposes not prohibited under this Convention', even where this involves production in appropriate quantities of potential chemical weapons agents, including ICAs. Consequently, in order to increase 'transparency of national programmes related to protective purposes', Article X obliges each state party to 'provide annually to the Technical Secretariat information on its programme' (see: OPCW, Chemical Weapons Convention, Article X).
67. OPCW, Chemical Weapons Convention, Article I(3).
68. Ibid., Article I(4).
69. Ibid., Articles II(9) (a), V(14), and XI(2) (c).
70. Ibid., Article II(1)a.
71. Ibid., Article II(2).
72. Ibid., Article II(2).
73. M. Meselson and J. Perry Robinson, 'New Technologies and the Loophole, Editorial', *Chemical Weapons Convention Bulletin* 23 (March 1994), Harvard Sussex Program, 1, http://fas-www.harvard.edu/_/hsp/bulletin/cwcb23.pdf (accessed 5 August 2014).
74. Although the CWC schedules currently list only one ICA: BZ (Schedule 2.a.), and two of its immediate precursors, 3-Quinuclidinol and Benzilic Acid (both Schedule 2.b.) (see: OPCW, Chemical Weapons Convention, Annex on Chemicals, B. Schedules of Chemicals, Schedule 2.), all toxic chemicals promoted as ICAs fall within the convention's ambit.
75. OPCW, Chemical Weapons Convention, Article II(9).
76. In addition to the Chemical Weapons Convention, the use of toxic chemicals in armed conflict is prohibited under the 1925 Geneva Protocol and customary international humanitarian law. For further discussion, see: ICRC, 'Toxic Chemicals as Weapons for Law Enforcement'; D. Loye, 'Potential Implications for International Humanitarian Law', in *Expert Meeting*, ed. ICRC, 40–2; F. Hampson, 'International Law and the Regulation of Weapons', in *Incapacitating Biochemical Weapons*, ed. Pearson, Chevrier, and Wheelis, 231–61; R. Coupland, 'Incapacitating Biochemical Weapons: Risks and Uncertainties', in *Incapacitating Biochemical Weapons*, ed. Pearson, Chevrier, and Wheelis, 225–23.
77. OPCW, Chemical Weapons Convention, Article III(1) a–c.
78. Ibid., Article I (2) and (4); Article IV and Article V.
79. Ibid., Article II(9)d.
80. A. Chayes and M. Meselson, 'Proposed Guidelines on the Status of Riot Control Agents and Other Toxic Chemicals Under the Chemical Weapons Convention', *Chemical Weapons Convention Bulletin* 35 (March 1997), Harvard Sussex Program, 13–8.
81. W. Krutzsch, 'Non-Lethal Chemicals for Law Enforcement', BITS Research Note 03.2, April 2003, Berlin Information Centre for Transatlantic Security; W. Krutzsch and A. Von Wagner, 'Law Enforcement Including Domestic Riot Control: The Interpretation of Article II, Paragraph 9(d)', cwc2008.files.wordpress.com/2008/04/krutzsch-von-wagner-law-enforcement.pdf (accessed 11 January 2015).

82. W. Krutzsch and R. Trapp, 'Article II: Definitions and Criteria', in *The Chemical Weapons Convention: A Commentary*, ed. W. Krutzsch, E. Myjer, and R. Trapp (Oxford: Oxford University Press, 2014), 73–104.
83. A. Von Wagner, 'Toxic Chemicals for Law Enforcement Including Domestic Riot Control Purposes Under the Chemical Weapons Convention', in *Incapacitating Biochemical Weapons*, ed. Pearson, Chevrier, and Wheelis, 195–208.
84. The only possible exceptions to this restriction recognised are those toxic chemicals used for judicially sanctioned execution, provided such chemicals are not on the convention's Schedule 1 list. See for example Chayes and Meselson, 'Proposed Guidelines on the Status of Riot Control Agents and Other Toxic Chemicals Under the Chemical Weapons Convention', 17–18.
85. Ibid., 17.
86. Krutzsch and Trapp, 'Article II: Definitions and Criteria', 102.
87. D. Fidler, 'Incapacitating Chemical and Biochemical Weapons and Law Enforcement under the Chemical Weapons Convention', in *Incapacitating Biochemical Weapons*, ed. Pearson, Chevrier, and Wheelis, 174.
88. D. Neil, 'Riot Control Agents and Incapacitating Chemical Agents Under the Chemical Weapons Convention', Defence R&D Canada, Technical Memorandum DRDC CORA TM 2007-22, June 2007.
89. Fidler, 'Incapacitating Chemical and Biochemical Weapons and Law Enforcement', 174.
90. Ibid., 175.
91. Ibid., 185.
92. See for example: OPCW, Statement by Ambassador Dominik M. Alder, Permanent Representative of Switzerland to the OPCW, Second Review Conference of the Chemical Weapons Convention, General Debate, The Hague, Netherlands, 8 April 2008.
93. OPCW, Conference of States Parties, Switzerland: Statement by Markus Borlin, Permanent Representative of Switzerland to the OPCW, General Debate, Statement at the Third Special Session of the Conference of the States Parties to Review the Operation of the Chemical Weapons Convention, 8 April 2013.
94. The text of national statements delivered, and relevant working papers submitted, by states parties to the Third Review Conference are available on the OPCW website.
95. OPCW, Conference of States Parties, Australia, Weaponisation of Central Nervous System Acting Chemicals for Law Enforcement, Nineteenth Session C-19/NAT.1, 1–5 December 2014, 14 November 2014, para. 5.
96. During the Third CWC Review Conference, certain states parties, i.e. Germany and Switzerland, explicitly declared that only riot control agents can be employed in their countries for law enforcement.
97. OPCW, Conference of States Parties, Australia, para. 6.
98. Ibid., para. 7.
99. Other potentially applicable norms are: the rights to health, and to liberty and security. For further discussion see: M. Crowley, 'The Use of Incapacitants in Law Enforcement', in *Weapons under International Human Rights Law*, ed. S. Casey-Maslen (Cambridge: Cambridge University Press, 2014), 357–81; L. Doswald-Beck, 'Assessing "Incapacitating Chemical Agents" under Human Rights Law', in 'Incapacitating Chemical Agents', ed. ICRC, 39–45; F. Hampson, 'Potential Implications for Human Rights Law, in *Expert Meeting*, ed. ICRC, 53–56.
100. See, for example, Universal Declaration of Human Rights, adopted and proclaimed by UN General Assembly Resolution 217 A (III), 10 December 1948, Article 3; International Covenant on Civil and Political Rights, adopted on 16 December 1966, Article 6; Convention on the Rights of the Child, adopted and opened for signature, ratification and accession by UN General Assembly Resolution 44/25 of 20 November 1989, Article 6.
101. African Charter on Human and Peoples Rights, adopted by Organisation of African Unity on 27 June 1981, Article 4; American Convention on Human Rights, signed at San Jose, Costa Rica, 22 November 1969, Article 4; European Convention on the Protection of Human Rights and Fundamental Freedoms, signed on 4 November 1950, Article 2. These obligations are binding upon those states party to the relevant agreements and their application has subsequently been clarified following judgments made by the relevant regional legal institutions.

102. W. Aceves, 'Human Rights Law and the Use of Incapacitating Biochemical Weapons', in *Incapacitating Biochemical Weapons*, ed. A. Pearson, M. Chevrier, and M. Wheelis, 286.
103. Fidler, 'Incapacitating Chemical and Biochemical Weapons and Law Enforcement', 175. See also: ICRC, 'Toxic Chemicals as Weapons for Law Enforcement', 3.
104. Leading human rights non-governmental organisations have also raised concerns about this use of an ICA weapon by the Russian Federation. See, for example, Human Rights Watch, 'Independent Commission of Inquiry Must Investigate Raid on Moscow Theater: Inadequate Protection for Consequences of Gas Violates Obligation to Protect Life', Press Release, 30 October 2002; Amnesty International, 'Rough Justice: The Law and Human Rights in the Russian Federation', October 2003 (AI Index EUR 46/054/2003).
105. 'Report of the Special Rapporteur, Asma Jahangir, Submitted Pursuant to Commission on Human Rights Resolution 2002/36', UN doc. E/CN.4/2003/3, 13 January 2003, 15, §34.
106. 'Concluding Observations of the Human Rights Committee: Russian Federation', UN doc. CCPR/CO/79/RUS, 6 November 2003, 4, §14.
107. Ibid.
108. Ibid., 4, §14.
109. Under Article 2 of the ECHR: ' 1. Everyone's right to life shall be protected by law. No one shall be deprived of his life intentionally save in the execution of a sentence of a court following his conviction of a crime for which this penalty is provided by law. 2. Deprivation of life shall not be regarded as inflicted in contravention of this Article when it results from the use of force which is no more than absolutely necessary: (a) in defence of any person from unlawful violence; (b) in order to effect a lawful arrest or to prevent the escape of a person lawfully detained; (c) in action lawfully taken for the purpose of quelling a riot or insurrection.'
110. European Court of Human Rights, *Finogenov and others* v. *Russia*, App. Nos 18299/03 and 27311/03, Judgment, 20 December 2011.
111. Ibid., §201.
112. Ibid., §202.
113. Ibid., §202.
114. Ibid., §203.
115. This term refers to the space for manoeuvre that the Strasbourg organs are willing to grant national authorities in fulfilling their obligations under the ECHR. For further discussion see, for example: The Margin of Appreciation, Council of Europe, Judicial Professions, The Lisbon Network, http://www.coe.int/t/dghl/cooperation/lisbonnetwork/themis/echr/paper2_en.asp (accessed 18 January 2015).
116. Ibid., §213.
117. Ibid., §232.
118. Ibid., §236.
119. See ibid., §§243–62, and §266.
120. See Ibid., §§277, 279, 281 and 282.
121. ICRC, 'Toxic Chemicals as Weapons for Law Enforcement', 3.
122. A. Kelle, 'The Message From Strasbourg', *Bulletin of the Atomic Scientists*, 23 February 2012; A. Kelle, 'Legally Incapacitated, Politically Outmaneuvered', *Bulletin of the Atomic Scientists*, 7 June 2012.
123. See in particular, European Court of Human Rights, *Finogenov and others* v. *Russia*, paras 162–4 and 228–9.
124. Ibid., para. 229.
125. European Court of Human Rights, press release issued by the Registrar of the Court, ECHR 270 (2012) 27.06.2012.
126. In the case of *Finogenov and others* v. *Russia*, the court ruled that Russia was to pay all 64 applicants a total award – as regards non-pecuniary damage – of €1,254,000, and €30,000, jointly, for costs and expenses. See ibid., §§285–96.
127. The African Court on Human and Peoples' Rights, the European Court of Human Rights and the Inter-American Courts of Human Rights.
128. The Human Rights Committee can also consider a case raised through individual petition, but can only reach non-binding conclusions in such instances. See: F. Hampson, 'International Law and the Regulation of Weapons', in *Incapacitating Biochemical Weapons*, ed. A. Pearson, M. Chevrier, and M. Wheelis, 243.
129. Ibid.

130. Universal Declaration of Human Rights, Article 5; ICCPR, Article 7; Convention against Torture and Other Cruel, Inhuman or Degrading Treatment or Punishment, adopted and opened for signature, ratification and accession by UN General Assembly Resolution 39/46, 10 December 1984; and the Convention on the Rights of the Child, Article 37(a).
131. See the 1981 African Charter on Human and Peoples' Rights, Article 5; ACHR, Article 5; ECHR, Article 3; European Convention for the Prevention of Torture and Inhuman or Degrading Treatment or Punishment, Strasbourg, 26 November1987; and the Inter-American Convention to Prevent and Punish Torture, adopted by the 15th Regular Session of the General Assembly of the Organisation of American States, 9 December 1985, OAS Treaty Series No. 67.
132. See, for example, ICCPR, Articles 4 and 7; Human Rights Committee, 'General Comment No. 29: States of Emergency (Article 4)', UN doc. CCPR/C/21/Rev.1/Add.11, 21 August 2001, §7.
133. United Nations, Convention against Torture, Article 1(1).
134. United Nations, Rome Statute of the International Criminal Court, A/CONF.183/9 of 17 July 1998, Article 8 (2) (a) (ii), as cited in J.M. Henckaerts and L. Doswald-Beck, eds, *Customary International Humanitarian Law: Rules, Volume I* (Cambridge: Cambridge University Press, 2005), Rule 90.
135. European Commission of Human Rights, *Greek* case (cited in Vol. II, Ch. 32, § 1339), as cited in Henckaerts and Doswald-Beck, *Customary International Humanitarian Law*, Rule 90.
136. United Nations, Body of Principles for the Protection of All Persons under Any Form of Detention or Imprisonment, Adopted by General Assembly Resolution 43/173 of 9 December 1988, Principle 6, Commentary.
137. United Nations, Commission on Human Rights, 'Torture and Other Cruel, Inhuman or Degrading Treatment', Report of the Special Rapporteur on the Question of Torture, Manfred Nowak, E/CN.4/2006/6, 23 December 2005, para. 38.
138. W. Aceves, 'Human Rights Law and the Use of Incapacitating Biochemical Weapons', in *Incapacitating Biochemical Weapons*, ed. A. Pearson, M. Chevrier, and M. Wheelis, 271.
139. The notion of 'degrading treatment' has been defined by the European Commission of Human Rights as treatment or punishment that 'grossly humiliates the victim before others or drives the detainee to act against his/her will or conscience'. European Commission of Human Rights, *Greek* case (cited in Vol. II, Ch. 32, § 1339), as cited in Henckaerts and Doswald-Beck, *Customary International Humanitarian Law*, Rule 90.
140. Royal Society, 'Brain Waves Module 3', 24.
141. Ibid., 24, n. 78.
142. Fidler, 'Incapacitating Chemical and Biochemical Weapons and Law Enforcement', 176.
143. Ibid.
144. Such as the Committee against Torture established under the UN Convention Against Torture (1984); or the European Committee for the Prevention of Torture and Inhuman or Degrading Treatment or Punishment and the European Court of Human Rights with regard to the European Convention for the Prevention of Torture and Inhuman or Degrading Treatment or Punishment (1989).
145. Given the nature of the toxic chemicals under consideration and the proposed contexts for their use, the applicability of the Single Convention on Narcotic Drugs, the Convention on Psychotropic Substances, and the Biological and Toxin Weapons Convention may also be applicable. For further discussion see: D. Crowley, 'Potential Implications for Disarmament and Other Areas of International Law', pp. 42–53, in *Expert Meeting*, ed. ICRC; ICRC, 'Toxic Chemicals as Weapons for Law Enforcement'.

Human rights and public health: towards a balanced relationship

Brigit Toebes

Department of International Law, Faculty of Law, the University of Groningen, the Netherlands

In international law there are many references to the protection of public health contrasting with other interests, including the interests of trade, commerce, intellectual property protection, transportation and warfare. Potentially, in such contexts, the 'right to health' as an economic and social right can be used as an additional collective claim to advance the health of the public, thus counterbalancing such interests as international and domestic trade and the conduct of warfare. While this approach has potential, it should be born in mind that public health measures potentially infringe on the civil and political rights of individuals, including their rights to privacy and freedom of movement. We are thus dealing with a complex relationship between public health, human rights and international law that is still ill-understood. An integrated approach to human rights, taking into account both civil and political and economic, social and cultural rights, seems the most balanced response to public health concerns.

Introduction

The protection of the health of the overall population is an important issue of public concern, both at domestic and international levels. Population health, or 'public health', is a vital concern that needs to be balanced against such interests as trade, industrial profit, intellectual property protection and military warfare (see Figure 1). For instance, the trade regime as agreed on by states creates a tension with the need to ensure access to affordable medicines, especially in the developing world. Furthermore, while the tobacco industry has an interest in selling its products, there is clear evidence that smoking is detrimental to health. Lastly, environmental pollution, climate change and military warfare have a devastating impact on the health of populations worldwide.

From a human rights perspective, it is important to consider whether the protection of public health is potentially also a human right, be it individual or collective in nature. Seen in this light, the 'right to health' can be a collective claim reflecting 'public health' and going against the interests of, for example, the tobacco, food and beverages industry (see Figure 1). Hence, as will be asserted below, the 'right to health' can potentially play a role in advancing the protection of 'public health' on the domestic and international plane.

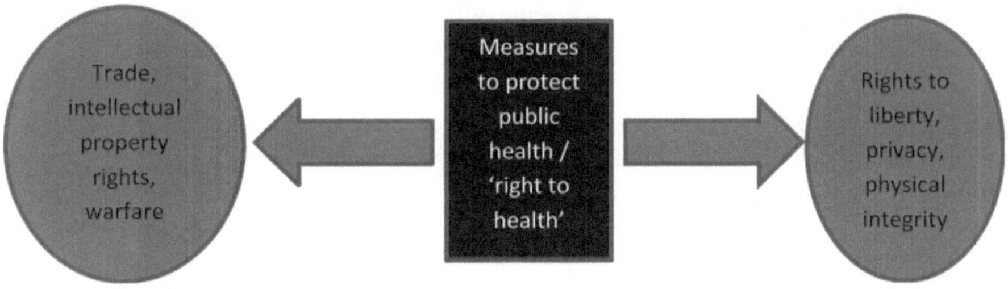

Figure 1. The tensions between the protection of public health and other interests

At the same time, the protection of public health, and the right to health for that matter, can be at odds with the interests of the individual. In other words, while the right to health potentially embraces claims to public health, this may also create a tension with the exercise of individual rights, including the rights to physical integrity, privacy and freedom of movement.[1] This tension will surface particularly when it comes to the protection against infectious diseases and other so-called 'health security threats'. For example, while the public at large has a right to be protected against the spread of infectious diseases, individuals have a right to be protected against unnecessary interferences with their privacy (see Figure 1). We are, thus, dealing with an important tension in human rights law that receives little attention in the literature.[2]

We need a better comprehension of how to address this tension, and what to do when the right to health is used to justify certain types of governmental health measures.[3] This ties in with recent calls for the adoption of a convention addressing global health. Driven by concern about the increasing global and domestic health inequalities, a number of scholars and civil society organisations have proposed the adoption of a Framework Convention on Global Health (FCGH), by the World Health Organization (WHO).[4] This network proposes that the FCGH be grounded in the right to health and as such that the right to health is positioned as a key norm in the global health law debate.[5] Thus, if we want to advance the importance of the right to health on the international plane, we need to ensure that we have a clear picture of its potential and of the possible clashes with other rights and interests.

In an attempt to create clarity with regard to these matters, in this contribution I will seek to lay bare the various connections between public health and human rights. To clarify the meaning of the concept of 'public health', I will start with an analysis of the historical evolution of this concept and of some subsequent international developments in this field. Subsequently, I will discuss the existing 'public health clauses' that are included in a range of treaties under international law, including in international trade law and international environmental law. In other words I will explain how the notion of 'public health' is embedded in these branches of international law. Subsequently I will bring the discussion back to human rights law by analysing whether the right to health also reflects claims to public health and what is the potential of such claims, so as to find out whether the 'right to health' as a human rights standard can reinforce the existing public health clauses under international law. As such I will scrutinise if, and if so how, the right to health can be a collective claim against the powerful forces of international trade, the private industry, and the interests of warfare. Subsequently I will look at some potential tensions in this approach. To do so, I will analyse the tensions between the urge to protect public health and the right of individuals to privacy, liberty and individual health protection. In this context I will discuss to what extent such rights can be limited by outlining briefly what the public health derogations and limitations in human rights law and international law more generally look like. This article will end with an evaluation of how to balance these interests, and of what can be the role of human rights law in this balancing act.

While the analysis in this article mainly builds on human rights standards and legal human rights discourse, it touches on several other disciplines, including domestic and international health law, social medicine, public health and medical ethics, as well as international trade law, international humanitarian law and international environmental law. It refers to human rights treaties that have been adopted at the United Nations (UN) as well as regional levels (in particular, the Council of Europe), in an integrated fashion. Rather than creating an exhaustive overview of the field, an attempt is made to scope and to define the field and to explain how the human rights framework can be better equipped to protect 'public health', taking into account the above-mentioned goals and tensions.

Public health and the global public health movement

Before we can discuss the connections between human rights and public health, a few words need to be devoted to the origins and meaning of the term 'public health'. When it comes to its origins, we see that a sense of community responsibility for the health of the public has existed since ancient civilisations. For example, through the ages civilisations have recognised that adequate sanitation is a pivotal factor for the improvement of public health.[6] The aggregate of such community efforts is usually indicated with the term 'public health'. According to Rosen, modern public health took its origins in nineteenth-century England, as the first modern industrial country.[7] An influential person at that time in England was Edwin Chadwick who, strongly influenced by the utilitarian philosopher Bentham, advocated that a healthy working class would benefit society at large.[8] He was involved in the adoption of a new Poor Law in Britain in 1834, which created a Poor Law Commission, which published a report emphasising the connection between environmental conditions (water supply, the removal of refuse) and disease.[9]

The issue of 'public health' increasingly also obtained an international dimension. Due to the developments in commerce and transportation, it had become necessary to coordinate the prevention of transmissible diseases at the international level. The first steps towards an international health organisation were also taken in the nineteenth century. A range of International Sanitary Conferences was organised which culminated in the establishment of the *Office International d'Hygiène Publique* (OIHP) in 1907.[10] This OIHP, which was subsequently placed under the auspices of the League of Nations, was complemented with another international health organisation, the 'Health Organization of the League of Nations', so as to more adequately deal with increasing global health problems. Until the creation of the UN, these two organisations existed side-by-side.[11]

In 1946, the World Health Organization was established and representatives of 61 States signed the Constitution of the World Health Organization (WHO). While the Constitution of the WHO does not define 'public health' explicitly, its website contains the following broad definition:

> Public health refers to all organized measures (whether public or private) to prevent disease, promote health, and prolong life among the population as a whole. Its activities aim to provide conditions in which people can be healthy and focus on entire populations, not on individual patients or diseases. Thus, [as opposed to 'medicine'] public health is concerned with the total system and not only the eradication of a particular disease.[12] (text between brackets added)

This definition indicates that 'public health' does not focus on individual patients or diseases and encapsulates many dimensions. Based on an overview of the WHO's public health campaigns it may embrace issues like vaccination and control of infectious diseases, motor-vehicle safety, occupational health, safe drinking water, maternal and child health, coronary heart disease and stroke, and prevention of smoking.[13]

While the primary focus of 'public health' lies at the domestic level, WHO also recognises that as a result of globalisation, forces that affect public health can and do come from outside state boundaries, and in that context it uses the term 'global public health'.[14] An important dimension of global public health is 'global health security' which focuses not only on the spread of infectious diseases, but also more generally on the detrimental health effects of man-made and natural disasters, including armed conflict, biological terrorism and nuclear disasters.[15] The new International Health Regulations (IHR, as revised in 2005) reflect this broader approach by focusing not only on a limited range of diseases but on a wider range of health security threats (see also the contribution by Zidar elsewhere in this special issue).

Without being exhaustive, another important new dimension of the WHO's concept of 'public health' concerns the focus on socio-economic health inequalities. In relation to this, there is an increasing emphasis on the so-called 'social determinants of health', i.e. the 'conditions in which people are born, grow, live, work and age'.[16] It is increasingly stressed that illness, chronic diseases and disability, as well as socio-economic health inequalities more generally, form important public health concerns. To quote Lawrence Gostin, a key scholar in this debate:

> (...) global efforts should be directed toward universal assurance of the essential conditions for health: population-level strategies drawn from the tool box of public health; fully affordable, accessible, high quality health care for all; and a wide range of policies beyond the health sector to address the social determinants of health.[17]

As such, Gostin establishes a link between public health and the need to provide good and accessible health care and other health-related services.

To bring this back to human rights law: this emphasis on 'health security' and on 'socio-economic health inequalities' raises the question of how the 'right to health', as also stipulated in the Constitution of the WHO, can strengthen and reinforce such claims on the international plane. Addressing the more narrow aim of the spread of infectious diseases potentially raises tensions with the civil and political rights of individuals. Fostering access to health services and tackling health inequalities, on the other hand, does not necessarily create such tensions but rather relies on a key component of the right to health that stands separately from civil and political human rights. As will be asserted in the conclusions to this contribution, if we want to address global public health properly from a human rights perspective, we should address both dimensions by taking an integrated approach to human rights, emphasising the importance of both civil and political rights and economic, social and cultural rights.

Claims to 'public health' under public international law

Before we can discuss how the 'right to health' reflects public health, we should explore how public health is reflected in several other branches of public international law. In international law there are many references to the protection of public health contrasting with other interests, including the interests of trade, commerce, intellectual property protection, transportation and warfare. A clear example is provided in the Framework Convention on Tobacco Control (FCTC), which stipulates in its preamble that the parties to this convention '[are] *Determined* to give priority to their right to protect public health'.[18] This is a robust expression of the desire of parties to give the protection of public health, and the state's duty to protect this interest, considerable weight in comparison to, in this case, the interests of the tobacco industry and trade-related interests of states. As will be discussed further below, the FCTC has played a crucial role in several domestic cases concerning tobacco control.

Without being exhaustive, this section will give some examples of existing public health clauses under international law.[19] Starting with the IHR that have been adopted within the framework of the WHO: they plainly reflect the potential tensions that may arise between the public health component of the right to health and the protection of individual civil and political rights. The IHR reflect the right to health where they are aimed at preventing, protecting against, controlling and providing a public health response to public health risks (Article 2). At the same time, the regulations take into account civil and political rights where they state that their implementation 'shall be with full respect for the dignity, human rights and fundamental freedoms of persons', thereby underscoring the importance of human rights protection during public health emergencies (Article 3-1). Throughout the document, several references are made to the civil and political rights of individuals. For example, Article 23, on 'health measures on arrival and departure', stresses the right to informed consent of travellers.[20] However, how these rights exactly come into play is not spelled out, and there is a clear need for further research in this field.[21]

The protection of public health also plays a role in international trade law, as regulated within the framework of the WTO.[22] Here, the protection of public health goes against freedom of trade, intellectual property protection, and generally the interests of commerce. The General Agreement on Tariffs and Trade (GATT),[23] which covers international trade in goods, permits member states in Article XX(b) GATT to take measures 'necessary to protect human, animal or plant life or health'. This provision recognises that members may wish to give priority to public health concerns.[24] As this provision was considered to be very important, a new agreement has been adopted which contains more specific rules for the protection of health, i.e. the Agreement on Sanitary and Phytosanitary Measures (SPS). This agreement regulates 'sanitary measures', which relate to human or animal health, and 'phytosanitary measures', which deal with plant health.

A number of WTO cases have considered defences under Article XX(b).[25] For example, in the case of *EC-Asbestos*, Canada opposed a French law which prohibited the manufacture, sale, distribution and import of chrysotile asbestos fibres and products containing this kind of asbestos. Canada argued that the French law discriminated against Canadian asbestos in favour of certain French substitute products. Both the Panel and Appellate Body of the WTO ruled that the European Commission had demonstrated that France's measure was necessary to protect human life or health.[26] Here we see how a claim to public health was invoked by one member to halt the import of a potentially harmful good into its country by another member.

Invoking these clauses may imply possible negative trade effects for other GATT members. As indicated by Lester et al., it is important to strike a balance between allowing members to protect public health or other social interests and preventing them from using these policies in such a way that they have a negative effect on trade and the interests of the other members.[27] It would be important that this clause is only invoked if there is a genuine threat to the health of the member's public.

Another framework under WTO law where public health issues are addressed concerns intellectual property law and the so-called TRIPS Agreement.[28] An important public health dimension of the TRIPS Agreement is that due to the patenting of medicines under this agreement, many drugs are practically unaffordable, especially to patients in the developing world. Contrary to other public health dimensions of trade law, this is an area where human rights scholars have stressed the tensions between this patent regime and the right to health.[29] Many scholars and non-governmental organisations (NGOs) have explored the potential role that the right to health can play in addressing these injustices.[30] In WTO circles this language has not been adopted, however a recognition of the problem was expressed in the DOHA Declaration:

> We agree that the TRIPS Agreement does not and should not prevent members from taking measures to protect public health. Accordingly, while reiterating our commitment to the TRIPS Agreement, we affirm that the Agreement can and should be interpreted and implemented in a manner supportive of WTO members' right to protect public health and, in particular, to promote access to medicines for all.[31]

Like with the Tobacco Framework Convention, DOHA contains a recognition of a right of member states to protect public health.

Another dimension of the TRIPS Agreement where a conflict with public health protection has arisen is tobacco control. In 2011 Australia introduced the Tobacco Plain Packaging Act (TPPA), which introduced the plain packaging of cigarettes, in other words the removal of all branding. The aim was to improve public health by discouraging smoking and to implement certain obligations under the Framework Convention on Tobacco Control (FCTC) of the WHO.[32] Australia became the respondent in five WTO disputes regarding the introduction of the TPPA, commenced by Ukraine, Honduras, the Dominican Republic, Cuba and Indonesia.[33] While several dimensions of WTO law play a role here, the TRIPS Agreement plays a key role in the case at issue. It is argued in the case that the Australian TPPA failed to protect trademarks registered outside Australia and placed unjustified encumbrances on the use of tobacco-related trademarks.[34] From a right to health perspective, the plain packages case is a clear example of a country wishing to protect the health of its population (Australia) against the trade interests (and potentially the right to development) of other nations.

With regard to the FCTC, another interesting case has arisen recently in the Netherlands, which also illustrates how the interests of public health can be weighed against the interests of trade. In September 2014 the Youth Smoking Prevention Foundation started legal proceedings against the Kingdom of the Netherlands to 'end the structural and excessive influence exerted by the tobacco lobby on government anti-smoking policies'.[35] The case is based on Article 5(3) of the FCTC and the ensuing guidelines, which require states parties to protect their anti-tobacco policies from commercial and other vested interests of the tobacco industry. In addition, the case relies on the right to health in the Dutch Constitution and international treaties that the Netherlands is a party to. Due to the monist system in the Netherlands, neither the FCTC nor the human rights instruments have to be transformed into domestic law before they can be invoked before the courts. No matter what the outcome of the case will be, it creates an interesting precedent for similar cases in which the interests of public health are balanced against the interests of international trade. It shows that the FCTC can potentially become a powerful instrument to give more weight to the protection of the health of the public. It raises the question of whether there is a need for more treaties addressing public health concerns, for example an instrument addressing the global increase in the incidence of chronic diseases and the dubious role of the food and beverage industry in this regard.[36]

Furthermore, in international environmental law, increasing attention is being given to the linkages between the environment and the protection of health.[37] Many multilateral environmental agreements contain references to the protection of health, including the Montreal Protocol on Protection of the Ozone Layer (1987), the Basel Convention on the Control of Transboundary Movements of Hazardous Wastes and their Disposal (1989), the Convention on Biological Diversity adopted in 1992, the Kyoto Protocol of the United Nations Framework Convention on Climate Change (1997), the Rotterdam Convention on the Prior Informed Consent Procedure for Certain Hazardous Chemicals and Pesticides in International Trade (1997), and the Stockholm Convention on Persistent Organic Pollutants (2002).[38] For example, the Stockholm Convention on Persistent Organic Pollutants stipulates as its main objective 'to protect human health and the environment from persistent organic pollutants'.[39] As indicated by Von Schirnding et al., environmental treaties can be used in the interest of promoting health.[40] Vice versa, the right to health can be used as a claim in support of the protection of the environment under international environmental law.

When it comes to the laws regulating armed conflicts, clearly there are many references to the protection of health. The Geneva Conventions and Additional Protocols contain many provisions regulating the safe and undisturbed delivery of medical services, the medical neutrality of medical personnel during armed conflicts, and the protection of the health of prisoners of war.[41] Yet most closely related to the protection of public health is Article 55 of Additional Protocol I (applicable during international armed conflicts), which focuses on the protection of the natural environment:

> Care shall be taken in warfare to protect the natural environment against widespread, long-term and severe damage. This protection includes a prohibition of the use of methods or means of warfare which are intended or may be expected to cause such damage to the natural environment and thereby to prejudice the health or survival of the population.[42]

The notion that weapons can cause severe damage to health is also underlying the weapons conventions, including the Chemical Weapons Convention and the Biological Weapons Convention.[43]

Lastly, in air law, we find several provisions on the protection of the health and safety of the persons on board aircraft. For example, Article 14 of the Convention on Civil Aviation addressing the prevention of the spread of diseases reads as follows:

> Each contracting State agrees to take effective measures to prevent the spread by means of air navigation of cholera, typhus (epidemic), smallpox, yellow fever, plague, and such other communicable diseases as the contracting States shall from time to time decide to designate, and to that end contracting States will keep in close consultation with the agencies concerned with international regulations relating to sanitary measures applicable to aircraft. (…)[44]

It is clear that measures taken on airports and on board aircraft to prevent the spread of infectious diseases may conflict with the civil and political rights of travellers. The tensions between the need to protect public health and civil and political rights will be discussed later.

The right to health as a public health claim against trade and other interests

We will now turn to the question of if, and if so how, the right to health can be positioned as an additional claim to public health in the above circumstances, reinforcing the existing public health claims under international law. In principle, the right to health reflects individual claims to health vis-à-vis governments. Such claims include access to specific health care services, medicines and the financial reimbursement for such services, as well as claims to the underlying determinants for health, including access to water, environmental health, occupational health and health-related information. The question arises whether, in addition to such individual claims, the right to health also embraces claims to 'public health' and, as such, requires governments to effectuate a national health policy and to enhance the health of the public at large. In light of the developments in the health field, this seems a very valid claim indeed. To quote Meier and Mori:

> Rather than relying solely upon an individual right to medical care, envisioning a collective right to public health – employing the language of human rights at the societal level – would alleviate many of the injurious health inequities of globalization.[45]

If the right to health is to become a key norm under global health law reflecting such claims to public health, it is important to consider how its implementation would turn out in a cases like the ones described above. In these examples the question arose whether public health measures could be taken which could then potentially conflict with such interests as international trade, intellectual property protection and warfare. Apart from the TRIPS debate, the right to health has not yet been positioned as an additional claim to public health going against such interests. For the right to health to be applied in such settings, it would be important that it is used for genuine public health concerns and not for protectionist reasons, so as to shield the domestic market from the import of competing products from abroad. In relation to this, the potential tensions with other rights should also be considered. The tension between public health and trade interests may, for example, translate into a tension between the right to health and the right to development. While, on the one hand, members invoking these public health clauses could frame this as a right to health claim, members barred from trading their goods based on such measures could possibly stress the right to development of their people, because they are barred from exporting their goods, which hampers their development. This tension could become particularly pressing in situations where a developed country invokes a public health claim against a (development claim) of a developing nation. The complex relationship between the WTO framework and the human rights framework in this respect is still under-researched.

In addition to such conceptual questions, there are also procedural issues that need to be addressed. The question arises how the right to health, as an individual right, can reflect collective public health claims. As we have framed human rights as individual rights, it will not be so easy to change the existing mechanisms and our understanding of them. This does not mean that our existing individual rights cannot lead to collective claims, however. As put by Galenkamp, we could perceive the right as materially conferred on individual members of a group, but procedurally looked after by the collectivity.[46] When it comes to judicial accountability, it seems possible to capture the interests of an affected group in the form of a 'bundle' or 'cluster' of individual rights.

It is, in this regard, of inspiration to consult the case law of the European Committee of Social Rights, the treaty-monitoring body of the (Revised) European Social Charter (ESC). Its collective complaint mechanism has enabled several international NGOs to defend the health-related interests of population groups.[47] As a collective complaint mechanism, it is able to represent a larger group of people, for example a group of undocumented migrants, or an indigenous population. The case law of this committee has touched on various health-related concerns, including access to health care for undocumented migrants, the occupational health concerns of miners in Greece, and the protection of the health of the Roma. For example, in the decision of *ECCR* v. *Bulgaria*, the committee explicitly addressed the notion of health inequalities with respect to the Roma in Bulgaria. It stated that Bulgaria had failed to:

> […] take reasonable steps to address the specific problems faced by Roma communities stemming from their often unhealthy living conditions and difficult access to health services.[48]

This is a clear claim to public health: the unhealthy living conditions were an important reason for the committee to conclude that the rights in the ESC had been violated. While the decisions of this committee are not legally binding, they are influential, and can have a spillover effect for national court cases addressing similar concerns.

We may conclude that some ingenuity is required for implementing the right to health as a norm that also encapsulates global and domestic public health concerns. As an individual human right, it typically addresses the health concerns of the individual. Nonetheless, there are possibilities for constructing the interests of a group as a 'bundle of rights', and for establishing judicial and quasi-judicial mechanisms that allow for collective complaints. Given the magnitude of global public health concerns, such mechanisms are much-needed.

The right to health as a health security claim against the rights of individuals

While, as was illustrated above, the right to health may feature as a claim to public health, there can also be a tension between this presumed public health component of the right to health and the civil and political rights of individuals, including their rights to security, liberty, physical integrity, privacy and family life, but potentially also their right to the best possible health care. While the spread of infectious diseases is the obvious and most pressing example of where this friction may arise, potential clashes may also occur in settings where biomedical research with human subjects is conducted and when it comes to the use of bio-banks, the testing of medicines, (forced) vaccinations, and the (unsolicited) storing of data.[49] The concrete measures that cause such tensions include detention, quarantine, and forced and unsolicited testing for diseases. It is clear that such acts may also be carried out beyond health care settings, for example in prisons and border detention centres.

This means that caution is to be exercised if the right to health (or a claim to 'public health') is used to justify certain types of governmental health measures.[50] While the state has an obligation to 'protect' health on the basis of the right to health, it should balance such measures against the rights and interests of individuals. This brings me to the question of whether, and if so to what extent, the scope and exercising of individual rights can be compromised for the sake of public health. With this I enter the field of human rights derogations and limitations, a complex field which has many dimensions.

To start with derogations from rights: both the European Convention on Human Rights (ECHR) and the International Covenant on Civil and Political Rights (ICCPR) provide for a system of derogations that allow states parties to adjust their obligations under the treaty in exceptional circumstances.[51] These measures can only be temporary in nature and are permitted only in exceptional circumstances, when the 'life of the nation is at stake', including armed conflicts, civil and social unrest, environmental and natural disasters, and potentially also public health emergencies.[52] Contrary to limitations, derogations lead to the content of the right being suspended completely. Nonetheless, both the ICCPR and the ECHR stipulate a limited set of rights that cannot be derogated from, including the right to life, the prohibition of torture and the prohibition of slavery.[53] This means that in situations of a declared emergency, the majority of the rights may be suspended, while a limited set of rights remains intact completely.

For the purposes of this contribution, it is important to speculate on the consequences of such a derogation in case of a 'public health emergency threatening the life of a nation'. On 8 August 2014, the WHO officially declared that the Ebola outbreak in West Africa constitutes an 'extraordinary event' and a public health risk to other states.[54] While the countries involved did not formally notify the United Nations Secretary General (UNSG) of a derogation from the rights in the ICCPR,[55] the question arises what would be the potential consequences of such a derogation from the perspective of the rights of individual patients. In this regard it is important to note that a derogation from the ICCPR and ECHR would imply that, in principle, the rights to liberty and security and privacy and family life can be suspended. In health care settings, such as in the case in the Ebola crisis, this means that the patients' rights of individuals could be overruled completely. This could lead to situations where severe and possibly unnecessary restrictions can be imposed on individuals. This tension deserves to be studied very critically by human rights scholars.

While derogations lead to rights being disregarded completely, limitations imply that the 'core of the right' should remain intact and may not be affected by a possible limitation. Rights in the ICCPR, ICESCR and ECHR may be limited for certain legitimate aims, as listed in the treaty, including national security, public safety, public order, the prevention of crimes, morals and health.[56] To enhance this balancing act within the framework of the ICCPR, the UN 'Siracusa Principles' on the limitations of rights provide some useful guidelines. This set of guidelines was drawn up by a group of 31 experts in international law in 1984. While it provides guidelines for the use of the limitations and derogations under the ICCPR, it may also have a wider reach. According to paragraph 10:

> 10. Whenever a limitation is required in the terms of the Covenant to be 'necessary', this term implies that the limitation:
>
> (a) is based on one of the grounds justifying limitations recognized by the relevant article of the Covenant,
> (b) responds to a pressing public or social need,
> (c) pursues a legitimate aim, and
> (d) is proportionate to that aim.

Moreover, paragraph 25 touches specifically on public health:

> Public health may be invoked as a ground for limiting certain rights in order to allow a State to take measures dealing with a serious threat to the health of the population or individual members of the population. These measures must be *specifically aimed at preventing disease or injury or providing care for the sick and injured.* [emphasis added]

And paragraph 26 adds:

> Due regard shall be had to the International Health Regulations of the World Health Organization.

The Siracusa Principles limit the application of the 'public health' clause to measures taken specifically to prevent the spread of diseases, and establish the link with the IHR.[57]

In addition, it is important to look at the ECHR, as the most authoritative human rights instrument in Europe. The case law of the European Court of Human Rights (ECtHR) increasingly pays attention to patients' rights, including rights to consent and privacy, in its case law.[58] Moreover as will be discussed below, the ECtHR has in a number of cases assessed how limitation clauses and limits to the rights to security and privacy come into play in health care settings and situations of detention.

Similar to the ICCPR, the ECHR stipulates that states may invoke so-called 'legitimate aims' or purposes laid down in the limitation clauses under Articles 8–11 of the convention and Article 2 of Protocol No. 4. The 'legitimate aims' clause embraces, among other aims, the protection of 'health or morals'. As pointed out by Van Dijk and Van Hoof, the Strasbourg organs have rarely found a violation of convention rights by reference to the 'legitimate aim' standard. One reason may be that the assessment of this standard is somewhat abundant, as it is normally carried out in conjunction with the third standard, 'necessary in a democratic society', and in particular with the application of proportionality.[59]

Nonetheless, as also discussed elsewhere in this special issue by Sanden and Bachmann, the ECtHR has in several cases considered the detention of a person with an infectious disease. Sanden and Bachman discuss a range of cases in which this issue is addressed. In the key case *Enhorn* v. *Sweden*, for example, the ECtHR considered the extent of the right to liberty and security of the person in Article 5(1) ECHR in light of the compulsory detention of a man infected with the HIV virus.[60] The court found that:

> the essential criteria when assessing the 'lawfulness' of the detention of a person 'for the prevention of the spread of infectious diseases' are whether the spreading of the infectious disease is dangerous to public health or safety, and whether detention of the person infected is the *last resort* in order to prevent the spreading of the disease, because *less severe measures have been considered* and found to be insufficient to safeguard the public interest.[61] (emphasis added)

By seeing detention for public health reasons as a 'last resort' the court seems to take a stricter approach than the Siracusa Principles. In this case, the court was not convinced that the detention of Mr Enhorn was a last resort, as less severe measures had not been considered.[62] It also noted that the Swedish authorities had failed to strike a fair balance between competing interests, because the detention amounted to one and a half years in total, which, in the court's opinion, was not sufficiently balanced to the needs of society in preventing the spread of the HIV virus.[63]

As mentioned above, the limitation of rights may also come into play when it comes to such public health concerns as biomedical research with human subjects, the use of biobanks, the testing of medicines, (forced) vaccinations, and the (unsolicited) storing of data. International human rights law still provides little guidance in such situations. An important European instrument that may provide direction or inspiration in this field is the European Convention on Human Rights and Biomedicine ('Oviedo Convention'), adopted by the Council of Europe in 1997, and its protocols on cloning, transplantation, biomedical research and genetic testing for health purposes.[64] When it comes to limitations, this instrument contains a limitation clause that is comparable to the clause in the ECHR, in Article 26. This provision, however, offers states parties fewer possibilities for restricting rights as it does not allow this clause to be placed on several Articles in the Biomedicine Convention, thus providing for an interesting mix between limitations and non-derogable rights.[65]

An important specific issue of concern is the ethical and legal issues surrounding the conduct of clinical trials with human participants in developing countries. Western organisations and companies have in recent years increasingly used the countries of the developing world as places for their trials.[66] Importantly, the above-mentioned protocol concerning biomedical research of the Council of Europe states in Article 3 that 'The interests and welfare of the human being participating in research shall prevail over the sole interest of society or science.'[67] In the absence of an enforcement mechanism for this treaty and its protocols, it is difficult to envisage how this instrument may work out in practice. Nonetheless, it would be worthwhile to carefully explore the scope and potential of this document for the purposes of protecting the rights of those exposed to such clinical trials, also – or especially – in the developing world.

Lastly some attention should be paid to the possibility of restricting the 'right to health' itself. For, as was suggested above, the right to health, if exercised collectively as a public health claim, potentially also clashes with the right to the best possible health care of individuals, or in other words their individual right to health. As such, the perceived collective dimension of the right to health potentially conflicts with the individual right to health of individuals. In a setting where an infectious disease is threatening to become a threat to public health, the medical needs of individual patients may be easily overlooked. There is an increasing emphasis in the literature on the notion that limitations to economic and social rights should not affect the 'core' or 'core obligations' inherent in the rights.[68] This would imply that when measures are taken for the interests of public health, the right of the individual to essential health services should not be affected. If we place this approach in the context of the recent Ebola crisis, this would imply that a quarantine which is to serve the health of the public should allow for a continued right to basic health care services for the quarantined individuals.

In addition, it is worthwhile to look at the system of limitations in the ICESCR, which includes the right to health. Can the right to health of the individual also be limited for the sake of the health of the public? Article 4 ICESCR contains the following limitation clause:

> The States Parties to the present Covenant recognize that, in the enjoyment of those rights provided by the State in conformity with the present Covenant, the State may subject such rights only to such limitations as are determined by law only in so far as this may be compatible with the nature of these rights and solely for the purpose of the general welfare in a democratic society.

The reference to the 'nature' of rights has similarities to the idea of a 'core' inherent in economic, social and cultural rights. General Comment 14 on the right to health explains that Article 4 is primarily intended to:

> (…) *protect the rights of individuals* rather than to permit the imposition of limitations by States. Consequently a State party which, for example, restricts the movement of, or incarcerates, persons with transmissible diseases such as HIV/AIDS, refuses to allow doctors to treat persons believed to be opposed to a government, or fails to provide immunization against the community's major infectious diseases, on grounds such as national security or the preservation of public order, *has the burden of justifying* such serious measures in relation to each of the elements identified in article 4.[69] (emphasis added)

Hence a restrictive interpretation of this provision and a burden of proof on the part of states to justify the measures taken. There is a clear indication that the right to minimum or basic health services should remain intact. Furthermore General Comment 14 explains that states have to justify the public health restrictions that they impose, *inter alia* by proving that such measures are in the interest of the legitimate aims pursued:

> Such restrictions must be in accordance with the law, including international human rights standards, compatible with the nature of the rights protected by the Covenant, in the interest of

legitimate aims pursued, and strictly necessary for the promotion of the general welfare in a democratic society.

This wording is very similar to the language and approach in the limitation clauses under the ICCPR.

All in all, there seems to be a general understanding in human rights law that restrictions taken for the sake of public health should not go against the nature or 'essence' of the rights of the individual, that they should be proportionate, pursue a legitimate aim and that they should be taken solely for the interests of a democratic society. These requirements are to be borne in mind when measures are taken that are to benefit the public health of society at large.

Public health and human rights: towards a balanced relationship

We are witnessing a number of serious challenges both in domestic and global health, including a change in disease patterns, some of which are lifestyle-related, as well as increasing health inequalities within and between states. What is more, many countries are struggling with the detrimental health effects of environmental degradation, climate change, international migration, urbanisation and internal conflicts. All this is affecting the health and well-being of individuals worldwide, and especially those who are marginalised and disadvantaged. From a human rights perspective, the question arises how human rights can affectively advance the health of the public, whilst respecting the rights of individuals.

It was illustrated above that the right to health plays an ambivalent, yet increasingly important, role in the protection of global and domestic public health. On the one hand, the right to health can potentially strengthen claims to health, so as to balance this interest against the interests of trade, intellectual property protection and warfare. It is important to pay more detailed attention to this potentially promising role of the right to health. While the right to health is primarily an individual right, possibly it could be conceived as a 'bundle' of individual rights exercised by a collectivity. Perceived this way, it could potentially act as a collective claim against, for example, the interests of the tobacco industry, the interests of warfare, or the negative effects of environmental pollution, or a specific polluting industry.

At the same time, where it concerns issues of health security, including preventing the spread of infectious diseases, there is a potential clash between the right to health, or public health claims, and the individual rights of patients and others. In such situations individuals have rights to privacy, liberty, but also to the best possible health care. We all watched in dread as West Africa attempted to address the tremendous challenges caused by the last and biggest outbreak of Ebola.[70] These and similar outbreaks raise huge dilemmas under human rights law. On the one hand, there is the need to protect public health, and along those lines, the legal obligation to protect the right to health of the public. On the other hand, there is a need to respect the individual rights of the patients and their family members.

It is interesting to see how Human Rights Watch (HRW), in response to the recent Ebola outbreak, takes an integrated approach towards human rights law by focusing on both economic, social and cultural rights and civil and political rights, thus emphasising that human rights are 'indivisible, interdependent and interrelated'.[71] On the one hand, it refers to the right to health by stressing the importance of the need to 'protect health workers from infection, limit the use of quarantines, address the gender dimensions of the outbreak, ensure security forces responding to the crisis respect basic rights (…)'. It states that 'donor governments, through international assistance and cooperation, should help these governments fulfill the right to health and efforts to address the epidemics broader impact'.[72] Simultaneously, HRW refers to civil and political rights by stressing that 'international human rights law requires that restrictions on human rights in the name of public emergency meet requirements of legality, evidence-based necessity, and proportionality'. In this context, it expresses its concern that quarantines imposed during this epidemic have frequently not met these standards.[73]

Such an integrated approach to human rights, taking into account both civil and political and economic, social and cultural rights, seems the most balanced response to public health concerns, in particular when it comes to health security threats. Should there be a clash between the rights as suggested above, then a careful balancing of the rights, in light of existing limitation and derogation clauses and existing guidelines, is in place. It is important to bear in mind that the more rigorous possibility of 'derogations' to the human rights system as a whole allows for the complete derogation of patients' rights, including the rights to liberty, privacy and family life. More research is needed to create coherence among these standards and to come to a more profound understanding of how these limitations can best be applied.

Acknowledgements

I would like to thank Laura Niada and Andraz Zidar for their helpful comments. In addition I am grateful to my colleagues from the International Law Department of the University of Groningen, in particular André de Hoogh and Antenor Hallo de Wolf, for their useful feedback. I also thank Caroline Gallagher for language suggestions to an earlier version of this article.

Disclosure statement

No potential conflict of interest was reported by the author.

Notes on contributor

Brigit Toebes is an associate professor and Rosalind Franklin Fellow at the Department of International Law of the Faculty of Law of University of Groningen in the Netherlands. She has published widely in the field of health and human rights, including books with Intersentia (e.g. *Health and Human Rights in Europe*, 2012). She is the Co-Chair of the Global Health Law Committee of the International Law Association and she has established a programme called Global Health Law Groningen which facilitates research on the interface between international law, human rights and the protection of health.

Notes

1. *Inter alia*, Brigit Toebes, Mette Hartlev, Aart Hendriks, and Janne Rothmar Herrmann, eds, *Health and Human Rights in Europe* (Cambridge: Intersentia, 2012), 101–2.
2. See, for example, Thérèse Murphey, *Health and Human Rights* (Oxford: Hart, 2013), in particular Chapter 2: 'Is Human Rights Prepared?', 58.
3. See, also, the interesting observations by Murphey, who speaks about 'human rights preparedness'. Ibid., *inter alia* at 72.
4. JALI Health, *Joint Action and Learning Initiative on National and Global Responsibilities for Health*, http://www.jalihealth.org/ (accessed 18 August 2014). See also *JALI/FCGH Research Questions*, January 2014 update, http://www.jalihealth.org/research/docs/JALI%20Research%20Questions.pdf (accessed August 2014).

5. Lawrence O. Gostin, *Global Health Law* (Cambridge, MA: Harvard University Press, 2014), 20–31.
6. George Rosen, *A History of Public Health* (Baltimore, MD: John Hopkins University Press, 1993), 2–3, originally published in 1958 by MD Publications Rosen.
7. Rosen, *A History of Public Health* (1993), 170. See also Brigit Toebes, *The Right to Health as a Human Right in International Law* (Antwerpen: Intersentia/Hart 1999), 8–11.
8. H.E. Sigerist, *Medicine and Human Welfare* (New Haven, CT: Yale University Press/Oxford University Press, 1941), 90.
9. Rosen, *A History of Public Health* (1993), 176 and 196–8.
10. H.D.C. Roscam Abbing, *International Organizations in Europe and the Right to Health Care* (Deventer: Kluwer, 1979), 91. See also Toebes, *The Right to Health as a Human Right in International Law*, 12.
11. Toebes, *The Right to Health as a Human Right in International Law*, 11–13.
12. WHO, *Public Health*, http://www.who.int/trade/glossary/story076/en/ (accessed May 2014).
13. Ibid.
14. Ibid.
15. WHO, 'The World Health Report 2007: A Safer Future-Global Public Health Security in the 21st Century', http://www.who.int/whr/2007/en/ (accessed September 2014). Sophie Harman, *Global Health Governance* (Routledge Global Institutions Series, No. 60, 2012), 19–23. See also Global Health Security Initiative, http://www.ghsi.ca/english/index.asp (accessed August 2014). See also Oskar N.T. Thoms and James Ron, 'Public Health, Conflict and Human Rights: Toward a Collaborative Research Agenda', *Conflict and Health* 1, no. 11 (2007).
16. WHO, *Social Determinants of Health*, http://www.who.int/social_determinants/en/ (accessed August 2014).
17. Gostin, *Global Health Law*, 412.
18. WHO Framework Convention on Tobacco Control, Preamble. It was adopted by the World Health Assembly on 21 May 2003 and entered into force on 27 February 2005, http://www.who.int/fctc/en/ (accessed September 2014).
19. While the treaties of the International Labour Organization also have relevance in this field, they have not been taken into consideration in this section.
20. Article 23(3), International Health Regulations (see also Article 31(2)). See also Articles 42 and 45(1) of the IHR.
21. See also the contribution by Zidar elsewhere in this special issue.
22. See also World Health Organization and World Trade Organization, *WTO Agreements & Public Health*, A joint study by the WHO and the WTO Secretariat, 2002, http://www.wto.org/english/res_e/booksp_e/who_wto_e.pdf (accessed September 2014); and Wemos/European Health Alliance/Physicians for Social Responsibility, *World Trade Organization: Implications for Health Policy*, April 2000.
23. General Agreement on Tariffs and Trade 1994 (GATT), http://www.wto.org/english/docs_e/legal_e/06-gatt_e.htm (accessed September 2014).
24. Article XX, sub-paragraph (b). World Health Organization and World Trade Organization, *WTO Agreements & Public Health*, 11.
25. Simon Lester, Bryan Mercurio, and Arwel Dabies, *World Trade Law*, 2nd ed. (Oxford: Hart, 2012), 380.
26. Ibid., 381–4.
27. Ibid., 364.
28. WTO, Agreement on Trade-Related Aspects of Intellectual Property Rights, adopted in 1994 at the Uruguay Round of GATT.
29. See, for example, Jennifer Sellin, *Access to Medicines: The Interface Between Patents and Human Rights: Does One Size Fit All?* (Antwerp: Intersentia, 2014).
30. See, for example, *Sur International Journal on Human Rights* 5, no. 8 (2008), http://www.surjournal.org/eng/conteudos/getArtigo8.php?artigo=8,artigo_chaves.htm (accessed September 2014). See also Report of the Special Rapporteur, Paul Hunt, 'Mission to the World Trade Organization', CESCR, UN Doc. E/CN.4/2004/49/Add.1, 1 March 2004. E/CN.4/2004/49/Add.1, http://www.who.int/medicines/areas/human_rights/E_CN_4_2004_49_Add_1.pdf (accessed September 2014).
31. DOHA Declaration, para. 4, http://www.wto.org/english/thewto_e/minist_e/min01_e/mindecl_trips_e.htm (accessed September 2014).

32. Parliament of Australia, *Flagpost, Australia's WTO Plain Cigarette Packing Case: An Update*, 8 July 2014, http://www.aph.gov.au/About_Parliament/Parliamentary_Departments/Parliamentary_Library/FlagPost/2014/July/WTO_plain_cigarette_packaging_case (accessed August 2014).
33. WTO, Dispute Settlement: *Dispute DS 434, Australia – Certain Measures Concerning Trademarks and Other Plain Packaging Requirements Applicable to Tobacco Products and Packing*, http://www.wto.org/english/tratop_e/dispu_e/cases_e/ds434_e.htm / (accessed August 2014).
34. Ibid.
35. Youth Smoking Prevention Foundation, information in English, http://www.stichtingrookpreventiejeugd.nl/2014/09/dutch-government-taken-to-court-for-illegal-contacts-with-tobacco-industry/. For the summons see http://www.stichtingrookpreventiejeugd.nl/wp-content/uploads/2014/09/08-09-2014-Dagvaarding-Stichting-Rookpreventie-Jeugd-v.-Staat-der-Nederlanden.pdf (accessed September 2014).
36. For an initiative see World Obesity Forum, *Recommendations towards a Global Convention to Protect and Promote Healthy Diets*, May 2014, http://www.consumersinternational.org/news-and-media/resource-zone/recommendations-towards-a-global-convention-to-protect-and-promote-healthy-diets/ (accessed September 2014).
37. Yasmin von Schirnding, William Onzivu, and Andronico O. Adede, 'International Environmental Law and Global Public Health', *Bulletin of the World Health Organization* 80, no. 12 (2002): 970–4.
38. Ibid., 970.
39. Article 1, Stockholm Convention on Persistent Organic Pollutants (2002).
40. Von Schirnding, 'International Environmental Law and Global Public Health', 970.
41. Brigit Toebes, 'Healthcare on the Battlefield: In Search of a Legal and Ethical Framework', *Journal of International Humanitarian Legal Studies* 4 (2013): 197–213.
42. Article 55, Additional Protocol I to the Geneva Conventions, adopted 8 June 1977.
43. Biological Weapons Convention, opened for signature on 10 April 1972; Convention on the Prohibition of the Development, Production, Stockpiling and Use of Chemical Weapons and on their Destruction, adopted 30 November 1992; Biological Weapons Convention, opened for signature on 10 April 1972.
44. Convention on Civil Aviation (Chicago Convention), adopted 7 December 1944.
45. Benjamin Mason Meier and Larisa M. Mori, 'The Highest Attainable Standard: Advancing a Collective Human Right to Public Health', *Columbia Human Rights Law Review* 37 (2005): 101–21, at 102, http://www.unc.edu/%7Emeierb/Meier%20&%20Mori,%20The%20Highest%20Attainable%20Standard%20%282005%29.pdf (accessed May 2014).
46. Marlies Galenkamp, 'Collective Rights', in *SIM Special No. 16* (Utrecht: Netherlands Institute of Human Rights, 1995), 53–102, at 70–1.
47. For an overview of all the decisions see the website of the European Committee of Social Rights: http://www.coe.int/t/dghl/monitoring/socialcharter/Complaints/Complaints_en.asp (accessed March 2014).
48. ECSR, *ECCR* v. *Bulgaria* (complaint no. 46/2007), para. 49. For an overview of all the decisions see the website of the European Committee of Social Rights: http://www.coe.int/t/dghl/monitoring/socialcharter/Complaints/Complaints_en.asp (accessed March 2014).
49. Mette Hartlev, 'Patients' Rights', in Toebes et al., *Health and Human Rights in Europe*, 111–44, at 125.
50. See also Murphey, *Health and Human Rights*, 58–84.
51. RULAC, *Derogations from Human Rights Treaties in Situations of Emergency*, http://www.geneva-academy.ch/RULAC/derogation_from_human_rights_treaties_in_situations_of_emergency.php (accessed September 2014). Derogation clauses are provided for in Article 4 of the ICCPR, Article 15 of the ECHR, and Article 27 of the American Convention of Human Rights (ACHR).
52. For an elaborate study on this matter see Anna-Lena Svensson McCarthy, *The International Law of Human Rights and States of Emergency* (The Hague: Martinus Nijhoff Publishers, 1998).
53. Art. 15 ECHR: Art. 2 (life), Art. 3 (torture), Art. 4.1 (slavery), Art. 7 (no punishment without law); Art. 4 ICCPR: Arts 6 (life), 7 (torture), 8 (slavery, paragraphs I and 2), 11 (contractual obligation), 15 (criminal offence), 16 (recognition before the law) and 18 (freedom of thought, conscience and religion).

54. WHO, 'Statement on the Meeting of the International Health Regulations Emergency Committee Regarding the 2014 Ebola Outbreak in West Africa', http://www.who.int/mediacentre/news/statements/2014/ebola-20140808/en/ (accessed September 2014).
55. See https://treaties.un.org/Pages/ViewDetails.aspx?src=TREATY&mtdsg_no=IV-4&chapter=4&lang=en (accessed September 2014).
56. The ICCPR can be limited in the interests of public health: 12(3) (freedom of movement), 18(3) (freedom of religion and belief), 19(2) (freedom of expression), 21 (peaceful assembly) and 22 (2) (freedom of association), and the following rights can be limited in the interests of public health in the ECHR: Arts 8–11. The ICESCR contains a general limitation clause (see below).
57. UN Commission on Human Rights, *The Siracusa Principles on the Limitation and Derogation Provisions in the International Covenant on Civil and Political Rights*, 28 September 1984, E/CN.4/1985/4, http://www.refworld.org/docid/4672bc122.html (accessed September 2014).
58. See also Hartlev, 'Patients' Rights'.
59. Van Dijk et al., *Theory and Practice of the European Convention on Human Rights*, 4th ed. (Antwerp: Intersentia, 2006), 339–40.
60. See also Alastair Mowbray, 'Compulsory Detention to Prevent the Spreading of Infectious Diseases', *Human Rights Law Review* 5, no. 2 (year): 387–91.
61. ECtHR 25 January 2005, *Enhorn* v. *Sweden*, no. 56529/00, para. 41.
62. Ibid., para. 55; Hartlev, 'Patients' Rights', 126.
63. Ibid., para 55; Hartlev, 'Patients' Rights', 126.
64. European Convention on Human Rights and Biomedicine (Oviedo Convention), adopted in Oviedo in 1997.
65. Articles 11–14, 16–17 and 19–21.
66. Michael Igoumenidis and Sophia Zyga, 'Healthcare Research in Developing Countries: Ethical Issues', *Health Science Journal* 5, no. 4 (2011): 243–50.
67. Article 3, Additional Protocol to the Convention on Human Rights and Biomedicine, concerning Biomedical Research.
68. For an elaborate discussion see Amrei Müller, *The Relationship between Economic, Social and Cultural Rights and International Humanitarian Law* (Leiden: Martinus Nijhoff Publishers: 2013), 124–8.
69. UN Committee on Economic, Social and Cultural Rights (CESCR), *General Comment 14 on the Right to the Highest Attainable Standard of Health*, UN Doc. E/C.12/2000/4, 11 August 2000, para. 28.
70. Centres for Disease Control and Prevention, '2014 Outbreak in West Africa', http://www.cdc.gov/vhf/ebola/outbreaks/guinea/ (accessed September 2014).
71. As emphasised in the Vienna Declaration and Programme of Action, as adopted by the World Conference on Human Rights in Vienna on 25 June 1993, http://www.ohchr.org/EN/ProfessionalInterest/Pages/Vienna.aspx (accessed January 2015).
72. Human Rights Watch, 'West Africa: Respect Rights in Ebola Response', 15 September 2014, http://www.hrw.org/news/2014/09/15/west-africa-respect-rights-ebola-response (accessed September 2014).
73. Ibid.

WHO International Health Regulations and human rights: from allusions to inclusion

Andraž Zidar

British Institute of International and Comparative Law, London, and Regent's University London, UK

As a response to an increasing threat of infectious diseases in the globalised world (e.g. SARS, H1N1 influenza, Ebola, MERS, Poliovirus), the World Health Organization adopted a reinvigorated version of the International Health Regulations in 2005. The regulations empower the WHO Director-General to proclaim a public health emergency of international concern and issue temporary recommendations of health measures to states parties. However, although the regulations and related health measures inevitably touch upon human rights of affected individuals, the regulations contain but a few allusions to the international human rights framework. The aim of this article is to include the international human rights regime in the system for the fight against infectious diseases under the regulations.

Introduction

In a contemporary world characterised by high mobility, economic interdependence and environmental degradation, infectious diseases represent one of most serious health dangers to humanity.[1] Highly infectious agents can spread very fast and, if not contained effectively, may affect a large number of people. The consequences of a global spread of a deadly infectious disease could be devastating.[2] This is not a mere hypothetical or abstract danger. The outbreak of the severe acute respiratory syndrome (SARS) in 2003 affected 29 countries, infecting 8,098 and killing 774 people.[3] The sense of urgency caused by the epidemic led to the reform of the WHO International Health Regulations (the regulations). In 2005, the WHO adopted a new version of the regulations, which strengthened the international mechanism for the prevention, protection and control of the international spread of infectious diseases.[4] According to Lawrence Gostin, the regulations have 'become arguably the most important global health treaty of the twenty-first century, with the WHO at the center of the governance regime'.[5]

In May 2011, the Review Committee on the functioning of the regulations stated that the 'world is ill-prepared to respond to a severe pandemic influenza or to any similarly global, sustained and threatening public-health emergency'.[6] Currently, the world is fighting another serious pandemic, Ebola. Figures in early 2015 showed that the disease had affected eight countries, predominantly in West Africa, infecting more than 21,000 individuals, of whom more than 8,000 have died.[7] It became obvious that the regulations alone could not orchestrate an efficient fight against infectious diseases in states with weak national health systems.[8] Consequently, another important legal and diplomatic move followed suit. Shortly after the WHO Director-General declared Ebola a public health emergency of international concern (PHEIC or international health emergency), the UN Security Council adopted Resolution 2177 (2014).[9] In the resolution, the Security Council proclaimed the unprecedented extent of the Ebola outbreak in Africa a threat to international peace and security and instructed all relevant actors to strengthen health capacities, coordination and responses in the fight against Ebola.[10]

Both the regulations and Resolution 2177 (2014) enhance the global legal framework and provide a basis for the political mobilisation of the international community in the fight against infectious diseases. However, a build-up of the global public health security[11] must not cloud the requirement that emergency health measures be compatible with international human rights.

The regulations contain several references to human rights. However, they are scant and very general.[12] Rather than providing a comprehensive framework for the protection of human rights, these provisions allude to something that is 'external' to regulations. Consequently, health and governmental officials may perceive the protection of human rights as ancillary during the implementation of health measures. The aim of this article is to integrate the international human rights regime in the legal framework under the regulations. The first section of the article will analyse the concept of the international health emergency and link it to the protection of human rights in times of emergency or crisis. The second section will consider in more detail the impact of health measures under the regulations on human rights and how human rights provisions inevitably limit the ambit of these measures.

International health emergency and human rights

The regulations are instrumental in providing a global framework for the prevention, detection and assessment of infectious diseases that may spread internationally and facilitating the coordination of responses to PHEIC.[13] The authority to declare a PHEIC resides in the Director-General of the WHO.[14] The delegation of such an executive power to the head of an international agency represents a notable increase in administrative powers, which is a novelty in global administrative law.[15] This novelty reflects the importance the international community assigns to the fighting of infectious diseases.

On the basis of the information received, in particular from the affected state party, the Director-General determines whether an event constitutes a PHEIC.[16] This procedure presupposes the participation of the country or countries concerned and the Emergency Committee, a body of experts set up for each particular outbreak of an infectious disease.[17] When making a decision, the Director-General must consider: (i) information provided by the state party; (ii) the decision instrument (algorithm) contained in Annex 2 of the regulations[18]; (iii) the advice of the Emergency Committee; (iv) scientific principles and scientific evidence; and (v) an assessment of the risk to human health, of the risk of international spread of disease and of the risk of interference with international traffic.[19] After the proclamation of the PHEIC, the Director-General issues necessary temporary recommendations, which are valid for three months.[20] The Director-General then communicates the determination of the international health emergency and any temporary recommendations, together with the views of the Emergency Committee, to states parties for implementation.[21]

It is clear from this overview, that the Director-General has principal responsibility in determining the PHEIC, as well as issuing temporary recommendations.[22] At the same time, it is important to underline the importance of procedural mechanisms and standards, in particular those that rely on scientific principles and evidence, for the decision-making process, as this significantly limits the ambit for arbitrary decisions.[23]

Given that the regulations explicitly state that their implementation shall be with full respect for human rights and fundamental freedoms of persons,[24] this process must be compatible with the regime of international human rights law, which encompasses the moral code of the international community.[25] This regime anticipates situations of instability in which public threats affect the protection of human rights. Such situations can be referred to as 'risk within rights'. [26] The international human rights law regime envisages two models that allow for incursions in human rights.[27] First, in some circumstances the enjoyment of a human right may be limited.[28] This model can be labelled as the 'limitations model'. Second, in emergency situations, states may derogate from their obligations under international human rights documents.[29] This model is more robust and can be called the 'derogations model'. The main difference between the two models is that the limitations model shrinks the framework of protection of human rights from the full to a limited scope, while the derogations model temporarily suspends the enjoyment of rights, except core rights that may never be derogated from.

In terms of the limitations model, the Universal Declaration of Human Rights (UDHR) characteristically stipulates that in the exercise of rights and freedoms, the individual 'shall be subject only to such limitations as are determined by law solely for the purpose of securing due recognition and respect for the rights and freedoms of others and of meeting the just requirements of morality, public order and the general welfare in a democratic society'.[30] Gradually, these requirements expanded to include public health as well.[31] Thus, authoritative guidelines in the *Siracusa Principles on the Limitation and Derogation Provisions in the International Covenant on Civil and Political Rights* (Siracusa Principles) list public health as a legitimate ground for limiting certain rights.[32] Public health may be invoked as a ground for allowing a state to take measures dealing with a serious health threat to the population or individual members of the population.[33] However, these 'measures must be specifically aimed at preventing disease or injury or providing care for the sick and injured'.[34]

Limitations are subject to a test that ensures that they are in conformity with human rights.[35] If a certain limitation is deemed necessary under the International Covenant on Civil and Political Rights (ICCPR), it must comply with the following criteria: (i) it must be based on one of the grounds justifying limitations (that is, public health); (ii) it must respond to a pressing public or social need; (iii) it must pursue a legitimate aim; and (iv) it must be proportionate to that aim.[36] In this assessment, the standard of proportionality is at the heart of the balancing test between legitimate social aims and the limitation of rights. More specifically, the standard of proportionality involves 'a delicate equation evaluating the importance of the social aim, the importance of the right guaranteed, and the degree of encroachment'.[37]

The derogations model, on the other hand, is more rigid in terms of its treatment of the seriousness of the danger and the scope and weight of incursions into rights. According to the ICCPR, a state party may take measures derogating from their obligations under the covenant in time of public emergency, which threatens the life of the nation.[38] The Siracusa Principles state that a threat to the life of the nation must be a situation of exceptional and actual or imminent danger that: (i) affects the whole of the population and the whole or part of the territory of the state; and (ii) threatens the physical integrity of the population, the political independence or the territorial integrity of the state or the existence or basic functioning of institutions indispensable for the protection of rights.[39] It is important to emphasise that if a public health emergency assumes such a magnitude, it can be invoked as a ground for the derogation of human rights.

Here, a question arises whether public health threats may be considered emergencies under Article 4 of the ICCPR. Several authors caution that the contemporary discourse on global public health is too prone to portraying health crises as 'emergencies', thus bringing them on a par with security threats.[40] This leads to the use of 'militarised' rhetoric, inaccurately implying security responses to essentially public health challenges.[41] However, the concept of a public emergency under Article 4 of the ICCPR was, from the outset, conceived very broadly to include not only security or political situations but also emergencies resulting from serious natural or environmental catastrophes that would threaten the life of the nation.[42] The emergency on the basis of health considerations is covered by this broader understanding of the public emergency provided that it fulfils all criteria, that is, that it represents a direct, exceptional and actual or imminent threat to the life of the nation.[43] The regulations define the PHEIC as an extraordinary event, which (i) constitutes a public health risk to other states through the international spread of disease and (ii) potentially requires a coordinated international response.[44] According to the WHO, this definition implies a health situation that is serious, unusual or unexpected; carries implications for public health beyond the affected state's national border; and may require immediate international action.[45] In this sense, the international health emergency may represent a public emergency for states in the context of ICCPR Article 4.

In contrast to the limitations model, derogation does not imply a proportionate limitation of an exercise of a specific right, but its full suspension.[46] However, a set of important restrictions and checks applies even to the derogations model. First, there are some rights that cannot be derogated in times of emergency.[47] Second, it is worth emphasising that even where rights are derogated as a result of an emergency, the rule of law continues to prevail and there is no 'legal vacuum'.[48] Third, all limitations must be envisaged for a temporary period of time and to the extent strictly required by the exigencies of the situation.[49] The predominant objective of a state proclaiming the state of emergency must be the restoration of the state of normalcy with full respect of human rights.[50] Finally, during the period of the state of emergency, the state is under the scrutiny of the international community.[51] When a state resorts to the possibility of derogation from human rights under ICCPR, it must immediately notify the UN Secretary-General and, through him or her, other states parties to the ICCPR of the provisions from which it has derogated and of the reasons for such measures.[52] All these checks guarantee that during times of emergency, states do not slide into a condition of lawlessness.

When compared to the human rights regime that deals with emergency threats – the limitations model and the derogations model – the regime under the regulations for addressing PHEIC looks more complex. The decision-making process in the derogations model and limitations models is essentially monocentric. Monocentric tasks require a decision or a set of sequential binary decisions in which a decision-maker opts for one or another solution.[53] In the derogations model, there is a decision whether the social instability amounts to the state of emergency and, if the answer is affirmative, which rights are suspended during the emergency. Similarly, the limitations model pursues monocentric decisions in a sequence: (i) is there a ground justifying limitations?; (ii) is there a pressing public need?; (iii) is there a legitimate aim?; and (iv) is the limitation proportionate to that aim?

In contrast, the regulations define the international health emergency in an open-ended way.[54] There are three main components in the understanding of the PHEIC, which makes decision-making a very complex process: (i) the concept of public health risk; (ii) implications for public health beyond the affected state's borders; and (iii) a coordinated international response led by the WHO. One of the main novelties of the revised regulations is that they rely on the 'all hazards' approach, which extends the reach of health risks beyond infectious diseases to include other health hazards such as biological, chemical and radio-nuclear hazards.[55] This classification implies that health risks originate from numerous sources: persons (e.g. SARS, MERS, Ebola); goods, food, water or animals (e.g. botulism, bovine spongiform encephalopathy); vectors (e.g. plague, yellow fever) and the environment (e.g. radio-nuclear releases, chemical spills, anthrax).[56] Such a multifaceted matrix of health threats means that each health emergency has a distinctive evolutionary dynamic that would inevitably follow a different pathogenesis. Consequently, the emergency mechanism has to be flexible and adaptable, which is precisely the philosophy behind the regulations.[57]

In addition to the mutable character of public health risk, the other two components of the PHEIC are very indeterminate as well. The fact that we are speaking of an *international* health emergency implies that various countries and regions may be affected at different times or at different intensities. Therefore, in the context of a particular health hazard, different risk assessment phases may apply to different countries and regions. Correspondingly, the international response coordinated and led by the WHO may also vary with regard to the intensity of health risks, their temporal dynamic and geographical implications.

All these elements make decision-making on an international health emergency a polycentric exercise. Polycentric tasks require 'the balancing of a large number of variable items against all others'.[58] In the field of adjudication, for example, polycentricity normally involves multiple affected parties and a fluid state of affairs.[59] With regard to public health governance, Fidler and Gostin speak of the emergence of 'unstructured plurality', which comprises multiplying actors, initiatives, organisations and financial resources.[60] Polycentric decision-making is a process that implies many variables that are constantly shifting and are, as such, indeterminate and elusive.

All previously mentioned components of decision-making under the international health emergency essentially presuppose a polycentric dynamic. As mentioned above, the concept of the health risk implies various health hazards of different origins, of which each has its own evolutionary dynamic. In addition, the spread of the disease may spill from one country to another, expand to other countries and shift among them. Again, this dynamic is very fluid and mutable. Finally, the response of the WHO must be adaptable and follow the evolution of the outbreak in terms of its pathogenesis and geographic spread.[61]

The juxtaposition of the emergency framework under the human rights model and the PHEIC framework under the WHO model raises the following questions: do the regulations rely on the limitations model or on the derogations model?; is polycentric decision-making compatible with the monocentric character of decisions under the international human rights regime? Overall, it seems that the flexible, polycentric character of the international health emergency scheme actually accommodates both the limitations model and the derogations model depending on the particular health pandemic and the situation in a particular country or region. The mechanism under the regulations must therefore allow for an application of different approaches to different situations.

Recent practice supports this conclusion. Since the adoption of the regulations, the Director-General has declared an international health emergency on three occasions with regard to the following infectious diseases: (i) H1N1 influenza ('swine flu') in April 2009[62]; (ii) Poliovirus in May 2014[63]; and (iii) Ebola in August 2014.[64] In the case of the H1N1 influenza, the Director-General did not recommend any of the specific health measures available under the regulations. Affected countries followed distinct courses; some declared a state of national emergency[65] while others did not, relying instead on the use of the limitations model.[66] However, in the cases of the Poliovirus and the Ebola pandemics, the Director-General recommended that affected states proclaim states of national emergency and adopt a set of health measures.[67]

It is important to bear in mind that the mechanism of international health emergency under the regulations and the restrictions imposed according to the human rights regime cover two distinct levels. International health emergencies (and subsequent) temporary recommendations are proclaimed at the level of the WHO. National emergencies, on the other hand, are declared at the national level by the competent national organ (usually the head of state). In order to achieve the universal application of the regulations for the protection of all people from the international spread of the disease,[68] efforts at the international and national levels have to be compatible and coordinated.

Human rights in an international health emergency

One of the main principles of the regulations enshrined in Article 3(1), is that the regulations should be implemented 'with full respect for the dignity, human rights and fundamental freedoms of persons'.[69] Although very broad in nature, this provision is important because it establishes a link between the regulations and the international human rights regime and integrates the latter in the legal framework of the regulations. Additionally, as the responsibility for the implementation of health measures under the regulations falls to states parties,[70] the link between the regulations and human rights imposes an obligation on states parties to ensure that such measures are compatible with human rights standards. The provision in Article 3(1) also points to the responsibility of the WHO to protect human rights in two ways: (i) health measures that are recommended by the Director-General should be in conformity with human rights[71]; and (ii) implementation of health measures by states on the basis of WHO recommendations should likewise respect human rights.[72]

However, Article 3(1) of the regulations does not precisely delineate the scope of the obligation to protect human rights. Therefore, its function is to serve as a guideline, a policy statement or an interpretive principle rather than a prescription. This interpretive ambiguity is resolved by the subsequent principle in Article 3(2), which requires that implementation of the regulations be guided by the Charter of the United Nations.[73] As several provisions in the Charter emphasise a need for the protection of human rights,[74] the Charter incorporates a wide *corpus juris* of human rights standards adopted in the UN framework and further developed by UN expert bodies.[75] For the purposes of this article, we shall refer primarily to two fundamental human rights documents to identify the scope of human rights under the regulations: the UDHR and the ICCPR. Although the UDHR does not have binding force, it has a great moral authority and norm-generating force and many of its provisions have now become a part of international customary law.[76] The UDHR greatly influenced the content of the ICCPR, as the most important binding document on civil and political rights at the international level.[77] Human rights standards in the ICCPR are further developed by the HRC as the monitoring mechanism under that treaty.[78]

There is one important and distinct quality in the regulations with regard to the protection of human rights; the international human rights framework requires that every measure infringing upon rights be based on certain criteria, such as a compelling public interest.[79] The regulations necessitate that health measures be based on scientific principles and the available scientific evidence.[80] This is important because the reliance on professional criteria and verifiable data significantly reduces a possibility for arbitrary decisions by the law enforcement personnel.

Another unique feature of the regulations is that they make a distinction between two contexts of application of human rights: (i) human rights norms that apply to persons in general[81]; and (ii) human rights norms that apply to travellers.[82] The regulations understand 'traveller' as a 'natural person undertaking an international voyage'.[83] This reflects the traditional aim of the regulations (and preceding legal instruments) to regulate international traffic (and trade) to prevent the spread of infectious diseases.[84] However, the above distinction is functional rather than conceptual.[85] In terms of the protection of rights, there are no differences between the context that applies to travellers and the one that applies to persons.

It is important to underline that the focus of the regulations is the protection of civil and political rights rather than economic, social and cultural rights.[86] This is understandable as health measures under the regulations apply in the context of the PHEIC and represent a public health response to the international spread of the disease. In order to contain the spread of the disease, they infringe upon rights that are connected with travel.[87] At the same time, however, the purpose of the regulations is to enhance the capacity of national health systems to combat infectious diseases.[88] This state obligation is closely connected to the right to health,[89] which means that the implementation of the regulations also falls in the scope of ICESCR and its monitoring procedures.

Unfortunately, the strengthening of capacity of national health systems – which is a precondition for the exercise of the right to health in individual cases – remains one of the unattained goals of the regulations, particularly in developing countries.[90] In the case of the recent Ebola epidemic, for example, one of the main factors contributing to the rapid spread of the disease was the weak and ineffective national health systems in Sierra Leone, Liberia and Guinea,[91] mainly on account of the enduring political and security instability in these countries.[92] Scarce resources in developing countries may also prove problematic in the sense of the protection of civil and political rights in the implementation of the regulations. Therefore, there should be a clear obligation of the international community to assist developing countries in strengthening their national health and human rights capacities.[93]

In part one we already made a distinction between the derogation model and the limitation model on the protection of international human rights and demonstrated that the regulations do not make a clear difference between them. However, we can identify contours of the two models with the help of relevant provisions in the ICCPR. The regulations make a number of references to components of human rights that have a non-derogable status. These references are the respect for dignity[94] and the principle of non-discrimination.[95] The requirement for the respect for dignity corresponds to the prohibition of torture and ill-treatment, including the prohibition of medical experimentation, under Article 7 of the ICCPR.[96] It likewise covers the right of detainees (including those detained on medical grounds) to be treated with humanity and dignity under ICCPR Article 10.[97] Similarly, the non-derogable quality of the right to equality and non-discrimination in ICCPR Article 4(1) restricts state measures during times of emergency, including the ones based on health concerns. Such measures are prohibited from discriminating solely on the basis of race, colour, sex, language, religion or social origin.[98] However, it has to be emphasised that the list of non-derogable rights is not limited to references in the regulations. Since on several instances the WHO's temporary recommendations have called upon states to proclaim the state of emergency,[99] it goes without saying that the national implementation of adequate measures should respect the non-derogation framework in the ICCPR.[100]

However, the measures that the Director-General can issue as temporary recommendations in the context of PHEIC[101] primarily fall within the limitations model of the regime under the ICCPR. The envisaged measures under Article 18 of the regulations predominantly interfere with three forms of human rights in the ICCPR: the right to privacy (Article 17)[102]; the right to liberty (Article 9)[103]; and the freedom of movement (Article 12).[104] We shall deal with these three rights in more detail later[105]; at this stage, it is useful to recall that incursions in these rights must fulfil certain criteria of the limitations model such as the balancing exercise of proportionality between the degree of the interference and the intended purpose.[106]

In addition to the above-mentioned rights, the regulations devise a specific procedural regime under which travellers may be placed under mandatory public health supervision. This regime must be compatible with the basic tenets of due process guarantees. In the following sections we shall therefore deal more specifically with: (A) the right to privacy; (B) the right to liberty; (C) the freedom of movement; and (D) the procedural framework for health measures against travellers.

A. The right to privacy

The main characteristic of the right to privacy is its multifaceted nature. This means that the private sphere of an individual is protected through different emanations of the right to privacy in various contexts that touch upon individual personality.[107] The right to privacy encompasses elements such as identity, integrity, intimacy, autonomy, communication and sexuality.[108] Conceptually, this is a reflection of the liberal tradition that sees individuals as autonomous subjects, sovereign over themselves and their actions, to the degree that they do not interfere with the rights of others.[109]

The regulations specify measures that interfere with privacy in more detail. Thus, pursuant to WHO recommendations, states parties can apply the following measures that can interfere with the individual's identity or intimacy: (i) the review of the travel history of travellers in affected areas; (ii) the review of proof of medical examination and laboratory analysis; and (iii) the tracing of contacts of suspect or affected persons.[110]

Still within the sphere of identity and intimacy, the regulations prescribe rules for the treatment and protection of personal data. A general principle for states parties is that data collected or received by a state party from another state party or the WHO must be kept confidential and processed anonymously as required by national law.[111] However, an exception to this rule allows states parties to disclose and process personal data when it is essential for the purposes of assessing and managing a public risk.[112] There is also an obligation on the part of the WHO to provide personal data to individuals. Upon request, the WHO must, as far as practicable, supply such personal data in an understandable form, without undue delay or expense and, if the data is inaccurate, allow for correction.[113]

The regulations also envisage the application of two health measures by state parties that fall in the sphere of autonomy and integrity of individuals,[114] namely: (i) the requirement to undergo medical examination, which may include physical examination; and (ii) the requirement of vaccination or other prophylaxis (i.e. medical preventative measures).[115] These measures deal with interference with the individual's autonomy for the benefit of the common good, which may include submitting a person to a health assessment or a health treatment.

Vaccination is a medical term that most commonly denotes the '[i]njection of a killed microbe in order to stimulate the immune system against the microbe, thereby preventing disease',[116] whereas, prophylaxis simply means the prevention of the disease.[117] The regulations define medical examination as 'the preliminary assessment of a person by an authorized health worker or by a person under the direct supervision of the competent authority, to determine the person's health status and potential public health risks to others'.[118] In addition, the regulations make an important distinction between an 'intrusive' and an 'invasive' medical examination. Intrusive medical examinations can possibly provoke discomfort through close or intimate contact or questioning.[119] On the other hand, invasive medical examination implies the puncture or incision of the skin or insertion of an instrument or foreign material into the body as well as the examination of a body cavity.[120]

The international regime for human rights provides the following insights on the meaning of the right to privacy. Article 12 of the UDHR states that no one 'shall be subjected to arbitrary interference with his privacy' and that everyone has 'the right to the protection of the law against such interference'. The ICCPR has very similar provisions in Article 17.[121]

All health measures envisaged by the regulations that interfere with the right to privacy must abide by the principle of proportionality. Health measures that inquire about personal activities, travels, prior medical treatment and contacts must be legitimate, based on the law and proportionate to the intended purpose.[122] The regulations apply these standards to the following documents: (i) certificates for vaccination or prophylaxis[123]; (ii) requirements concerning vaccination and prophylaxis for specific diseases[124]; (iii) a model maritime declaration of health[125]; and (iv) the health part of an aircraft general declaration.[126] Furthermore, rules for the treatment and protection of personal data processed by states parties and the WHO must likewise follow standards on the protection of privacy. A comparison between standards developed by the HRC on this issue and the regulations show that the latter are in compliance with the ICCPR standards.[127] Finally, measures of medical examination (intrusive or invasive), vaccinations and other prophylactic measures must comply with the assessment of proportionality. It is important that states parties, where applicable under the regulation procedures, assess the presence of a public health risk on the basis of scientific principles and available scientific evidence.[128]

B. The right to liberty

Health measures under the regulations that have an impact on the right to liberty include three levels: (i) the placement of suspect persons under public health observation; (ii) the imposition of a quarantine or other similar health measures for suspect persons; and (iii) the submission of affected persons to isolation and treatment where necessary.[129] Public health observation involves the monitoring of the health status of a person over time in order to determine the risk of the disease transmission. Quarantine means the restriction of activities and/or separation from others to prevent the possible spread of infection or contamination. Its aim is to neutralise the risk if the person, who was exposed to an infectious disease but is asymptomatic, would subsequently become infectious.[130] Finally, isolation involves the separation of ill or contaminated persons to prevent the spread of infection or contamination.[131] Thus, all three forms of health measures represent a limitation on the liberty of person, with an intensity increasing from public health observation (lesser degree) to isolation (greater degree).[132]

Article 3 of the UDHR only briefly touches on the right to liberty, stating '[e]veryone has the right to life, liberty and security of person'. The ICCPR has a more elaborate provision that covers various aspects of the right to liberty. ICCPR Article 9(1) stipulates that '[e]veryone has the right to liberty and security of person' and goes on to prescribe that no one should be subject to arbitrary or unlawful deprivation of liberty.[133] For the purposes of this article, we shall focus only on those aspects of the right to liberty that apply to non-criminal cases.

The right to liberty under ICCPR Article 9 protects a rather narrow scope and has to be distinguished from the more philosophical meaning of liberty that pertains to human freedom in general. Article 9 relates to the freedom of bodily movement in the narrowest sense and covers the forceful detention of a person at a certain, narrowly bounded location.[134] In addition, Article 9 does not prohibit deprivation of liberty in absolute terms; what is prohibited are situations that would make deprivation arbitrary or unlawful.[135] At the same time, it should be noted that although the right to liberty is not a non-derogable right under the ICCPR, the fundamental guarantee against arbitrary detention is non-derogable, and even more so in connection to the protection of non-derogable rights.[136]

Standards imposed by the ICCPR and other related documents with regard to the right of liberty are important because they place limitations on health measures of public health observation, quarantine and isolation.[137] First, these health measures must be based on lawful grounds and should not be arbitrary.[138] The deprivation of liberty due to infectious diseases is different from other instances of deprivation in that the period of detention is contingent on epidemiologic or other medical factors. This means that the minimum period of detention should be as long as necessary to eliminate reasons for the spread of a particular disease.[139] Second, at the time of the deprivation of liberty, the individual concerned should be informed of the reasons for the deprivation of liberty and other rights.[140] In the context of health measures for the prevention of infectious diseases, this measure must be based solely on health concerns. A detained individual who is a foreigner must be provided with an interpreter.[141] Third, the detained person must have a right to *habeas corpus*, that is, he or she must be able to take proceedings before the court or other competent tribunal.[142] The court should decide about the complaint without any delay.[143] In addition, a person detained on health grounds must have the right to a counsel to be able to defend himself or herself.[144] Ideally, the court should hear the detained person and decide on the lawfulness of detention. Should this prove problematic, adequate modern technologies (video and audio equipment) could facilitate communication between the detainee and the court. In situations of mass complaints, procedures should be developed to allow the court to group and decide similar cases together and to avoid serious judicial backlogs.[145] Fourth, medically detained persons should also have, whenever circumstances allow, the possibility of seeking a second opinion on their medical condition.[146] It goes without saying that a person detained on the basis of infectious diseases should have adequate medical examination, care and treatment.[147] Whenever a detained person is moved to another facility, he or she should be able to notify family and other appropriate persons, receive their visits and have means to communicate with the outside world.[148] Again, modern technologies should facilitate such communication.[149] It is also imperative that there be a proper registration procedure in place to store all relevant data related to the health detention and to make the data available to all concerned, including relatives.[150] Finally, anyone who has been the victim of unlawful detention should have an enforceable right to compensation.[151]

C. The freedom of movement

The regulations envisage several health measures, on the basis of WHO recommendations to states parties, which can affect the freedom of movement. States parties can: (i) refuse entry of suspect and affected persons; (ii) refuse entry of unaffected persons to affected areas; and (iii) implement exit screening and/or restrictions on persons from affected areas.[152]

The scheme of the above health measures corresponds to the legal framework of the freedom of movement provisions in universal human rights documents. UDHR Article 13 stipulates that everyone 'has the right to freedom of movement and residence within the borders of each state' and 'the right to leave any country, including his own, and to return to his country'. ICCPR Article 12 follows the same framework.[153] First, everyone who is living lawfully within the territory of a state has the right of movement and freedom to choose his or her residence.[154] Second, everyone is free to leave any country, including his or her own.[155] Finally, a person must not be arbitrarily deprived of the right to enter his or her own country.[156]

However, the ICCPR draws an important distinction between the movement within the state and when leaving the country, on the one hand, and the movement when entering the home country, on the other. With regard to the first two components, the ICCPR allows for such restrictions on the basis of laws which are necessary for the protection of national security, public order (*ordre public*), public health or morals or the rights and freedoms of others.[157] Public health and the rights and freedoms of others are two grounds for restrictions that apply to infectious diseases.[158] However, any restriction on this basis must fulfil precise requirements of necessity and proportionality.[159]

A comparison between the regulations and human rights standards on the freedom of movement leads to the following insights. The regulations envisage control when entering and exiting a particular country as well as the movement within that country. In this way, the regulations cast a wide territorial net to monitor the movement of potentially suspect individuals. As mentioned earlier, health measures under the regulations correspond to the human rights framework; the refusal of entry of unaffected persons to affected areas falls within the scope of movement within the territory of a state. The implementation of exit screening and/or restrictions on persons from affected areas, on the other hand, corresponds to the freedom of leaving a country. The greatest discrepancy is with regard to the denial of entry into a country of suspect and affected persons. As we saw previously, the ICCPR gives a right to enter a particular country only to persons who have a strong attachment to that country, such as its nationals or residents.[160] While the regulations deal with a broader scope in that they regulate entry of *any* individual into a particular country, one must understand this provision from the point of view of an efficient control of infectious diseases rather than as an extension of the freedom of movement.[161]

Specific health measures that touch upon the right to movement include confinement to a restricted area; guarded home confinement[162]; and cordon sanitaire (a guarded line that prevents anyone from leaving).[163] Often law enforcement officials, including the military, are deployed to enforce these measures.[164] If ordered, such measures must conform to the requirements for restrictions of the right to movement, including necessity and proportionality. It is essential that there is an efficient system of checks and controls in place to monitor activities of law enforcement forces.[165] Since these measures can easily lead to the deprivation of other human rights, including the right to health, right to food, the right to water and the right to shelter,[166] the government must ensure that restrictions of the freedom of movement do not transform into massive violations of human rights.

D. Procedural framework for health measures regarding travellers

The Regulations articulate several measures that apply specifically to travellers. These measures can be subsumed in two sets. The first set pertains to the review of an individual's information connected to travelling. A state may review: (i) information concerning the planned destination; (ii) information concerning the individual's itinerary; and (iii) the individual's health documents if required under the regulations.[167]

However, much more interesting is another state prerogative that the regulations envisage. Pursuant to evidence obtained through such a review, or through other means,[168] states can trigger an examination procedure of a suspect or already affected traveller. The regulations first envisage what can be called a 'soft approach' and if that mechanism is not effective, the state can proceed to a 'robust approach', which reduces the scope of human rights protection offered to an individual.

In case of a public health risk, the regulations initially prescribe that medical examination, vaccination and prophylaxis or health measures be carried out on travellers only with their prior, express and informed consent, or – in case of minors or other incapable persons – that of their parents or guardians.[169]

Still echoing a softer approach, the regulations contend that invasive medical examination, vaccination or other prophylaxis are not required, for any traveller, as a condition of entry to the territory of a state party.[170] Nevertheless, states parties may require an individual to undergo these measures in the following cases: (i) when it is necessary to determine the existence of a public health risk; (ii) as a condition of entry if an individual is seeking temporary or permanent residence; (iii) as a condition of entry if states parties require the higher level of health protection than WHO recommendations; and (iv) on an arrival and departure and with prior express informed consent and information about risks associated with these measures.[171] If an individual refuses to comply, the state party may decide to deny entry to that individual.[172]

However, if there is evidence of an imminent public health risk, the traveller is not allowed to walk away. At this point, the state may compel the traveller to undergo the following measures[173]:

(i) the least invasive and intrusive medical examination to achieve the public health objective;
(ii) vaccination or other prophylaxis; or
(iii) additional health measures that prevent or control of the spread of disease, including isolation, quarantine or public health observation.[174]

The existence of 'an imminent public risk' represents a turning point from a soft to a robust state approach, which results in serious incursions into the human rights of travellers that can affect their human dignity, the right to privacy and the right to liberty. It is important to emphasise that in the above decision-making framework, the regulations omit standards of 'informed' and 'express consent'. This means that state authorities are not obliged to abide by these two standards before applying the above health measures.

The above mechanism inevitably opens up a question of its compatibility with human rights standards. Since the regulations are relatively silent on this point, both approaches need to be further interpreted in a way to incorporate all relevant standards of human rights and, in particular, the guarantees of due process.[175]

Generally, we could make a distinction between compulsory health measures that touch upon the right to privacy (the least invasive and intrusive medical examination[176] and vaccination or other prophylaxis) and those that touch upon the right to liberty (isolation, quarantine and public health observation).

With regard to health measures that interfere with the right to liberty, it is useful to recall guarantees mentioned previously: the right to be informed of the reasons for detention; the right to bring proceedings before the court; the right to a counsel; the right to seek the second medical opinion; the right to communicate with the family and the outside world; and the right to humane conditions of detention. All these rights apply to travellers who would be compelled to undergo isolation, quarantine and public health observation.

In the context of the right to privacy, the compulsory application of medical examination, vaccination and other prophylaxis represent an incursion in the autonomy of an individual. Because these measures are compulsory – there is no free and informed consent – they should be subject to due process guarantees inherent in Article 17 of the ICCPR.[177] However, since the incursion into the right to privacy is less intense than interference in the right to liberty, due process guarantees could meet a lower threshold in this context. More specifically, due process rights with regard to the right to privacy should include, at minimum, the following: the right to be notified of the decision to administer a compulsory health measure; a right to make a complaint to an independent expert body that could reassess necessity and reasonableness of the health measure; and the right to a counsel or a human rights defender.

Conclusion

The aim of this article was to analyse the regulations in the context of the international human rights regime. We can conclude that the regulations are fully compatible with international human rights standards; however, these standards must be included in the functioning of the WHO and states parties to the regulations.

We have seen that the approach behind the international health emergency is polycentric in nature, which allows it to accommodate two monocentric emergency models of the human rights regime: the derogations model and the limitations model. If states parties to the regulations decide to invoke such models in the context of the international health emergency, all conditions and guarantees from international human rights law apply.

Furthermore, health measures and procedures inherent in the regulations must comply with all relevant international human rights standards. In general, all measures must respect various components of human dignity, in particular the freedom from torture and other forms of ill-treatment (including medical experimentation without a free consent) and humane treatment of detained persons, as well as the right to equality and non-discrimination. Specific health measures must comply with corresponding human rights. Thus, the review of personal information, the treatment and protection of data and the requirement to undergo medical examination or vaccination must be compatible with the right to privacy. In addition, public health observation, quarantine and isolation must correspond to the standards of the right to liberty. Measures that limit entry to, exit from and movement within a state have to fulfil requirements of the freedom of movement. Finally, the procedural framework that applies to travellers must respect all relevant due process guarantees, whether in the context of a 'soft' or a 'robust' application of health measures by states.

This article made a move from mere allusions to human rights in the regulations towards their full inclusion in the implementation of health measures under that framework. The next essential task is to include these standards in training and education of public and health officials and ensure that these standards will be applied in practice, that is, at the operational level of national public health systems.[178]

Acknowledgements

The author wishes to thank Chanu Peiris for her assistance in the course of preparing this article as well as Robert McCorquodale, the editors of the special edition and an anonymous reviewer for their useful suggestions.

Disclosure statement

No potential conflict of interest was reported by the author.

Notes on contributor

Andraž Zidar is the Dorset Senior Research Fellow in Public International Law at the British Institute of International and Comparative Law and a Visiting Lecturer in International Law and International Humanitarian Law at Regent's University London. He is the author and co-editor of three books and numerous articles or book chapters on human rights, international law, diplomacy and international relations.

Notes

1. Margaret Chan, 'Message from the Director General', in *World Health Report 2007: A Safer Future: Global Public Health Security in the 21st Century* (Geneva: World Health Organization, 2007), vi–vii.
2. At present, catastrophic scenarios feature in movies such as 'Outbreak' (1995) and 'Contagion' (2011) (see http://www.imdb.com). These scenarios, which are based on scientific parameters, are not unlikely to occur in the real world.
3. Lawrence Gostin, *Global Health Law* (Cambridge, MA: Harvard University Press, 2014), 35.
4. Mary Wheelan, *Negotiating the International Health Regulations*, Global Health Programme Working Paper No. 1 (Geneva: The Graduate Institute, 2008), 5–6. The International Health Regulations (IHR) were adopted by resolution WHA58.3 at the Fifty-eighth World Health Assembly on 23 May 2005. They came into force on 15 June 2007 (see WHO, *International Health Regulations* (Geneva: World Health Organization, 2008), 1). The regulations were not the first legal instrument against infectious diseases. There is a long tradition of international law-making on such instruments and the previous version of the regulations dated back to 1969. For more on the regulations, see Gostin, *Global Health Law*, 177–204; and David P. Fidler, 'From International Sanitary Conventions to Global Health Security: The New International Health Regulations', *Chinese Journal of International Law* 4 (2005): 325–92.
5. Gostin, *Global Health Law*, 178.
6. WHO, *Implementation of the International Health Regulations (2005)*, Report of the Review Committee on the Functioning of the International Health Regulations (2005) in relation to Pandemic (H1N1) 2009, 5 May 2011, A64/10, 12.
7. See WHO, 'Ebola Situation Report', 21 January 2015, http://www.who.int/csr/disease/ebola/situation-reports/en/.
8. See Lawrence O. Gostin, 'Ebola: Towards an International Health Systems Fund', *The Lancet*, 4 September 2014, 1–3.
9. See UNSC, Resolution 2177 (2014), 18 September 2014.
10. See Gian Luca Burci and Jakob Quirin, 'Ebola, WHO, and the United Nations: Convergence of Global Public Health and International Peace and Security', *ASIL Insight* 18, no. 25 (2014): http://www.asil.org/insights/volume/18/issue/25/ebola-who-and-united-nations-convergence-global-public-health-and; Louis Balmond, 'Le Conseil de sécurité et la crise d'Ebola: entre gestion de la paix et pilotage de la gouvernance globale', *QIL*, no. 10 (2014): 5–25; and Gian Luca Burci, 'Ebola, the Security Council and the Securitization of Public Health', *QIL*, no. 10 (2014): 27–39.
11. See WHO, *World Health Report 2007*, 34–67. According to the WHO report, global public health security means proactive and reactive activities 'to minimize vulnerability to acute public health events that endanger the collective health of populations living across geographical regions and international boundaries'. It includes the strengthening of international and national public health systems (ibid., ix, 57).
12. The protection of human rights was one of the important issues during negotiations on the regulations. However, agreed provisions did not go beyond general references to human rights (cf. Wheelan, *Negotiating the International Health Regulations*, 9). Fidler suggests that this solution reflects the traditional attitude of the WHO of being reluctant to confront member states on human rights protection for fear of losing their cooperation on important

public health matters (David P. Fidler, *International Law and Infectious Diseases* (Oxford: Clarendon Press, 1999), 219).

13. WHO, *World Health Report 2007*, ix.
14. The current Director-General is Margaret Chan.
15. See, for example, Jan Klabbers, *An Introduction to Institutional Law* (Cambridge: Cambridge University Press, 2009), 315–17; and Stefan Elbe, *Security and Global Health* (Cambridge: Polity Press, 2010), 59–60. In comparative terms, this authority is similar to the executive prerogative of heads of state or government to proclaim a state of emergency. See Oren Gross and Fionnuala Ní Aoláin, *Law in Times of Crisis: Emergency Powers in Theory and Practice* (Cambridge: Cambridge University Press, 2006); and Jaime Oraá, *Human Rights in States of Emergency in International Law* (Oxford: Clarendon Press, 1992).
16. IHR, Art. 12 (1).
17. For more details about this procedure see IHR, Arts 12, 48 and 49.
18. This decision-making process is part of an elaborate and precise algorithm contained in Annex 2 of the regulations ('Decision instrument for the assessment and notification of events that may constitute a public health emergency of international concern'). It includes consideration of three respective events that can lead to the international health emergency: (i) an infection caused by smallpox, poliomyelitis, a new subtype of human influenza or SARS; (ii) any event of potential international public health concern, including those of unknown causes or sources; and (iii) an infection due to cholera, pneumonic plague, yellow fever, viral haemorrhagic fevers, West Nile fever and other comparable diseases.
19. IHR, Art. 12 (4).
20. Procedures on the determination of the PHEIC and issuance of temporary recommendations are based on IHR Article 49 and thus very similar. In practice, decisions on the PHEIC and temporary recommendations usually make part of the same decision-making process (see below notes 63 and 64).
21. IHR, Art. 49 (6).
22. Cf. David P. Fidler and Lawrence O. Gostin, 'The New International Health Regulations: An Historic Development for International Law and Public Health', *The Journal of Law, Medicine & Ethics* 34 (2006).
23. See IHR, Art. 12(4).
24. IHR, Art. 3(1).
25. On moral justifications of the international human rights regime see Samantha Besson, 'Justifications', in *International Human Rights Law*, ed. Daniel Moeckli, Sangeeta Shah, and Sandesh Sivakumaran (Oxford: Oxford University Press, 2014), 39–41. The most important international legal instruments are the Universal Declaration of Human Rights (UDHR), the International Covenant on Civil and Political Rights (ICCPR), the International Covenant on Economic, Social and Cultural Rights (ICESCR), the European Convention on Human Rights (ECHR), the American Convention on Human Rights (ACHR) and the African Charter on Human and People's Rights (ACHPR).
26. Thérèse Murphy, *Health and Human Rights* (Oxford and Portland: Hart Publishing, 2014), 73.
27. The most illustrative document on this point is the *Siracusa Principles on the Limitation and Derogation Provisions in the International Covenant on Civil and Political Rights*, Annex to the document of the UN Commission for Human Rights, 28 September 1984, E.CN.4/1985/4. These are non-binding principles prepared by a group of human rights experts at the meeting in Siracusa, Italy, from 30 April to 4 May 1984. Although the Siracusa Principles do not represent a formal source of international law, they are frequently referred to by international organs and represent an authoritative text on standards for limitations and derogations of rights under the ICCPR.
28. Frédéric Mégret, 'Nature of Obligations', in *International Human Rights Law*, ed. Moeckli, Shah, and Sivakumaran, 110.
29. Ibid.
30. UDHR, Art. 29(2). The ICESCR likewise includes the limitations model in Article 4, albeit in slightly different terms.
31. See ICCPR, Arts 22(2) and 29(2).
32. See above note 27.
33. *Siracusa Principles*, para. 25.
34. Ibid.

35. Mégret, 'Nature of Obligations', 111.
36. *Siracusa Principles*, para. 10.
37. Mégret, 'Nature of Obligations', 112.
38. ICCPR, Art. 4(1); and *Siracusa Principles*, para. 39.
39. Ibid.
40. See David P. Fidler and Lawrence Gostin, *Biosecurity in the Global Age* (Stanford, CA: Stanford University Press, 2008), 7–8; and Stefan Elbe, *Virus Alert: Security, Governmentality, and the AIDS Pandemic* (New York: Columbia University Press, 2009), 1–26.
41. Alex de Waal, 'Militarizing Global Health', *Boston Review* (11 November 2014), http://www.bostonreview.net/world/alex-de-waal-militarizing-global-health-ebola.
42. Manfred Nowak, *U.N. Covenant on Civil and Political Rights: CCPR Commentary* (Kehl am Rhein: Engel, 1993), 79. See also Human Rights Committee (HRC), *General Comment No. 29: States of Emergency (Article 4)*, 31 August 2001, CCPR/C/21/Rev.1/Add.11, para. 5.
43. See Nowak, *CCPR Commentary*, 78–9; and *Siracusa Principles*, para. 39.
44. IHR, Art. 1(1).
45. WHO, 'IHR Procedures Concerning Public Health Emergencies of International Concern (PHEIC)', http://www.who.int/ihr/procedures/pheic/en/.
46. Nevertheless, the assessment on whether the exigencies of the situation require derogation from a certain right is subject to the principle of proportionality (see *General Comment No. 29*, para. 4).
47. Pursuant to Art. 4(2) of ICCPR, the non-derogable rights are: the right to life; freedom from torture and other forms ill-treatment; freedom from slavery, slave trade and servitude; right not to be imprisoned on the basis of a contractual obligation; the principle of legality; the right to be recognised as a person before the law; and freedom of thought, conscience and religion. To these, the HRC added certain humanitarian law or peremptory norms, the principle of non-discrimination of protected categories (race, colour, sex, language, religion or social origin), as well as certain aspects of the procedural and judicial guarantees (see *General Comment No. 29*, paras 8, 11–15. See also *Siracusa Principles*, paras 58–9, 67–70). For non-derogable rights in regional contexts see ECHR, Art. 15 and ACHR, Art. 27.
48. *Siracusa Principles*, paras 61, 64; and *General Comment No. 29*, para. 16.
49. ICCPR, Art. 4(1), *Siracusa Principles*, paras 51–7; and *General Comment No. 29*, para. 2.
50. *General Comment No. 29*, para. 1.
51. Cf. Mégret, 'Nature of Obligations', 113; and *Siracusa Principles*, paras 44–7, 71–6. It is worrying that states that adopted derogation measures in the context of the current Ebola outbreak have not communicated these derogations to the UN Secretary-General (see https://treaties.un.org/Pages/ViewDetails.aspx?src=TREATY&mtdsg_no=IV-4&chapter=4&lang=en).
52. ICCPR, Art. 4(3), *Siracusa Principles*, paras 51–7; and *General Comment No. 29*, para. 17.
53. It was Lon L. Fuller who introduced – on the basis of Michael Polanyi's work – the distinction between monocentric and polycentric decision-making in legal theory. Although Fuller does not provide a precise definition of monocentricity, it can be deduced that it involves judicial decision-making on the basis of whether one wins the case or not, or whether one's right is recognised, and other decisions on the basis of dichotomy between positive and negative (see Lon L. Fuller, 'Adjudication and the Rule of Law', *American Society of International Law Proceedings* 54 (1960): 2–4, 5–6; and Lon L. Fuller, 'The Forms and Limits of Adjudication', *Harvard Law Review* 92 (1978): 404–5).
54. See above note 44.
55. Gostin, *Global Health Law*, 185; Fidler, 'From International Sanitary Conventions to Global Health Security', 351, 358, 365–6; and Fidler and Gostin, *Biosecurity in a Global Age*, 137–8, 154–5. The WHO subsequently urged member states to integrate an 'all-hazards' approach into their health emergency and disaster risk programmes with the WHA Resolution 64.10, adopted on 24 May 2011.
56. Gostin, *Global Health Law*, 185.
57. Cf. ibid.
58. Michael Polanyi, *The Logic of Liberty: Reflections and Rejoinders* (Chicago: Chicago University Press, 1951), 191.
59. Fuller, 'Forms and Limits of Adjudication', 397.
60. Fidler and Gostin, *Biosecurity in the Global Age*, 236–7, 250–2; and Fidler, 'From International Sanitary Conventions to Global Health Security', 387.

61. On the fluidity of territorial borders with regard to infectious diseases see Daniel Bethlehem, 'The End of Geography: The Changing Nature of the International System and the Challenge to International Law', *European Journal of International Law* 25 (2014): 16–17.
62. WHO, 'Swine Influenza', 25 April 2009, http://www.who.int/mediacentre/news/statements/2009/h1n1_20090425/en/.
63. See WHO, 'WHO Statement on the Meeting of the International Health Regulations Emergency Committee concerning the International Spread of Wild Poliovirus', 5 May 2014, http://www.who.int/mediacentre/news/statements/2014/polio-20140505/en/.
64. See WHO, 'WHO Statement on the Meeting of the International Health Regulations Emergency Committee Regarding the 2014 Ebola Outbreak in West Africa', 8 August 2014, http://www.who.int/mediacentre/news/statements/2014/ebola-20140808/en/. The Director-General and the Emergency Committee are closely surveying the spread of Middle East respiratory syndrome coronavirus (MERS-CoV). However, the Director-General has not yet declared it to be a PHEIC (see WHO, 'WHO Statement on the Seventh Meeting of the IHR Emergency Committee regarding MERS-CoV', 1 October 2014, http://www.who.int/mediacentre/news/statements/2014/7th-mers-emergency-committee/en/).
65. For WHO updates regarding the swine influenza see http://www.who.int/csr/disease/swineflu/updates/en/. For a list of countries declaring national emergencies see James G. Hodge, 'Global Legal Triage in Response to the 2009 H1N1 Outbreak', *Minnesota Journal of Law, Science & Technology* 11 (2010): 612–23.
66. See updates under WHO, 'Swine Influenza'.
67. 'WHO Statement on the Meeting of the International Health Regulations Emergency Committee concerning the International Spread of Wild Poliovirus' and 'WHO Statement on the Meeting of the International Health Regulations Emergency Committee Regarding the 2014 Ebola Outbreak in West Africa'.
68. IHR, Art. 3(3).
69. IHR, Art. 3(1).
70. See IHR, Arts 3(4) and 42.
71. This obligation is derived from the norms on the responsibility of international organisations. See Draft Articles on the Responsibility of International Organizations (DARIO), adopted by the International Law Commission at its sixty-third session, in 2011, and submitted to the General Assembly as a part of the commission's report covering the work of that session (A/66/10, para. 87). In particular see DARIO Articles 3–6, 10 and 17. DARIO is a 'soft law' instrument, not legally binding for international organisations. Nevertheless, many of its provisions reflect international customary law and the relevance of other norms will be tested in practice by states, international organisations, courts and other actors in international law.
72. There is an emerging view, which is still subject to a wider acceptance, that international organisations are responsible for decisions they adopt, including the respect for human rights. Article 17(1) of DARIO prescribes the responsibility of an international organisation for acts of its members following its binding decision while Article 17(2) identifies such a responsibility following a (non-binding) authorisation (see Antonios Tzanakopoulos, *Disobeying the Security Council: Countermeasures against Wrongful Sanctions* (Oxford: Oxford University Press, 2011), 21–3, 49, 53; Jan Wouters, Eva Brems, Stefaan Smis and Pierre Schmitt, eds, *Accountability for Human Rights Violations by International Organisations* (Antwerp: Intersentia, 2010); and August Reinisch, 'The Challenging International Legal Framework for Dealing with Non-State Actors', in *Non-State Actors and Human Rights*, ed. Philip Alston (Oxford: Oxford University Press, 2005), 40, 46).
73. IHR Article 3(2) likewise refers to the constitution of the WHO.
74. See Preamble and Articles 1, 55 and 56 of the UN Charter. Notably, Article 55 stipulates that the UN shall promote 'universal respect for, and observance of, human rights and fundamental freedoms for all without distinction as to race, sex, language, or religion'.
75. Ilias Bantekas and Lutz Oette, *International Human Rights Law and Practice* (Cambridge: Cambridge University Press, 2013), 147–8.
76. Ibid., 20–2 and 62–3; Philip Alston and Ryan Goodman, *International Human Rights* (Oxford: Oxford University Press, 2013), 142; and Ed Bates, 'History', in *International Human Rights Law*, ed. Moeckli, Shah, and Sivakumaran, 30–2.
77. See Alston and Goodman, *International Human Rights*, 158–62.

78. Carlos Fernández De Casadevante Romani, *International Law of Victims* (Heidelberg: Springer, 2012), 123; and Anne F. Bayefsky, *The UN Human Rights Treaty System: Universality at the Crossroads* (The Hague: Kluwer Law International, 2001), 5, 99, 168.
79. Fidler, 'From International Sanitary Conventions to Global Health Security', 382.
80. See IHR, Arts 17(c) and 43(2). The regulations define scientific principles as 'the accepted fundamental laws and facts of nature known through the method of science' and scientific evidence as 'information furnishing a level of proof based on the established and accepted methods of science' (IHR, Art. 1(1)). However, it was not until late nineteenth century that scientific evidence prevailed as a criterion for the administration of public health measures, on the basis of ground-breaking scientific discoveries about microbes (see Fidler, *International Law and Infectious Diseases*, 21 *et seq.*, 217–18).
81. See IHR, Arts 3(1), 18, 45.
82. See IHR, Arts 23, 30–2.
83. IHR, Art. 1(1).
84. See Gostin, *Global Health Law*, 183–4, 196.
85. We can exclude such an interpretation with a reference to Article 3(1), which spells out a principle that the implementation of the regulations have to be in 'full respect for the dignity, human rights and fundamental freedoms of people'. Hence, any distinction as to persons in the regulations means these specific categories have to fall under 'persons' and within the general framework for the protection of human rights.
86. Fidler likewise points to the tension between the focus on civil and political rights and the need to strengthen national health systems in the fight against infectious diseases (see Fidler, *International Law and Infectious Diseases*, 172, 179 *et seq.*).
87. The focus of the regulations on civil and political rights is traditional since public health measures limit civil and political rights connected to liberty of individuals in the widest sense (see ibid., 171, 194, 218).
88. The regulations require states parties to develop capacities with regard to information and public health response (see IHR, Arts 5–8, 13 and Annex 1).
89. Article 12(2)(b) of the IESCR explicitly states that for the full realisation of the right to health states must take steps necessary for 'the prevention, treatment and control of epidemic … diseases'. For the link between civil and political rights and the right to health see Brigit Toebes, 'Towards an Improved Understanding of the International Right to Health', *Human Rights Quarterly* 21, no. 3 (1999): 661–9.
90. Kumanan Wilson, John S. Brownstein, and David P. Fidler, 'Strengthening the International Health Regulations: Lessons from the H1N1 Pandemic', *Health Policy and Planning* 25 (2010): 506–7; and Editorial, 'Ebola: What Lessons for the International Health Regulations?', *The Lancet* 384 (11 October 2014): 1321.
91. The Executive Board of the WHO addressed these issues and called upon member states and the international community to enhance the effective response to Ebola preparedness, contribute to long-term health strengthening, and improve implementation of the regulations. See Executive Board, Resolution 'Ebola: Ending the Current Outbreak, Strengthening Global Preparedness and Ensuring WHO's Capacity to Prepare for and Respond to Future Large-scale Outbreaks and Emergencies with Health Consequences', 25 January 2015, EBSS3.R1, in particular paras 11, 12, 29, 48.
92. See Alicia Ely Yamin, 'Ebola, Human Rights, and Poverty – Making the Links', *Open Global Rights*, 23 October 2014, https://www.opendemocracy.net/openglobalrights-blog/alicia-ely-yamin/ebola-human-rights-and-poverty-making-links; and 'Violation by Omission? The Case of Human Rights in Public Health Emergencies', *The Graduate Institute*, 11 December 2014, http://graduateinstitute.ch/home/research/centresandprogrammes/globalhealth/news/past-news.html/_/news/ghp/news-8.
93. See 'Violation by Omission?' (remarks by Gorik Ooms) and OHCHR, 'Fact Sheet No.3 (Rev.1), Advisory Services and Technical Cooperation in the Field of Human Rights', http://www.ohchr.org/Documents/Publications/FactSheet3Rev.1en.pdf.
94. See IHR, Art. 3(1), and Art. 32(1), including (a).
95. See IHR, Art. 42 and 32(1) (b).
96. See Nowak, *CCPR Comentary*, 126–41.
97. *General Comment No. 29*, 5.
98. Cf. *General Comment No. 29*, 4; and Bantekas and Oette, *International Human Rights*, 74.

99. See above note 67.
100. See ICCPR, Art. 4, *General Comment No. 29*; and Nowak, *CCPR Commentary*, 72–93.
101. See IHR, Art. 18(1).
102. Some aspects of the right to privacy concerning the treatment of personal data are addressed also in Article 45.
103. It must be emphasised that certain aspects of ICCPR Article 9 enjoy the status of non-derogable rights that cannot be limited under the limitations model. The fundamental guarantee against arbitrary detention is non-derogable, as well as procedural guarantees for the protection of non-derogable rights (see HRC, *General Comment No. 35, Article 9: Liberty and Security of Person*, 16 December 2014, CCPR/C/GC/35, 19–20; and *Siracusa Principles*, para. 70).
104. With regard to ICCPR Article 12, the principle of proportionality applies solely to Articles 12 (1) and (2).
105. For a similar classification see Fidler and Gostin, 'The New International Health Regulations', 87–8.
106. For the balancing exercise and the standard of proportionality in the jurisprudence of the HRC see: with regard to the right to privacy *Toonen* v. *Australia*, 31 March 1994 (No. 488/1992), paras 8.3, 8.5; with regard to the right to liberty *M.M.M. et al.* v. *Australia*, 23 October 2013 (No. 2136/2012), para. 10.3; and with regard to the right to movement *Sayadi and Vinck* v. *Belgium*, 22 October 2008 (No. 1472/2006), para. 10.5.
107. See US Supreme Court, *Griswold* v. *Connecticut*, 7 June 1965, 381 U.S. 479 (1965), Opinion of the court delivered by Justice Douglas. See also Michael O'Flaherty, 'Sexual Orientation and Gender Identity', in *International Human Rights Law*, eds. Moeckli, Shah, and Sivakumaran, 306–7.
108. See Nowak, *CCPR Commentary*, 294–9.
109. John Stuart Mill, *On Liberty* (Kitchener: Batoche Books, 2001[1859]), 14. See also Nuffield Council on Bioethics. *Public Health: Ethical Issues* (London: Nuffield Council on Bioethics, 2007), 14–16.
110. IHR, Art. 18(1).
111. IHR, Art. 45(1).
112. However, in doing so states parties – as well as the WHO – must observe certain rules. They must ensure that the personal data is: (i) processed fairly and lawfully; (ii) adequate, relevant and not excessive in relation to the purpose; (iii) accurate and, where necessary, kept up to date; inaccurate data must be erased or rectified; and (iv) not kept longer than necessary (IHR, Art. 45(2)).
113. IHR, Art. 45(3).
114. See Nowak, *CCPR Commentary*, 295–6, 297–8; and Fidler and Gostin, *Biosecurity in the Global Age*, 198.
115. See IHR, Art. 18.
116. See http://www.medicinenet.com/script/main/art.asp?articlekey=5925. See also *Public Health: Ethical Issues*, 53 and the term vaccine at: http://www.who.int/topics/vaccines/en/.
117. See http://www.medicinenet.com/script/main/art.asp?articlekey=12063.
118. The regulations go on to specify that medical examination 'may include the scrutiny of health documents, and a physical examination when justified by the circumstances of the individual case (IHR, Art. 1(1)).
119. Ibid.
120. The regulations further specify that the following measures are considered non-invasive: 'medical examination of the ear, nose and mouth, temperature assessment using an ear, oral or cutaneous thermometer, or thermal imaging; medical inspection; auscultation; external palpation; retinoscopy; external collection of urine, faeces or saliva samples; external measurement of blood pressure; and electrocardiography' (ibid.).
121. See also Nowak, *CCPR Commentary*, 290–1; and HRC, *M.R.* v. *Germany*, 23 July 2008 (No. 1482/2006), para. 10.1.
122. See HRC, *Toonen* v. *Australia*, paras 8.3, 8.5, 8.6. On the principle of proportionality concerning the right to privacy see also HRC: *Van Hulst* v. *Netherlands*, 1 November 2004 (No. 903/1999), paras 7.6, 7.10; and *Raihman* v. *Latvia*, 28 October 2010 (No. 1621/2007), para. 8.3.
123. IHR, Annex 6.
124. IHR, Annex 7.
125. IHR, Annex 8.

126. IHR, Annex 9.
127. See HRC, *General Comment No. 16: Article 17 (Right to Privacy)*, adopted 8 April 1988, HRI/GEN/1/Rev.9 (Vol. I) 191, para. 10.
128. See IHR, Arts 43(2), 23(2) and 31(2)(c).
129. IHR, Art. 18(1). When referring to the measure of quarantine the line continues with the text 'or other health measures for suspected persons'. It seems reasonable to interpret that expression in relation to quarantine.
130. Lesley A. Jacobs, 'Rights and Quarantine During the SARS Global Health Crisis: Differentiated Legal Consciousness in Hong Kong, Shanghai, and Toronto', *Law & Society Review* 41, no. 3 (2007): 513, 521.
131. IHR, Art. 1(1). See also 'Fact Sheet on Isolation and Quarantine', 20 January 2004, Centres for Disease Control and Prevention, Department of Health and Human Services, http://www.cdc.gov/sars/legal/fs-legal.pdf; and Geoff Manaugh and Nicola Twilley, 'Ebola and the Fiction of Quarantine', 11 August 2014, *The New Yorker*.
132. These measures may include voluntary staying at home or guarded home confinement. Sometimes it is not easy to delineate these measures from those falling within the context of the freedom of movement.
133. ICCPR, 9(1).
134. Nowak, *CCPR Commentary*, 160; and Sangeeta Shah, 'Detention and Trial', in *International Human Rights Law*, ed. Moeckli, Shah, and Sivakumaran, 261.
135. Ibid., 159–60, 167–8; Shah, 'Detention and Trial', 263–4; and *General Comment No. 35*, 3.
136. *General Comment No. 35*, 19–20.
137. In particular those provisions of Article 9 that do not pertain to criminal proceedings.
138. See *General Comment No. 35*, 3, 4, 7; and jurisprudence of the HRC: *Van Alphen* v. *The Netherlands*, 23 July 1990 (No. 305/1988), para. 5.8, *Gorji-Dinka* v. *Cameroon*, 17 March 2005 (No. 1134/2002), para. 5.1; and *Kulov* v. *Kyrgyzstan*, 26 July 2010 (No. 1369/2005), para. 8.3.
139. For example, the incubation period for yellow fever is three to six days, for viral haemorrhagic fevers (e.g. Ebola) it can be up to 21 days, while anthrax develops in one to seven days (see Centres for Disease Control and Prevention, *CDC Health Information for International Travel 2014: 2014 Yellow Traveller's Book*, http://wwwnc.cdc.gov/travel/page/yellowbook-home-2014).
140. See Shah, 'Detention and Trial', 265; and HRC, *Wenga and Shandwe* v. *DR Congo*, 17 March 2006 (No. 1177/2003), para. 6.2. See also *Body of Principles for the Protection of All Persons under Any Form of Detention or Imprisonment*, General Assembly, 9 December 1988, A/RES/43/173, Principle 10 (the *Body of Principles for the Protection of All Persons under Any Form of Detention or Imprisonment* is a set of soft law norms adopted by the UN General Assembly which further extrapolates the substance of the right to liberty).
141. *General Comment No. 35*, 8; and *Body of Principles*, Principle 14. In addition, foreigners have a right to communicate with consular or diplomatic agents of their respective countries or, if they are refugees, with a representative of the appropriate international organisation (ibid., Principle 16(2)).
142. *General Comment No. 35*, 12–14; *Body of Principles*, Principles 32 and 11; and Shah, 'Detention and Trial', 266. See also jurisprudence of the HRC: *Fijalkowska* v. *Poland*, 26 July 2005 (No. 1062/2002); paras 8.3, 8.4; *Ahani* v. *Canada*, 29 March 2004 (No. 1062/2002), para. 10.2; and *Mika Miha* v. *Equatorial Guinea*, 8 July 1994 (No. 414/1990), para. 6.5.
143. Under the relevant Canadian legislation, a suspected individual can be held for 48 hours. If held for longer, the executive decision is automatically subject to a judicial review. Judges must hear such cases within one day (Erin M. Page, 'Balancing Individual Rights and Public Health Safety during Quarantine: The U.S. and Canada', *Case Western Reserve Journal of International Law* 38 (2006–2007): 535–6).
144. See *Body of Principles*, Principles 11(1), 17 and 18; and *Fijalkowska* v. *Poland*, para. 8.4.
145. Cf. George J. Annas, Wendy K. Mariner and Wendy E. Parmet, *Pandemic Preparedness: The Need for a Public Health – Not a Law Enforcement/National Security – Approach* (New York: American Civil Liberties Union, 2008), 33. Ries suggests that there should be a possibility of 'class quarantine orders' to put suspected individuals under quarantine (Nola M. Ries, 'Quarantine and the Law: The 2003 SARS Experience in Canada', *Alberta Law Review* 43 (2005): 547). Although this is a viable option, access to the court should be provided to those affected by such orders.

146. See *Body of Principles*, Principle 25.
147. Cf. IHR, Art. 32(c); and *Body of Principles*, Principle 24.
148. See *Body of Principles*, Principles 16 and 19. The Canadian SARS experience demonstrates that persons who were quarantined and were barred from social contacts experienced a serious sense of isolation (see Ries, 'Quarantine and the Law', 538–9).
149. The regulations mention that authorities should provide 'means of necessary communication if possible in a language that they can understand' (IHR, Art. 32(c)).
150. Ibid., Principle 12; and *General Comment No. 35*, 17.
151. *General Comment No. 35*, 15–16; and Shah, 'Detention and Trial', 266. See HRC, *Bolaños* v. *Ecuador*, 26 July 1989 (No. 238/1987), para. 10; and *Mulezi* v. *Democratic Republic of the Congo*, 8 July 2004 (No. 962/2001), para. 8.
152. IHR, Art. 18(1).
153. The ACHR has a similar scheme for the right to movement in Article 22 (Freedom of Movement and Residence).
154. ICCPR, Art. 12(1). See HRC, *Lovelace* v. *Canada*, 30 July 1981 (No. R.6/24), paras 15 and 18.
155. ICCPR, Art. 12(2). See HRC, *El Ghar* v. *Libyan Arab Jamahiriya*, 29 March 2004 (No. 1107/2002), para. 7.3.
156. ICCPR, Art. 12(4). See infra note 161.
157. ICCPR, Art. 12(3).
158. That public health is such a ground is self-evident. In addition, the category of the rights and freedoms of others is likewise relevant in the context of the spread of infectious diseases (e.g. HIV/AIDS). However, every case needs to be evaluated on an *ad hoc* basis to avoid social stigma because of the disease (Nowak, *CCPR Commentary*, 215, 217). See also a judgment in the case *Enhorn* v. *Sweden*, European Court of Human Rights, 25 January 2005 (Application No. 56529/00); and Robyn Martin, 'The Exercise of Public Health Powers in Cases of Infectious Disease: Human Rights Implications', *Medical Law Review* 14 (2006): 132–43.
159. HRC, *General Comment No. 27: Freedom of Movement (Article 12)*, 1 November 1999, CCPR/C/21/Rev.1/Add. 9, 4; and HRC, *Sayadi and Vinck* v. *Belgium*, para. 10.5; and Nowak, *CCPR Commentary*, 217.
160. Nowak, *CCPR Commentary*, 219–21. See also jurisprudence of the HRC: *Lichtensztejn* v. *Uruguay*, 31 March 1983 (No. 77/1980), para. 8.3; *Stewart* v. *Canada*, 1 November 1996 (No. 538/1993), paras 12.2–12.9; *Madafferi* v. *Australia*, 26 July 2004 (No. 1011/2001), para. 9.6.
161. For an opposite view see Barbara von Tigerstrom, 'The Revised International Health Regulations and Restraint of National Health Measures', *Health Law Journal* 13 (2005): 64–5.
162. This measure can likewise represent a limitation of the right to liberty.
163. Fidler, *International Law and Infectious Diseases*, 26–7; Annas, Mariner, and Parmet, *The Need for a Public Health Approach*, 33; Kathleen S. Swendiman and Jennifer K. Elsea, *Federal and State Quarantine and Isolation Authority* (Washington DC: The Library of Congress, 2005), 18–19; Lawrence Gostin, Daniel Lucey, and Alexandra Phelan, 'The Ebola Epidemic: A Global Health Emergency', *JAMA* 312, no. 1 (2014): 1095; and Donald G. McNeil, 'Using a Tactic Unseen in a Century, Countries Cordon Off Ebola-Racked Areas', *The New York Times*, 12 August 2014, http://www.nytimes.com/2014/08/13/science/using-a-tactic-unseen-in-a-century-countries-cordon-off-ebola-racked-areas.html?_r=0.
164. Gostin, Lucey, and Phelan, 'The Ebola Epidemic', 1095.
165. Human Rights Watch, 'West Africa: Respect Rights in Ebola Response', 15 September 2014, http://www.hrw.org/news/2014/09/15/west-africa-respect-rights-ebola-response. Fidler and Gostin speak of the need for the rule of law in the context of the biosecurity governance (see Fidler and Gostin, *Biosecurity in the Global Age*, 195–203).
166. This was particularly the case during the Ebola epidemic. See McNeil, 'Using a Tactic Unseen in a Century'; Solomon Sogbandi, 'Living with Ebola in Freetown: "It Feels like the Whole Country is in Quarantine"', *Amnesty International UK/Blogs*, 6 November 2014, http://www.amnesty.org.uk/blogs/global-voices/living-ebola-freetown-it-feels-whole-country-quarantine; and Joseph Amon, 'What Turns a Few Cases of Disease into Thousands?', *Human Rights Watch*, 12 September 2014, http://www.hrw.org/news/2014/09/12/what-turns-few-cases-disease-thousands.
167. IHR, Art. 23(1)(a)(i) and (ii).
168. One can envisage data collection through data sharing with WHO and other states (see IHR, Art. 45).

169. IHR, Art. 23(3).
170. IHR, Art. 31(1).
171. Ibid. At this point, the regime under the regulations gets circular with cross-references to articles that served as a point of departure. Consequently, it becomes increasingly difficult to decipher the clear intent behind some provisions.
172. IHR, Art. 31(2).
173. The regulations also use the expression that the state may 'advise' the traveller to undergo this treatment, pursuant to his or her express informed consent. Yet again, cross-references get circular, which enhances the compulsory character of this provision.
174. IHR, Art. 31(2).
175. Fidler and Gostin, 'The New International Health Regulations', 88; and Hodge, 'Global Legal Triage in Response to the 2009 H1N1 Outbreak', 610.
176. An important point here is that the requirement of 'the least invasive and intrusive' applies only to medical examination and not to other, more serious health measures such as vaccination, quarantine and isolation (Hodge, 'Global Legal Triage in Response to the 2009 H1N1 Outbreak', 610).
177. Any interference with the right to privacy must be lawful and non-arbitrary and there should be protection of the law against such interference. See ICCPR, Art. 17(1) and 17(2). See also *General Comment No. 16*, 1–2.
178. Fidler and Gostin, 'The New International Health Regulations', 87.

Some scepticism on the right to health: the case of the provision of medicines

Laura Niada-Avshalom

Student Affairs, University of Westminster, London, UK

Medicines exist to treat a great number of illnesses, but they can be costly and unaffordable. This article analyses the obligations of states to provide medicines originating from International Covenant on Economic, Social and Cultural Rights (ICESCR) article 12 on the right to health, which arguably stipulates a right to medicines. Given the limited resources available, it is asked which medicines states shall provide and prioritise. The article then asks whether the provision of medicines by states *ought to* be guided by the right to health. In order to answer this question, multidisciplinary perspectives including health policy, bioethics and socio-legal studies are considered. The article concludes that the ICESCR right to health and medicines entails legal, moral and political flaws. The indeterminacy of the duties corresponding to the right and its penchant for public health and the collective dimension are found to be particularly problematic. Thereby the article proposes to contribute to critical perspectives on human rights, with a particular emphasis on economic, social and cultural rights.

1. Introduction

Medicines can help prevent, treat or alleviate a variety of illnesses.[1] Unfortunately access to medicines can be insufficient for people in all parts of the world. The World Health Organization (WHO) has estimated that in sub-Saharan Africa 47% of people lack access to 'essential' medicines,[2] which are already a selection of medicines (the identification of essential medicines is discussed below in section 2.3), while they are affected by 25% of the world's burden of disease (the concept of the burden of disease is discussed below in section 3.1).[3] In developed countries as well individuals can lack access to medicines. In the United Kingdom (UK), for example, public health care is provided by the National Health Service (NHS), which is funded from general taxation.[4] The NHS provides for free or for a subsided price a selection of medicines, identified according to cost-effectiveness assessments undertaken by the National Institute for Health and Clinical Excellence (NICE). Therefore, it does not provide certain costly therapies, including certain cancer medicines, for which it is often criticised.[5]

Considering the worldwide problems of access to medicines and medicine financing this article asks in section 2 whether states are bound to provide access to medicines under international human rights law.[6] The International Covenant on Economic, Social and Cultural Rights (ICESCR), adopted by the United Nations (UN) General Assembly, is studied in particular. It is demonstrated that the 'right of everyone to the enjoyment of the highest attainable standard of physical and mental health' enshrined in ICESCR article 12 includes a right to medicines, which requires the provision of medicines by states. More specifically, the provision of 'essential' medicines is a core, non-derogable obligation, hence there is a minimum obligation to provide essential medicines.[7]

As with many economic, social and cultural rights, however, the realisation of access to medicines requires resources which are scarce. Thus, considering the apparent gap between health needs and resources within states this article enquires in sections 2.2 and 2.3: according to the right to medicines, who is to get which medicines? Which medicines are 'essential'? What diseases and health conditions should be targeted? The most prevalent? Those which are cost-effective to treat? The most severe? Should certain groups such as children, pregnant women and the poor be given priority? It will be shown that the ICESCR framework, which includes General Comment No. 14 on the right to health and No. 3 on the nature of states parties' obligations of the Committee on Economic, Social and Cultural Rights (CESCR), does not give a precise answer about priorities in health care. With a broad and inclusive approach it simultaneously refers to interventions of public health that would benefit a population as a whole; attention for specific groups within a population; and to entitlements for the individuals. Despite the indeterminacy, the public health dimension seems to be seen with particular favour.

The article subsequently asks in section 3 the normative (prescriptive) question: 'Should the human right to medicines be utilised to take decisions on the provision of medicines?' In order to answer this question, the duties originating from the ICESCR on the provision of health care and medicines are analysed and questioned through multidisciplinary perspectives which include medical, public health, ethical, economic, social and political considerations. Furthermore, the theoretical contributions of socio-legal studies (in particular, Luhmann) and sociology (in particular, Foucault and Agamben on biopower and security) are utilised as critical-analytical tools to better answer this normative question.

Ideally, the right to medicines would legally bind states to undertake a defined principled conduct that would lead to the best access to medicines. Conversely, this article concludes that the prescriptions of the right to medicines (the human right to health in relation to medicines) are not an adequate tool to take decisions on the provision of medicines. The indeterminacy and the penchant for public health are particularly problematic. Indeterminacy involves abundant room of manoeuvre, and thence discretion, for states to determine what action to take on access to medicines. The penchant for public health involves attention to the population as a whole, and thence numbers, rather than to the individual. Thus the utilisation of the human right to health in relation to medicines is demonstrated to entail legal, moral and political flaws. Therefore the article attempts to contribute to the critique of human rights, and particularly economic, social and cultural rights, by looking at the specific case of the right to health in relation to access to medicines and the legal, moral and political problems of its implementation.

2. The ICESCR framework on access to medicines

2.1 *There is a right to medicines in the ICESCR*

The ICESCR, which binds 162 states parties from all world regions,[8] is studied in this article as it can be deemed to be one of the most significant sources of the international human right to health and medicines.[9] In analysing what the ICESCR entails, the General Comments of the CESCR, the treaty monitoring body, will receive particular attention as, even if not binding *per se*, they can be considered 'authoritative interpretations' of the covenant.[10] Article 12 of the ICESCR enshrines the human right to health, namely 'right of everyone to the enjoyment of the highest attainable standard of physical and mental health' providing that:

1. The States Parties to the present Covenant recognize the right of everyone to the enjoyment of the highest attainable standard of physical and mental health.
2. The steps to be taken by the States Parties to the present Covenant to achieve the full realization of this right shall include those necessary for:
   (a) The provision for the reduction of the stillbirth-rate and of infant mortality and for the healthy development of the child;
   (b) The improvement of all aspects of environmental and industrial hygiene;
   (c) The prevention, treatment and control of epidemic, endemic, occupational and other diseases;
   (d) The creation of conditions which would assure to all medical service and medical attention in the event of sickness.[11]

Access to medicines is a necessary component of the health interventions named in paragraphs 2 (a), (c) and (d). It has to be established what policies states shall undertake to support access to medicines. The ICESCR does not mention direct intervention of states in health care. States have to take steps for '[t]he *creation of conditions* which would assure to all medical service and medical attention … '.[12] In general the ICESCR rights are to be realised, vaguely, 'by all appropriate means, including particularly the adoption of legislative measures'.[13]

The CESCR General Comment No. 14: the Right to the Highest Attainable Standard of Health (General Comment 14) instead prescribes conduct for states in a more expansive way. The CESCR holds that according to the ICESCR states have tripartite obligations to *respect*, *protect*, and *fulfil* the human right to health,[14] and some of these are especially pertinent to access to medicines.[15] States have duties to *respect* the human right to health by refraining from interfering in the equal access to treatment[16]; *protect* by 'controlling the marketing of medical equipment and medicines by third parties'[17]; and *fulfil* by 'ensur[ing] the provision of health care, including immunization programmes against the major infectious diseases … '.[18] Furthermore, the CESCR clearly identifies the provision of essential medicines as one of the measures to be taken under article 12(2)(d) which, the committee maintains, 'includes the provision of equal and timely access to basic preventive, curative, rehabilitative health services and … the provision of essential drugs … '.[19]

These CESCR prescriptions too, however, are quite indeterminate. In effect the CESCR ultimately states that '[t]he most appropriate feasible measures to implement the human right to health will vary significantly from one State to another. Every State has a margin of discretion in assessing which measures are most suitable to meet its specific circumstances.'[20] Furthermore, judicial enforceability is not prescribed in mandatory terms by the CESCR.[21] The CESCR is apparently more assertive with regard to the so-called minimum core obligations, as it is shown below.

Another element of uncertainty regards the fact that the ICESCR stipulates that the rights recognised in the covenant have to be realised progressively, to the maximum of the state's available resources:

> Each State Party to the present Covenant undertakes to take steps, individually and through international assistance and co-operation, especially economic and technical, to the maximum of its available resources, with a view to achieving progressively the full realization of the rights recognized in the present Covenant by all appropriate means, including particularly the adoption of legislative measures.[22]

The question arises about *how slowly* the steps can be undertaken without constituting violations of the covenant. The wording 'achieving progressively' may be seen as an excuse for delaying the parties' conduct for the realisation of the rights. It is noteworthy that the concern about the formula had been expressed during the *travaux préparatoires* by some representatives who argued that it introduced uncertainty in the liability of states for the realisation of the ICESCR rights.[23] The CESCR in its comment states that the concept of progressive realisation in fact 'imposes an obligation to move as expeditiously and effectively as possible towards that goal'.[24] The CESCR phrasing is however still indeterminate. Reference to the 'maximum of available resources' also implies contingency. Studying the ICESCR *travaux préparatoires*, Alston and Quinn note that some representatives interpreted the expression generously. In particular, the Lebanese representatives, Azkoul, specified that the 'maximum of available resources' refer to the real resources of a country and not to budgetary appropriations.[25] Nevertheless, with a view to other comments, Alston and Quinn conclude that 'it is clear from the *travaux* that States parties are presumed to have considerable discretion in determining what resources are in fact available for use in economic, social, and cultural right-related concerns'.[26]

ICESCR article 12 also possibly concedes some delay in the implementation of the human right to health: in paragraph 1, the covenant utilises the term 'highest attainable standard' which is ambiguous.[27] Toebes and Hestermeyer note that the French version of article 12 recites: '*meilleur état de santé ... qu'elle soit capable d'atteindre*'. Thus, it would only refer to the biological preconditions of the individual.[28] The CESCR, more expansively, states that it 'takes into account both the individual's biological and socio-economic preconditions and State's available resources'.[29] Paragraph 2, article 12 prescribes certain 'steps' that the parties shall undertake, thereby contemplating a gradual implementation.[30]

Nonetheless, in General Comment No. 3: The Nature of States Parties Obligations (General Comment 3), the CESCR expresses the view that 'a minimum core obligation to ensure the satisfaction of, at the very least, minimum essential levels of each of the rights is incumbent upon every State party'.[31] Short of these minimum core obligations the covenant 'would be largely deprived of its raison d'être'.[32] Importantly, according to the CESCR, the provision of 'essential drugs' is on its own a core, non-derogable obligation.[33] This means that states bear the burden of proof to demonstrate that they do not have the resources to satisfy it.[34] Moreover, according to a former Special Rapporteur on the Right to Health, the obligation should be satisfied immediately.[35] The CESCR however does not list 'essential drugs' in General Comment 14. The identification of essential medicines is discussed below in section 2.3.

Thus, according to the doctrine around the ICESCR, states shall 'promote', 'facilitate' and 'provide' access to medicines.[36] The view that the human right to health in the ICESCR can imply obligations for states parties with regard to medicines is upheld, *inter alia*, by national courts.[37] It can arguably be said, therefore, that access to the medicines needed for health is a human right under the ICESCR. This view is also maintained by former Special Rapporteur on the Right to Health, Professor Hunt, who explicitly reported on the 'human right to medicines',[38] and international lawyers.[39] Hence, this article refers to a human right to medicines.

Having established this, it is noted that the provision of medicines through public health financing requires revenue collection, pooling of resources and purchasing of interventions.[40] With regard to collection and pooling, as is the case of other economic, social and cultural rights sanctioned in the ICESCR, it is not clear how many resources should be raised, and from whom. The ICESCR framework refers to 'available resources': if they are to be understood as the real resources of a country and not as budgetary appropriations there is considerable room for manoeuvre.[41] How many resources can the state raise from the public? How much can the state allocate to medicines, considering other economic, social and cultural rights in society? The CESCR itself refers to other core needs which naturally compete with the provision of 'essential' medicines such as the needs 'of essential foodstuffs, of essential primary health care, of basic shelter and housing, or of the most basic forms of education'.[42] More generally other needs, rights, interests and freedoms of individuals have to be curtailed in order to fully respond to the medicine needs of a population. For example, a country's taxpayers may be required to contribute to the provision of medicines at the national level through taxes, that which would affect their private property. Short of a collection of resources that would satisfy all medicine needs in a country, states need to prioritise the distribution of medicines. The ICESCR guidance on the prioritisation of health interventions is analysed in section 2.2, while section 2.3 looks specifically at the identification of the 'essential' medicines mentioned by the CESCR.

2.2 *The provision of health care between public health and individual right*

The ICESCR right to health framework does not indicate what specific policies states should implement and how to prioritise between health interventions. Instead, it refers to several dimensions of interventions. It can be said that some of them relate to public health while others relate to (individual) medical care.[43] This section discusses which, if any, is to prevail.

The WHO defines public health as

> all organized measures (whether public or private) to prevent disease, promote health, and prolong life among the population as a whole. Its activities aim to provide conditions in which people can be healthy and focus on entire populations, not on individual patients or diseases.[44]

Three out of four dimensions referred to by the ICESCR can be seen as public health interventions, namely, child health (article 12(2)(a)), environmental and industrial hygiene (article 12(2)(b)), and the management of epidemic, pandemic, occupational and other diseases (article 12(2)(c)).[45] Furthermore, within medical interventions, the CESCR states that essential primary health care is a minimum core obligation that should be realised immediately.[46] Primary health care is often identified in the public health field as a typical public health policy.[47] Primary health care however is *a* particular element of health assistance to be implemented in the context of health systems.[48]

Thus, the ICESCR seems to hold a penchant for public health. Accordingly Tomasevski remarks that 'in defining the obligations of States that correspond to the human right to health, priority is accorded [by international human rights law such as that originating from the ICESCR] to *public* health measures'.[49] It is also noted that the very concept of the human right to health has been traced to early public health measures.[50] Attention to curative approaches that would address other personal medical care needs is nonetheless provided for by the ICESCR. Indeed the steps referred by the ICESCR for the members to follow include, although somewhat hesitantly, '[t]he creation of conditions which would assure to all medical service and medical attention in the event of sickness'.[51] The same article also binds members to take steps for the treatment of different kinds of diseases.[52]

Together with the question of the identification of the health policies states are required to implement – public health or medical care measures – lies the question of the identification of right-holders, namely, if these are individuals, groups, or the whole population. On the one hand the ICESCR refers to the highest attainable standard of health, which includes a personalised approach to health needs, referring to the biological preconditions of the individual.[53] The CESCR further suggests that article 12 of the ICESCR provides for an entitlement, not only a freedom to be healthy.[54] However, according to the CESCR, both the individual and collective dimensions are recognised by the human right to health:

> [r]egardless of whether groups as such can seek remedies as distinct holders of rights, States parties are bound by both the collective and individual dimensions of article 12. Collective rights are critical in the field of health; modern public health policy relies heavily on prevention and promotion which are approaches directed primarily to groups.[55]

The importance attributed to the collective dimension is also apparent when the CESCR states that 'investments should not disproportionately favour expensive curative health services which are often accessible only to a small, privileged fraction of the population, rather than primary and preventive health care benefiting a far larger part of the population'.[56] Thus curative health services that would benefit a smaller 'privileged' part of the population should yield to primary and preventative interventions that would benefit a larger population.

Lastly, the CESCR identifies certain groups as deserving particular attention.[57] In particular, with regard to vulnerable and marginalised groups the committee maintains, *inter alia*, that the 'vulnerable members of society' must be protected 'even in times of severe resources constraints', by the adoption of relatively low-cost targeted programmes.[58] The former Special Rapporteur on the Right to Health also recommends special attention to the vulnerable and marginalised.[59] Thus, the ICESCR right to health addresses the individual as well as the collective population and particular groups.

2.3 *The identification of 'essential' medicines and health interventions prioritising according to the ICESCR regime*

This section studies more closely the provision of 'essential medicines'. As mentioned in section 2.1 the provision of essential medicines is deemed by the CESCR to be a core, non-derogable obligation.[60] What are 'essential' medicines? How are they different to other medicines? Does this concept solve the problems of prioritisation of access to medicines?[61]

Fundamentally, essential medicines are a selection of prioritised medicines. But the CESCR does not directly identify which medicines are essential. It refers instead to the medicines 'from time to time defined under the WHO Action Programme on Essential Drugs', a document which corresponds to the WHO Model List of Essential Drugs.[62] In effect, the sources referred to by the CESCR are open-ended. As the WHO itself maintains, the WHO Model List of Essential Medicines is purely indicative and does not relate to the health problems of individual countries.[63] The WHO's list is indeed meant to guide the development of national and institutional essential medicine lists (EMLs). Once identified at the national level, essential medicines are to be included in the national EML.[64] The lists generally contain between 200 and 400 medicines and can serve as a guide for medicine supply in the public sector, medicine benefits within reimbursement schemes, medicine donations, local production and be linked to national clinical guidelines used for training and supervision.[65] The aim of the lists is to concentrate resources and rationalise the use of medicines in a country, i.e. to use of 'fewer drugs more effectively'.[66]

Fundamentally, WHO recommends States to identify essential medicines as:

> [...] those that satisfy the priority health care needs of the population. They are selected with due regard to public health relevance, evidence on efficacy and safety, and comparative cost effectiveness...exactly which medicines are regarded as essential remains a national responsibility.[67]

Accordingly, it appears that essential medicines are to be identified with consideration of the public health impact as those responding to the burden of disease of the population and taking into account their cost-effectiveness. Thus, they are not simply the most cost-effective within their therapeutic class; they also represent a selection of the health problems to be tackled, and this demands momentous decisions. For instance, the WHO has long excluded treatment for HIV/AIDS from the lists, as vocally lamented by campaigners.[68] Similarly, anti-retrovirals (medicines to treat HIV) have for a long time not been present in the EMLs of South Africa, one of the countries hardest hit by the AIDS pandemic.[69] Patented medicines tend not to be included in the WHO essential medicines list.[70] For instance, the most recent list includes no patented anti-cancer drugs.[71] It can be noted that, even in developing countries, cancer kills more people than AIDS, malaria and tuberculosis combined.[72] Thus, whilst attempting to address 'public health' needs, the limitation to essential medicines fails to respond to the medical needs of many individuals.

The collective approach is reflected by the liability of states in relation to access to essential medicines. According to the CESCR a state is *prima facie* failing to discharge its obligations under the ICESCR if '*any significant number of individuals*' is deprived of essential medicines.[73] In fact the use of domestic courts by individuals to redress individual claims relating to access to medicines as part of the right to health is not common worldwide. An exception is the growing jurisprudence of such cases in Central and Latin America.[74]

While this article does not specifically discuss the justiciability of the right to medicines[75] it is relevant to look into the South African *Minister of Health* v. *TAC* case. The case is probably the only domestic court case dealing with the provision of medicines in sub-Saharan Africa (where, as seen in the introduction, access to medicines is particularly inadequate) and it explicitly addresses the issue of provision of medicines as an individual entitlement and a core obligation.[76] The case concerned the provision of the medicine nevirapine to pregnant HIV-positive women so that they could prevent the transmission of AIDS to their foetuses. Nevirapine was offered to the government by the manufacturing companies free of charge for five years, but the government announced it would introduce the medicine only in certain pilot sites. The non-governmental organisation Treatment Action Campaign (TAC) consequently launched a constitutional challenge, alleging a violation of the right to access health care.[77]

In this case, the Constitutional Court of South Africa asserted its competence (subject-matter jurisdiction) on the realisation of the human right to health, which is a constitutional right in South Africa.[78] The court however refused to recognise individual entitlements, maintaining that, considering the available resources, the rights involved did not generally create an individual entitlement to any specific resources.[79] It is noteworthy that the court did not endorse the view of the CESCR and the African Commission in relation to the obligations of states to realise immediately a minimum core of the human right to health and medicines, ruling instead that it is not possible to give everyone access even to a 'core' service immediately.[80] The court also stated that courts are not institutionally equipped to determine what the minimum core standards should be.[81] Nonetheless, the identification of a core service was in fact acknowledged by the court to be 'possibly…relevant to reasonableness under section 26(2)', as previously recognised in *Grootboom*.[82] Ultimately the TAC's case succeeded because the government's action was deemed by the court to be 'unreasonable'.[83]

Thus, with the possible exception of certain cases in Central and Latin America, the core obligation to provide essential medicines is not matched by a legally enforceable individual entitlement to specific medicines. The concept of essential medicines, conversely, is used within public health to respond to the health needs of a *population* with regard to the cost-effectiveness of interventions.

3. Should the human right to medicines be utilised to take decisions on the provision of medicines?

As seen in section 2, the right to health enshrined in the ICESCR refers to dimensions of health interventions which span public health and medical care. The ICESCR demands action that would target the population at large, addressing the environment, working conditions and infectious diseases. As far as health care is concerned, primary and preventative care seem to be preferred, although an individual medical care approach and entitlement can be inferred. Moreover, groups such as children and vulnerable and marginalised people are given special consideration. In relation to the special case of the provision of essential medicines, the priority health care needs of a population are to be taken into account, with due regard to public health relevance.

It could be argued that the ICESCR's broad and inclusive approach to health is ideal as it covers different dimensions of health policy. Instead, it is argued in this article that these provisions are problematic and contradictory. Human rights cases and literature highlight some problems. With regard to the reference to individual medical care, the notion of an entitlement to health care and medicines – not even 'essential' medicines – is generally not welcomed by domestic courts, as the discussion of the *Minister of Health* v. *TAC* case has illustrated. With regard to the reference to the public health dimension, the human rights literature warns about the 'double-edged sword' of public health. Public health policies may demand the limitation of the right to health, privacy and autonomy of the individual in favour of the collective interest.[84] Within human rights law the protection of public health may constitute legitimate grounds for limiting civil and political rights such as the freedom of movement,[85] the freedom of expression,[86] the right to assembly[87] and the freedom of association.[88] Thus Toebes remarks that the human right to health is essentially private: it pertains to individuals or groups rather than the public and should not be a tool for states to take public health measures.[89] (In this special issue Toebes explores further the complex and difficult relationship between public health and human rights.)

Section 3 of this article attempts to demonstrate why the ICESCR's broad approach to health may not be desirable by utilising a multidisciplinary perspective which adds to human rights law considerations. Section 3.1 analyses various principles of health care prioritisation identified in the health policy literature that largely correspond to the dimensions of health interventions recommended by the ICESCR. It is demonstrated that such principles can hardly be taken as universally valid precepts. On the contrary, they are subject to discussion and critique in the literature with regard to their medical, public health, ethical, economic, social and political implications. These results are consequently interpreted through the contributions of Luhmann, Agamben and Foucault in section 3.2.

3.1 *The prioritisation of health interventions: aggregate status of a population, individual need and equity*

Three main principles or goals are generally identified in the health policy literature as informing choices of health intervention prioritisation, namely: the health improvement of the aggregate status of a population; the response to individual medical needs; and the promotion of equity.[90] These three principles match to some extent the main prescriptions indicated by the right to health in the ICESCR, respectively directed to the collective, public health dimension; the individual; and special groups.

The focus on the aggregate health status of a population (which corresponds to the ICESCR prescriptions on the collective, public health dimension) entails that greatest attention should be dedicated to the health conditions which are most prevalent and most threatening for a population. The benefits to a population can be measured in terms of reduction of the national 'burden of disease', often measured through aggregate disability-adjusted life-years (DALYs) or quality-adjusted life-years (QALYs).[91] Resources are then to be allocated on the basis of cost-effectiveness analysis, in order to discover the highest health impact per resource spent.[92] This is the principle that the UK's NICE (see section 1) uses and the WHO and the World Bank recommend for African and developing countries to adopt in health interventions prioritisations.[93]

The WHO Commission on Macroeconomics and Health specifically recommends improvement of the aggregate health of a population as a means to an end, seeing the reduction of the burden of disease, estimated as DALYs saved, as a measure that would boost low-income countries' economies.[94] The commission reckons that each DALY saved delivers a monetary value of US$563 in these countries.[95] The commission then advocates investing in vertical (disease-oriented) programmes that would save the most DALYs with the lowest cost.[96]

Besides the technical difficulties of estimating DALYs or QALYs, the aggregate approach is at odds with other moral principles. To begin with, it contrasts with the 'rule of rescue', that is, the 'imperative...to rescue identifiable individuals facing avoidable death, without giving too much thought to the opportunity cost of doing so'.[97] The rule of rescue suggests that identifiable patients should be favoured over non-identifiable patients (the statistical people) while this runs counter to QALY reasoning and prevention policies.[98] (Examples of the use of the rule of rescue are expensive searches for people lost at sea or on the mountains as well as offering intensive care to patients with small chances of survival.[99]) Next, the emphasis on the aggregate health status of a population brought to the extremes suggests the concentration of public health interventions in densely populated regions, where economies of scale are probable and more 'benefit' is to be reaped given the greater number of individuals served at one time.[100] Also, it may induce exclusion of the elderly from health care, as their life expectancy is shorter and thence their life has lower value.[101] QALY calculations deliver lesser importance to palliative care than that attributed by otherwise shared sensitivity.[102] Arguably, particular attention may be morally required to those who are particularly badly off with regard to their health or those for whom no alternative treatment is available, while QALYs forsake such concerns.[103] Also, 'double jeopardy', which occurs when other conditions subsist which otherwise impair the quality of life or that make treatment more difficult, may need to be considered.[104]

Another critique of the choice of burden of disease as the representation of population health needs is that it derives most of its appeal from a prudential – as opposed to moral – stance. Sheaff argues that under a prudent course of action the individual, who is uncertain of the types of ill health that might befall him, assumes that the relative size of different care groups indicates the relative probability that he will need that kind of care in the future.[105] From this, 'population health needs' would be construed. However, Sheaff recommends that the needs of the care groups composed by those exposed to particular risks, or whose risks cannot affect the 'living' others (such as genetic diseases) should be elaborated from an impartial or objective standpoint, that is, through an ethical approach, lest being neglected.[106]

The second main principle that can inform decisions on the prioritisation of medical interventions at the population level is medical need, which occurs 'when an individual has an illness or disability for which there is an effective and acceptable treatment'.[107] (This principle corresponds to the ICESCR prescriptions on medical services and individual entitlement.) Brauman, from Médecins Sans Frontières (MSF), eloquently contrasts the paradigm of health-care prioritising based on medical needs of the individual to the paradigm of public health. Brauman criticises the public health model for being too 'rationalistic' as it considers, in health decision-making, non-medical issues and long-term medical outcomes. Moreover, the public health model presupposes the questionable exactitude and validity of epidemiological predictions.[108] Instead, he supports the 'humanitarian' model, asserting as 'primary obligation…to give direct medical treatment to people who require medical attention'.[109]

This principle however faces the practical, economic problem that the health needs of a people can be infinite: to be put into practice it also requires some sort of prioritisation and ranking.[110] Indeed if this approach were accepted by courts admitting claims on entitlements to medicines, the results would be financially ruinous for the health systems. It can be recalled here that, as mentioned in section 2.3, Central and Latin America are characterised by the success of individuals or groups in litigating access to medicines as part of the right to health.[111] This expansion has led some authors to question whether the award of medicines through the courts in those cases affects the fairness of resources allocations.[112] For example, a study on Costa Rica revealed that 70% of cases where access to medicines not otherwise supplied by the state was awarded regarded 'either low priority or experimental [medicines] and can be described as providing "marginal" health benefits for very severe conditions at a high cost to the health care system'.[113]

The principle of the promotion of equity introduces other dimensions in the distribution of health resources. (This principle is similar to the prescriptions of the ICESCR framework relating to the vulnerable and marginalised.) The principle derives from Rawls' 'Difference Principle' of justice which requires that the basic social and economic institutions of society be arranged so as to maximise the expectations of the worst-off representative group. According to Rawls, 'the justice of a society can be seen in how it treats its least fortunate members'.[114] This can be seen to refer to a range of personal circumstances of individuals including their personal health, social, psychological and financial standing. For example, Hammer and Berman see 'equity' in relation to health care policy in developing countries as referring to income.[115] Accordingly, an equity-oriented policy views health care as an instrument for reducing poverty: 'It places the emphasis on who benefits from public spending on health, arguing that it should differentially be the poor (or other groups defined in terms of social or economic disparities), not necessarily those who suffer from diseases for which the most cost-effective treatments are available.'[116] This approach would therefore focus on those diseases and treatments which place the largest burden (financial, productivity loss, household stress) on the poor.[117] Overall, the equity approach, while arguably responding to principles of distributive justice, may be questionable as a sole guide for *health* policy. On what basis exactly should equity be measured? Can the concern for equity satisfy the purpose of a right to health and medicines? If to be used as an auxiliary principle, to what extent and how should it be implemented?

It can be concluded that no prioritisation principle is perfect. This section demonstrated that the health policy prioritisation principles reviewed – and hence the corresponding provisions of the ICESCR – ought not to be implemented without a careful consideration of the practical and moral problems they entail. For example, attention to the aggregate status of the population does not seem to be fitting for a human, individual right as it does not necessarily respond to the health needs of individuals. To some extent it also does not indicate a moral course of action. In certain instances it is used for policies which see the health of a people as a means to an end (e.g. economic growth and development). The principle of individual need does not successfully address the problem of finite resources. The principle of equity is not solely concerned with health, and this can be a confusing approach for a right to health. In addition, such principles conflict with each other.

3.2 *Human rights fundamentalism, biopower and security: a reading of Luhmann, Agamben and Foucault*

This section proposes to interpret the findings presented above through some theoretical contributions which inspire a critical analysis of the right to medicines. While other authors offer important insights,[118] explicit use is made here of Luhmann's critique of human rights[119] as well as the concepts of biopolitics and biopower elaborated by Foucault and Agamben.[120]

Within his elaborate theorisation of social systems, Luhmann presents a compelling critique of human rights. Three sets of considerations are highlighted here as relevant to this study. The first set relates to the observation by Luhmann that human rights are presumed by their proponents to be the ultimate utopia, the programme of humanity.[121] But, Luhmann remarks, there are as many values as stars in heaven and they can actually collide between each other.[122] From a legal point of view, therefore, the inscription of human rights in the positive law can result in a law which lacks clarity and is contradictory.[123] Luhmann further argued that the 'fundamentalist' use of human rights is to beware of.[124] Luhmann called 'human rights fundamentalism' the idea that human rights are natural, indispensable, based on principles, and are supposed to have unlimited validity.[125] Instead, there is nothing 'fully independent of consequences' in human rights.[126]

This set of considerations applies to the analysis of ICESCR rights. The right to health framework tries to address several approaches of health care prioritisation, appealing to different moral principles. However, the approaches conflict with each other. The right to medicines is also not very clear in what it actually prescribes – what states are bound to do and what individuals or groups (or both) are entitled to claim. Moreover, the provisions in the ICESCR framework have 'side-effects', for example when they require resources which have an opportunity cost; overlook responses to non-prioritised health needs; or limit other rights, freedoms or interests.

In a second set of considerations, Luhmann notes that human rights are utilised to include individual human beings in the legal system.[127] This is paradoxical as subjective rights are legally valid only as 'objective rights', that which entail forgoing the unity and uniqueness of the individual:

> Human rights are always generalized; I cannot claim them simply 'as myself', but only, for instance, as a woman, as a worker, or as a member of a racial minority. In that way, one has actually to disavow one's unique individuality in order to be able to rely on human rights. A subject can only claim them 'objectively' in the form 'as X'.[128]

Thus, the right to medicines is bound to the legal (human rights) need for generalisation and universality. As a result it overlooks the special medical needs of individuals.

The third set of considerations regards the political consequences of human rights. Luhmann noted that human rights have a complex relationship with politics. In their utopian 'communication', human rights are meant to control the assault of the state.[129] At the same time, in order to realise their utopia, human rights attribute roles and powers to the very actors that bear human-rights duties (states as well as, in some cases, non-state actors).[130] Therefore, while human rights are ideally meant to control the power of the state, they can in fact entrench the state's (and other actors') power to take decisions relating to sensitive, morally problematic issues.

The philosopher Agamben specifically elaborates on the power conferred on states through the human rights which relate to people's lives. Agamben notes that the state obtains legitimate *bio*power for intervening in public health and the health of the 'bare lives' from the inscription of the bare life (*zoē*) in the juridico-political order which take place in human rights declarations:

> Declarations of rights represent the originary figure of the inscription of natural life in the juridico-political order of the nation-state. The same bare life that in the ancien régime was politically neutral and belonged to God as creaturely life and in the classical world was (at least apparently) clearly distinguished as zoē from political life (bios) now fully enters into the structure of the state and even becomes the earthly foundation of the state's legitimacy and sovereignty.[131]

The concept of biopower was originally elaborated by Foucault. Foucault traces the birth of biopower in the eighteenth century with the rationalisation of the problems posed to the public governance by the phenomena deriving from a population, such as health, hygiene, nativity, longevity and races.[132] According to Foucault, biopower is distinguished from traditional sovereignty, as while the latter entails the 'right to *take* life or *let* live' ('*de faire mourir ou de laisser vivre*'), the former is the 'power to *foster* life or *disallow* it to the point of death' ('*faire vivre ou rejeter dans la mort*').[133] As Foucault identified it, power – thence to be called biopower – is not addressed anymore at 'deduction' [*prélèvement*] but is exerted positively on life, aiming at managing, growing, multiplying it and exerting precise controls and regulations on it.[134] Thus Foucault stated: 'By [biopower] I mean a number of phenomena that seem to me to be quite significant, namely, the set of mechanisms through which the basic biological features of the human species became the object of a political strategy, of a general strategy of power…'[135]

Foucault's notion of 'security' further sensitises on the potential problems of the exercise of biopower.[136] According to Foucault, security is a form of power based on the growth and production of a population.[137] Thus, the health of a population is ultimately instrumental to security and translates into more biopower. Under the security approach, 'population' is not conceived of as a collection of individual juridical subjects but as 'a set of elements in which we can note constants and regularities even in accidents…and with regard to which we can identify a number of modifiable variables on which it depends'.[138] Moreover, the security paradigm follows 'normalisation' rather than 'normation'. While according to normation, 'there is an originally prescriptive character of the norm and the determination and the identification of the normal and the abnormal becomes possible in relation to this posited norm',[139] according to normalisation different immanent normalities are observed within the population as a whole and a norm is fixed on the basis of these normalities: '[t]he norm is an interplay of differential normalities. The normal comes first and the norm is deduced from it'.[140]

It was shown in section 2 that to a great extent the human right to medicines framework favours interventions that aim to improve the *aggregate* status of the population through a public health approach rather than the health of the individual. Therefore, it arguably nurtures biopower, security and *normalisation* of populations, for instance when it aims to provide a minimum service and health status to the widest population or when the health of a population is seen as a means to an end of economic growth and development, as suggested by the WHO Commission on Macroeconomics and Health.[141] In general, the action of states on the lives and deaths of their citizens constitutes the exercise of biopower, which is all the more consolidated as states are called to exert it to implement human rights.

4. Concluding remarks: flaws from the legal, moral and political points of view

This article has shown that the ICESCR framework (the ICESCR and the CESCR General Comments) encompasses a human right to health which imposes on states the duties to respect, protect and fulfil access to medicines (right to medicines). So should the human right to medicines, as per the ICESCR framework, be utilised to take decisions on the provision of medicines? This article's research has exposed several legal, moral and political problems relating to the actual implementation of the obligations to fulfil the provision of medicines.

The provision of medicines requires the collection of national resources. It is not clear from the human rights framework of the ICESCR what resources should be raised from the population for health needs and what proportion of those resources should be dedicated to answering medicine needs. Short of a collection of resources that would satisfy all medicine needs in a country, states need to prioritise the distribution of medicines. It has been shown that the framework of the right to health does not provide a clear algorithm that would guide health choices in regard to the provision of medicines. The ICESCR indicates several broad dimensions but overall it seems to have a penchant for a public health and primary health care that would improve the aggregate status of the population rather than specific individual curative needs.

Thus, from a legal point of view, the right is weak as it depends on the utilisation of resources while courts are hesitant to accept that a human right creates an individual entitlement to any specific resource. The hesitance exists even for claims to access to 'essential' medicines, which is described by the CESCR as a core obligation under the ICESCR.[142] On the other hand were the right to medicines to be enforced as a collective right it would reinforce the collective (population or group), rather than empower the individual vis-à-vis the collective.[143] Always from a legal point of view, the right to health prescribes public health interventions, but within human rights law public health measures do at times conflict with and limit other human rights and freedoms (including civil and political rights).[144] This complies with Luhmann's assertion that human rights law lacks clarity and is contradictory. The uncertainty and open-endedness of the right to medicines contribute to its poor applicability and enforceability.

From a moral point of view, the right to medicines may not promote the 'right' decisions on the provision of medicines. The ICESCR framework seems to include several principles of health distribution at the same time (aggregate status of the population, individual medical need and equity). This can be seen as the presumption of human rights to be the ideal 'programme of humanity'.[145] However, these principles can hardly be assumed as absolute prescriptions and are subject to critique and elaboration within medical, public health, ethical, economic, social and political and other perspectives.

Generally, the aggregate, public health approach is at variance with the principles of medical, individual need. Favouring the consideration of the aggregate status of the population the right to medicines framework seems to care more for numbers than for individuals. It may be decided, for example, that the human right to health care and medicines does not apply for those who suffer from rare or expensive conditions.[146] Little is said by the ICESCR framework about the gravity of the condition or suffering endured. Furthermore, as argued by Sheaff, the consideration of the aggregate burden of disease corresponds to a prudential, rather than ethical, approach. Thus, it is hard to overcome the paradox of a human right to health which is not possible to award comprehensively and is in effect exclusive. Why are people suffering from rare, expensive conditions not entitled to have their human right to health realised in contexts of limited resources? Is this even a right? In fact, is a human right the most appropriate tool to improve and realise access to medicines?

From a political point of view, the right to medicines may not promote emancipation and oppose state power, as human rights are meant to do; rather, it may entrench biopower as the state is invested by the human rights framework of the authority to take decisions on whose life is to be fostered and whose life or health is, perhaps, to be sacrificed. Moreover, like other economic and social rights, the right to medicines is to be realised progressively, and states enjoy a 'margin of discretion' with regard to the ways of realisation of the right.[147] For a more specific case, it has been shown, the identification of essential medicines is ultimately a state choice. This margin of discretion of the state virtually concedes perpetual legitimacy to the shortcomings of state action. Human rights, consequently, are also inadequate to redress the use of power in relation to health care and access to medicines. Indeed, as Luhmann noted, '[a] subjective right offers a guarantee of freedom in a double sense: for the holder and for those against whom those rights are ineffective'.[148] Also, with specific regard to health, it is recalled that the human right to health envisages the protection of public health, and this can constitute legitimate grounds for states to limit human rights.[149] The favour of the right to medicines for public health also fosters biopower by entrenching 'security' – the state power based on the growth and production of a population.[150]

In conclusion, it is argued that the human right to health in relation to medicines *is not sufficiently human*. As observed by Philippopoulos-Mihalopoulos, Luhmann's system theory suggests that 'human rights are predicated precisely on the exclusion of human flesh and blood from society – otherwise the discourse would revert to a situation of total inclusion'.[151] Too much, it was showed, *cannot* be decided according to the human right to health and medicines. Thus, it is suggested that health policies should be critically analysed through a multidisciplinary approach that includes medical, public health, ethical, economic, social and political considerations adopted by the people through active democracy, participation and accountability – rather than being decided through an ambitious but un-delivering right to medicines.[152]

Acknowledgments

This article is based on my PhD thesis, titled 'The Human Right to Medicines in Sub-Saharan Africa' (University of Westminster, 2010). I am thankful to Dr Brigit Toebes and Richard Earle for having read drafts of my article and having provided insightful and thorough comments. I am also thankful to Dr Brigit Toebes and to Dr Myriam Feinberg for their work and support in relation to the editing of this publication.

Disclosure statement

No potential conflict of interest was reported by the author.

Notes on contributor

Laura Niada is working as Learning Adviser and Visiting Lecturer at the University of Westminster, London. She researches in the areas of international law, human rights, the third world and development.

Notes

1. The term 'medicine' is used as a synonym of 'drug'. The term 'medicine' is often being replaced in the public health literature as the term drug can denote an 'illicit drug'.
2. World Health Organization, *The World Medicines Situation* (Geneva: World Health Organization, 2004), 62.
3. World Health Organization, *World Health Report 2003* (Geneva: World Health Organization, 2003), 120.
4. National Health Service, *NHS Constitution for England* (United Kingdom: Department of Health, 2013), arts 1 and 2.
5. Michael D. Rawlins and Anthony Culyer, 'National Institute for Clinical Excellence and its Value Judgments', *British Medical Journal* 329, no. 7459 (2004): 224; Sarah Boseley, 'Drugs Watchdog Condemns Roche for High Price of Breast Cancer Therapy', *The Guardian*, 8 August 2014, http://www.theguardian.com/society/2014/aug/08/drugs-watchdog-nice-roche-breast-cancer-nhs-limit (accessed 21 August 2014); Press Association, 'Nice Decision on Prostate Cancer Drug is a "Kick in the Teeth" for Patients', *The Guardian*, 15 August 2014, http://www.theguardian.com/society/2014/aug/15/nice-prostate-cancer-drug-abiraterone (accessed 21 August 2014).
6. Access to medicines is defined as having essential medicines continuously available and affordable at public or private health facilities or drug outlets that are within a one hour walk of the population. See United Nations Development Group, *Indicators for Monitoring the Millennium Development Goals* (New York: United Nations, 2003). Accordingly, access to medicines entails two main components: availability and affordability. Availability implies the physical presence of medicines, while affordability relates to the individuals' resources to acquire medicines.
7. Committee on Economic, Social and Cultural Rights (CESCR), *General Comment 14: The Right to the Highest Attainable Standard of Health*, UN Doc. E/C.12/1999/5, 2000, para. 47.
8. Office of the High Commissioner for Human Rights (OHCHR), 'Status of Ratification Interactive Dashboard', http://indicators.ohchr.org/ (accessed 28 September 2014).
9. For other sources of the right to medicines such as the African Charter on Human and Peoples' Rights, and other human rights, such as the right not to be subjected to torture, inhuman and degrading treatment, or the right to life, and customary international law, see Laura Niada, 'The Human Right to Medicines in Relation to Patents in Sub-Saharan Africa: Some Critical Remarks', *The International Journal of Human Rights* 15, no. 5 (2011): 700–727.
10. Sigrun I. Skogly and Mark Gibney, 'Transnational Human Rights Obligations', *Human Rights Quarterly* 24 (2002): 791. A few considerations may justify such authority. The committee is a body of independent experts which was established under ECOSOC Resolution 17 (1985) to carry out the monitoring functions assigned to the United Nations Economic and Social Council (ECOSOC) in Part IV of the ICESCR. See OHCHR, 'Committee on Economic, Social and Cultural Rights – Sessions', 2008, http://www2.ohchr.org/english/bodies/cescr/sessions.htm. The committee has been active in elaborating General Comments on various ICESCR provisions and on how to better implement the covenant; issuing reporting guidelines

for the ICESCR parties, relating to issues and policies on which states have to focus their attention; analysing states' implementation of the covenant and expressing 'concluding considerations' on them. Laura Niada, 'Hunger and International Law: The Far-Reaching Scope of the Right to Food', *Connecticut Journal of International Law* 22, no. 1 (2006): 149.

11. International Covenant on Economic, Social and Cultural Rights (ICESCR), UN Doc. A/6316 (1966), entered into force 23 March 1976, article 12.
12. ICESCR article 12(2)(d) (my emphasis).
13. Ibid., article 2(1).
14. CESCR, *General Comment 14*, paras 33–6.
15. Ibid., para. 33.
16. Ibid., para. 34.
17. Ibid., para. 35.
18. Ibid., para. 36.
19. CESCR, *General Comment 14*, para. 17. On the equivalence between the terms medicines and drugs see note 1.
20. Ibid., para. 53.
21. The CESCR recommends remedies for the violation of the right to health in non-mandatory terms. Ibid., para. 59.
22. ICESCR article 2(1).
23. See Philip Alston and Gerard Quinn, 'The Nature and Scope of States Parties Obligations Under the International Covenant on Economic, Social and Cultural Rights', *Human Rights Quarterly* 9, no. 2 (1987): 156–229.
24. Committee on Economic, Social and Cultural Rights (CESCR), *General Comment 3: The Nature of State Parties Obligations*, United Nations Economic and Social Council, UN Doc. E/1991/23, annex III at 86, 1991, para. 9.
25. United Nations, UN Doc. E/CN.4/SR.271, 1952, 5.
26. Alston and Quinn, 'States Parties Obligations', 180. On the identification of the ICESCR maximum available resources and a discussion on the taxation necessary to realise economic, social and cultural rights see also Diane Elson, Radhika Balakrishnan, and James Heintz, 'Public Finance, Maximum Available Resources and Human Rights', in *Human Rights and Public Finance: Budgets and the Promotion of Economic and Social Rights*, ed. Aoife Nolan, Rory O'Connell, and Colin Harvey (Oxford: Hart Publishing, 2013), 13–40. On progressive realisation, maximum available resources and minimum core see also Rory O'Connell and others 'A Human Rights Framework Part 1: Exploring Article 2(1) ICESCR Obligations', in *Applying An International Human Rights Framework to State Budget Allocations: Rights and Resources*, ed. Rory O'Connell and others (London: Routledge, 2014), 61–86.
27. ICESCR article 12(1).
28. Brigit Toebes, *The Right to Health as a Human Right in International Law* (Oxford: Intersentia/Hart, 1999), 45–6; Holger P. Hestermeyer, 'Access to Medication as a Human Right', *Max Planck Yearbook of United Nations Law* 8 (2004): 127.
29. CESCR, *General Comment 14*, para. 9.
30. ICESCR article 12(2).
31. Ibid., para. 10.
32. Ibid.
33. CESCR, *General Comment 14*, para. 43(d) and 47.
34. CESCR, *General Comment 14*, 47. O'Connell and others define minimum core obligations as the 'bottom or floor from which states should endeavor to go up'. O'Connell and others, *International Human Rights Framework*, 80.
35. The former Special Rapporteur makes clear that 'the right to health encompasses access to non-essential and essential medicines. While a State is required to progressively realise access to non-essential medicines, it has a core obligation of immediate effect to make essential medicines available and accessible throughout its jurisdiction.' Paul Hunt, 'Report to the General Assembly (Maternal Mortality and Access to Medicines)', UNDoc.A/61/338, 2006, para. 58. See also para. 38.
36. CESCR, *General Comment 14*, para. 33.
37. In the *Viceconte* case the Argentinean Federal Court of Appeals also referred to the ICESCR in order to appreciate the social right to health and to assert the state obligation to manufacture the hemorrhagic fever vaccine as requested by the plaintiffs. See Argentina, Federal

Administrative Court of Appeals, 1998, Viceconte, Mariela c. Estado Nacional (Ministerio de Salud y Ministerio de Economía de la Nación) s/ Acción de Amparo, 2 June 1998 para. 5.

38. See Hunt, 'Report to the General Assembly (Maternal Mortality and Access to Medicines)', para. 40. Paul Hunt served as UN Special Rapporteur on the Right to Health from 2002 to 2008.
39. Hestermeyer, 'Access to Medication as a Human Right', 125; Alicia E. Yamin, 'Not Just a Tragedy: Access to Medications as a Right under International Law', *Boston University International Law Journal* 21, no. 2 (2003): 325–371.
40. World Health Organization, *World Health Report 2000* (Geneva: World Health Organization, 2000), 95.
41. United Nations, UN Doc. E/CN.4/SR.271, 5.
42. CESCR, *General Comment 3*, para. 10.
43. Roughly, primary care is the first point of consultation, secondary care is specialist and tertiary care is specialised on referral.
44. WHO, *Public Health*, http://www.who.int/trade/glossary/story076/en/ (accessed 21 September 2014). See also Brigit Toebes, 'Human Rights and Public Health: An Unsettled Relationship', *International Journal of Human Rights* 19, no. 4 (2015): this issue (Special Issue: 'Human Rights and Public Health', ed. Brigit Toebes and Laura Niada). The American Public Health Association has synthesised the many definitions and perspectives on public health and identified six basic principles of contemporary public health theory and practice (APHA): (a) emphasis on collective responsibility for health and the prime role of the state in protecting and promoting the public's health; (b) focus on whole populations; (c) emphasis on prevention, especially the population strategy for primary prevention; (d) concern for the underlying socio-economic determinants of health and disease, as well as the more proximal risk factors; (e) multidisciplinary basis which incorporates quantitative and qualitative methods as appropriate; and (f) partnership with the populations served. World Bank, *Public Health and World Bank Operations* (Washington, DC: International Bank for Reconstruction and Development/World Bank, 2002), 5.
45. ICESCR article 12(2)(a), (b) and (c). See also Toebes, noting within this special issue that 'WHO's public health campaigns…may embrace issues like vaccination and control of infectious diseases, motor-vehicle safety, occupational health, safe drinking water, maternal and child health, coronary heart disease and stroke, and prevention of smoking'. Toebes, 'Human Rights and Public Health', X.
46. CESCR, *General Comment 14*, paras 19, 43, note omitted.
47. World Bank, *Public Health and World Bank Operations*, 5
48. Again, primary health care is not a clear concept, as also recognised by the CESCR. CESCR, *General Comment 14*, endnote 9. As the WHO acknowledges in its *World Health Report 2000*, the implementation of primary health care has been problematic, also because its meaning is in fact ambiguous. WHO, *World Health Report 2000*, 13.
49. Katrina Tomasevski, 'Health Rights', in *Economic, Social and Cultural Rights: A Textbook*, ed. Asbjørn Eide, Catarina Krause, and Rosas Allan (The Hague: Kluwer Law International, 1995), 125 (italics in original).
50. Toebes, *Right to Health*, 8–14; Hestermeyer, 'Access to Medication as a Human Right', 111; Toebes, 'Human Rights and Public Health', X. [on Chadwick etc.]
51. ICESCR article 12(2)(d).
52. ICESCR article 12(2)(c).
53. ICESCR article 12(1). See above section 2.1.
54. CESCR, *General Comment 14*, paras 4, 8; Toebes, *Right to Health*, 51–2. See also Tomasevski, 'Health Rights', 125.
55. CESCR, *General Comment 14*, para. 59, footnote 30.
56. CESCR, *General Comment 14*, para. 19, note omitted.
57. See also Laura Niada, 'The Human Right to Medicines in Sub-Saharan Africa' (PhD dissertation, University of Westminster, 2010), 161–4.
58. CESCR, *General Comment 3*, para. 12.
59. Niada, 'The Human Right to Medicines', 161–4.
60. CESCR, *General Comment 3*, para. 10; CESCR, *General Comment 14*, 43, 47.
61. On the relationship between the concept of progressive realisation and the concept of minimum core obligation see Amrei Muller, *The Relationship between Economic, Social*

and Cultural Rights and International Humanitarian Law: An Analysis of Health-Related Issues in Non-International Armed Conflicts (Leiden: Martinus Nijhoff Publishers, 2013), 85. (Muller argues that a minimum core obligation is compatible with the concept of progressive realisation enshrined in article 2(1) ICESCR as the 'obligation to progressively realise ESC rights is hardly thinkable without a domestic minimum standard to start from'.)

62. CESCR, *General Comment 14*, para. 43(d) and note 5.
63. WHO, 'The Selection and Use of Essential Medicines', *Technical Report Series 920*, no. 54 (2003): 55.
64. WHO, *How to Develop and Implement a National Drug Policy* (Geneva: WHO, 2000), 7.
65. WHO and Health Action International (HAI), *Measuring Medicine Prices, Availability, Affordability and Price Components*, 2nd ed. (WHO and HAI, 2008), 28, 34.
66. Ibid., 28.
67. WHO, 'The Selection and Use of Essential Medicines', 54. On the use of this definition see Niada, 'The Human Right to Medicines', 174.
68. Richard Laing and others, '25 years of the WHO Essential Medicines Lists: Progress and Challenges', *Lancet* 361 (May 17, 2003): 1725. Some anti-retrovirals, however, have been introduced in the most recent versions of the WHO EML, relaxing the requirements of cost-effectiveness. Ibid.
69. South African Standard Treatment Guidelines and Essential Drugs List for Primary Health Care 2003. See also Mickey Chopra and others, '"Nothing New": Responses to the Introduction of Antiretroviral Drugs in South Africa', *AIDS* 20, no. 15 (2006): 1975–7. But see South African Standard Treatment Guidelines and Essential Drugs List Hospital Level Adults 2012.
70. Love recalls that only 14 (12 on the core list and two on the complimentary list) of the total 312 medicines on the [2005] EDL are under a United States patent. James P. Love, 'Letter Asking WHO Review of the Essential Drugs List (EDL) as it Relates to Patented Products', 2006, http://www.cptech.org/blogs/ipdisputesinmedicine/2006/12/letter-asking-who-review-of-essential.html. Reportedly, less than 5% of medicines on the WHO's essential drugs list are subject to patent protection. Roya Ghafele, *Perceptions of Intellectual Property: A Review* (London: Intellectual Property Institute, 2008), 16.
71. Love, 'Letter'.
72. *The Economist*, 'Worse than AIDS', 1 March 2014.
73. CESCR, *General Comment 3*, para. 10 (italics added).
74. Hogerzeil and colleagues for example have identified and analysed 71 completed court cases from 12 low-income and middle-income countries in which individuals or groups had claimed access to essential medicines with reference to the right to health in general, or to specific human rights treaties ratified by the government. They found that in 59 cases access to essential medicines as part of the fulfilment of the right to health could indeed be enforced through the courts. Most cases came from Central and Latin America, with South Africa being the only African case identified. Hans V. Hogerzeil and others, 'Is Access to Essential Medicines as Part of the Fulfilment of the Right to Health Enforceable through the Courts?', *Lancet* 368 (July 22, 2006): 305.
75. For a discussion on the justiciability of economic, social and cultural rights see for example Michael Dennis and David Stewart: 'Justiciability of Economic, Social, and Cultural Rights: Should There Be an International Complaints Mechanism to Adjudicate the Rights to Food, Water, Housing, and Health?', *American Journal of International Law* 98 (2004): 462–515; Hestermeyer, 'Access to Medication as a Human Right', 125; Alicia E. Yamin, 'Not Just a Tragedy: Access to Medications as a Right under International Law', *Boston University International Law Journal* 21, no. 2 (2003).
76. In the *Soobramoney* case the South African Constitutional Court permitted the individual enforcement of access to treatment, but the claim was based on access to emergency medical treatment rather than health care. South Africa, Constitutional Court, 1997, *Soobramoney* v. *Minister of Health (KwaZulu-Natal)*, Case No. CCT 32/97, 27 November 1997. See also Joan Fitzpatrick and Ron C. Slye, 'Republic of South Africa v. Grootbroom, Case No. CCT 11/00. 2000 (11) BCLR 1169. Constitutional Court of South Africa, 4 October 2000. *Minister of Health* v. *Treatment Action Campaign*. Case No. CCT 8/02', *American Journal of International Law* 97 no. 3 (2003): 678.
77. For a background of the case see ESCR-Net, 'Minister of Health v Treatment Action Campaign (TAC)', http://www.escr-net.org/docs/i/403050 (accessed 9 October 2014).

78. South Africa, Constitutional Court, 2002, *Minister of Health* v. *Treatment Action Campaign* [TAC], Case No. CCT 8/02, 5 SA 721 (CC), 5 July 2002, paras 5, 25. South Africa, Constitution of the Republic of South Africa, Act No. 108 of 1996, articles 27(1), 28(1).
79. *Minister of Health* v. *TAC*, paras 32, 37. On the reasonableness of the intervention see also ibid., para. 125.
80. Ibid., para. 35. It has to be noted that South Africa has not ratified the ICESCR. OHCHR, 'Status of Ratification'. It has however signed the covenant and the court does refer to the treaty in its ruling. Ibid., *Minister of Health* v. *TAC*, paras 26–33.
81. *Minister of Health* v. *TAC*, para. 37.
82. Ibid., para. 34.
83. Ibid., para. 67.
84. Robert Beaglehole and Ruth Bonita, *Public Health at the Crossroads: Achievements and Prospects* (Cambridge: Cambridge University Press, 2004), 264–6; Joseph C. D'Oronzio, 'Keeping Human Rights on the Bioethics Agenda', *Cambridge Quarterly of Healthcare Ethics* 10, no. 3 (2001): 223–226; Tomasevski, 'Health Rights', 125. For instance, vaccinations may be imposed that could have side-effects. O'Neill remarks that while (the new) medical ethics is centred on autonomy, it has 'relatively little to say about public health, where interventions are often (and sometimes necessarily) compulsory'. Onora O'Neill, 'Public Health or Clinical Ethics: Thinking beyond Borders', *Ethics and International Affairs* 16, no. 2 (2002): 36.
85. International Covenant on Civil and Political Rights (ICCPR) UN Doc. A/6316 (1966), entered into force 23 March 1976, article 12.
86. ICCPR article 19.
87. ICCPR article 21.
88. ICCPR article 22. See also Toebes, 'Human Rights and Public Health'.
89. Toebes, *Right to Health*, 275.
90. This account draws liberally from Hammer and Berman, who identify three goals and principles of public health policy in developing countries: improving aggregate health status, relieving equity/poverty, and improving individual welfare. Jeffrey S. Hammer and Peter Berman, 'Ends and Means in Public Health Policy in Developing Countries', *Health Policy* 32, nos 1–3 (1995): 29.
91. DALYs are defined as 'a measure of the future stream of healthy life (years expected to be lived in full health) lost as a result of the incidence of specific diseases and injuries', i.e. a sum of 'both premature mortality (years of life lost because of premature mortality or YLL) and disability (years of healthy life lost as a result of disability or YLD, weighted by the severity of the disability)'. International Bank for Reconstruction and Development (IBRD)/The World Bank, *The Global Burden of Disease and Risk Factors* (International Bank for Reconstruction and Development (IBRD)/The World Bank, 2006), 3. QALYs, i.e. quality-adjusted life-years, are the inverse form of DALYs. Ibid., 48.
92. Hammer and Berman, 'Ends and Means', 31.
93. Commission on Macroeconomics and Health, *Macroeconomics and Health: Investing in Health for Economic Development* (Geneva: WHO, 2001); World Bank, *World Development Report 1993: Investing in Health* (New York: Oxford University Press, Publication 1993); WHO, *Tough Choices: Investing in Health for Development: Experiences from National Follow-up to the Commission on Macroeconomics and Health* (Geneva: WHO, 2006).
94. The report of the Commission on Macroeconomics and Health gives recommendations for the utilisation of resources domestically in developing countries and for the disbursement of foreign aid.
95. Commission on Macroeconomics and Health, *Macroeconomics and Health*, 12.
96. Ibid., 69.
97. John McKie and Jeff Richardson, 'The Rule of Rescue', *Social Science and Medicine* 56 (2003): 2407.
98. Ibid.; Tony Hope, John Reynolds, and Sian Griffiths, 'Rationing Decisions: Integrating Cost-Effectiveness with Other Values', in *Medicine and Social Justice: Essays on the Distribution of Health Care*, ed. Rosamond Rhodes, Margaret P. Battin, and Anita Silvers (New York: Oxford University Press, 2002), 146.
99. McKie and Richardson, 'The Rule of Rescue', 2407.
100. Hammer and Berman, 'Ends and Means', 36.

101. Especially, if DALYs are considered. Hope, Reynolds, and Griffiths, 'Rationing Decisions', 146.
102. Ibid.
103. Ibid.
104. Ibid.
105. Rod Sheaff, *The Need for Healthcare* (London: Routledge, 1996), 176.
106. Ibid., 169.
107. Kenyon J. Mason and Graeme T. Laurie, *Mason and McCall Smith's Law and Medical Ethics* (Oxford: Oxford University Press, 2006), 428. The definition of need for medical care is taken from Anthony J. Culyer, *Need and the National Health Service* (Oxford: Martin Robertson, 1976).
108. In fact, collecting epidemiological data can be extremely impracticable in some circumstances: Niada, 'The Human Right to Medicines', Chapter 2.
109. Rony Brauman, 'Questioning Health and Human Rights', *MSF Article*, 2 April 2004. Brauman is a doctor at MSF. In this article, he refers, in particular, to humanitarian work in health care.
110. Mason and Laurie, *Mason*, 428. See also Nick Bosanquet, 'A "Fair Innings" for Efficiency in Health Services', *Journal of Medical Ethics* 27 (2001): 228. DALYs and QALYs may also be utilised to estimate the benefits of a health intervention to individuals.
111. Hogerzeil and others, 'Is Access to Essential Medicines'; Ole Frithjof Norheim and Bruce M. Wilson, 'Health Rights Litigation and Access to Medicines: Priority Classification of Successful Cases from Costa Rica's Constitutional Chamber of the Supreme Court', *Health and Human Rights 2014* 16, no. 2 (2014), http://www.hhrjournal.org/2014/10/02/health-rights-litigation-and-access-to-medicines-priority-classification-of-successful-cases-from-costa-ricas-constitutional-chamber-of-the-supreme-court/ (accessed 19 October 2014). See also Alicia Yamin and Siri Gloppen, eds, *Litigating Health Rights: Can Courts Bring More Justice to Health?* (Cambridge, MA: Harvard University Press, 2011).
112. Norheim and Wilson, 'Health Rights Litigation'; Yamin and Gloppen, *Litigating Health Rights.*
113. Norheim and Wilson, 'Health Rights Litigation'.
114. Dan W. Brock, 'Priority to the Worse Off in Health-Care Resource Prioritization', in *Medicine and Social Justice: Essays on the Distribution of Health Care*, ed. Rosamond Rhodes, Margaret P. Battin, and Anita Silvers (New York: Oxford University Press, 2002), 362–372.
115. Hammer and Berman, 'Ends and Means', 34.
116. Ibid., 31.
117. Ibid.
118. The theoretical framework of this article is inspired by different contributions including: the critical approaches to law and human rights of Arendt, Douzinas and Luhmann; the critique of 'modernity' by Bauman and Luhmann; Luhmann's social systems theory; the critique of positivism and quantification in science and public life of Marcuse and Porter; public health and medical ethics. Hannah Arendt, *The Human Condition* (Chicago: University of Chicago Press, 1958); Hannah Arendt, *The Origins of Totalitarianism* (London: Andre Deutsch, 1986); Costas Douzinas, *The End of Human Rights* (Oxford: Hart, 2000); Niklas Luhmann, *Law as Social System* (Oxford: Oxford University Press, 2004); Niklas Luhmann, *I Diritti Fondamentali come Istituzione* (Bari: Edizioni Dedalo, 2002/1965); Zygmunt Bauman, *Modernity and the Holocaust* (Ithaca, NY: Cornell University Press, 1993); Niklas Luhmann, *Social Systems* (Stanford, CA: Stanford University Press, 1995); Niklas Luhmann, *Observations on Modernity*, trans. William Whobrey, eds Timothy Lenoir and Hans U. Gumbrecht (Stanford, CA: Stanford University Press, 1998); Herbert Marcuse, *One-Dimensional Man* (London: Routledge, 2002[1964]); Theodore M. Porter, *Trust in Numbers: The Pursuit of Objectivity in Science and Public Life* (Princeton NJ: Princeton University Press, 1995); Lilani Kumaranayake and Damian Walker, 'Cost-Effectiveness Analysis and Priority-Setting: Global Approach Without Meaning?', in *Health Policy in a Globalising World*, ed. Kelley Lee, Kent Buse, and Suzanne Fustukian (Cambridge: Cambridge University Press, 2002), 140–156; Vicente Navarro, 'Assessment of the World Health Report 2000', *Lancet* 356 (2000), 1598–1601; Vicente Navarro, 'Can Health Care Systems Be Compared Using a Single Measure of Performance?', *American Journal of Public Health* 92, no. 1 (2002), 31–34; Sheaff, *Need for Healthcare.*
119. Luhmann, *Law as Social System*; Luhmann, *I Diritti Fondamentali.*

120. Giorgio Agamben, *Homo Sacer. Sovereign Power and Bare Life*, trans. Daniel Heller-Roazen (Stanford, CA: Stanford University Press, 1998); Michel Foucault, *L'Histoire de la Sexualite, I, La Volonté de Savoir* (Paris: Gallimard, 1976). See also Didier Fassin, 'Entre Politiques du Vivant et Politiques de la Vie: Pour une Anthropologie de la Santé', *Anthropologie et Sociétés* 24, no. 1 (2000); Didier Fassin, 'Humanitarianism as a Politics of Life', *Public Culture* 19, no. 3 (2007): 499–520; Mariella Pandolfi, 'L'Industrie Humanitaire; Une Souveraineté Mouvante et Supracoloniale: Réflexion sur l'Expérience des Balkans', *Multitudes* 3 (2001): 97–105; Mariella Pandolfi, '"Moral Entrepreneurs", Souverainetés Mouvantes et Barbelés', *Anthropologie et Sociétés* 26, no. 1 (2002): 29–51; Mariella Pandolfi, 'Contract of Mutual (In)Difference: Governance and the Humanitarian Apparatus in Contemporary Albania and Kosovo', *Indian Journal of Global Legal Studies* 10 (2003): 369–381.
121. Niklas Luhmann, *Die Gesellschaft der Gesellschaft* (Frankfurt am Main: Suhrkamp, 1997), 992–3.
122. Niklas Luhmann, 'Are There Still Indispensable Norms in our Society?', *Soziale Systeme* 14, no. 1 (2008): 28, 29 (Special Issue: '"Tragic Choices": Luhmann on Law and States of Exception', ed. William Rasch).
123. Luhmann, *Law as Social System*, 483.
124. Luhmann, *Die Gesellschaft*, 1022, translated in Hans-Georg Moeller, 'Human Rights Fundamentalism', *Soziale Systeme* 14, no. 1 (2008): 139 (special issue '"Tragic Choices": Luhmann on Law and States of Exception', ed. William Rasch).
125. Ibid.
126. Luhmann, 'Indispensable Norms', 19.
127. Ibid., 414.
128. Niklas Luhmann, 'Das Paradox der Menschenrechte und drei Formen seiner Entfaltung', in *Soziologische Aufklärung* (Opladen: Westdt, Verlag, 1995), 231, trans. in Moeller, 'Human Rights Fundamentalism', 131.
129. On Luhmann's use of the term communication see Luhmann, *Social Systems*, 59.
130. Luhmann, *I Diritti Fondamentali.*
131. Agamben, *Homo Sacer*, 127.
132. Michel Foucault, *Dits et Ecrits, 1976–1988*, Vol. 2 (Paris: Gallimard, 2001), 818.
133. Foucault, *L'Histoire*, 138.
134. Ibid., 136.
135. Michel Foucault, *Security, Territory, Population (Lectures at the College De France)* (Basingstoke: Palgrave Macmillan, 2007).
136. Foucault, *Dits et Ecrits*, 818; Foucault, *Security.*
137. Foucault, *Security.* In this context, security can be seen as both an end of biopower and a means of biopower to perpetuate itself.
138. Ibid., 74.
139. Ibid., 57.
140. Ibid., 63.
141. See section 3.1.
142. *Minister of Health* v. *TAC*, paras 32, 37.
143. On the relationship between human rights, group rights, and people's rights see Peter Jones, 'Human Rights, Group Rights, and People's Rights', *Human Rights Quarterly* 21 (1999): 80–107. On the use of collective complaints in relation to the right to health see also Toebes, 'Human Rights and Public Health'.
144. Toebes, *Right to Health.*
145. Luhmann, *Die Gesellschaft*, 992–3.
146. CESCR, *General Comment 14*, para. 19 (note omitted).
147. See also CESCR, *General Comment 14*, para. 53.
148. Luhmann, *Law as Social System*, 418. See also ibid., 151, 165.
149. Tomasevski, 'Health Rights', 125.
150. Foucault, *Security.*
151. Andreas Philippopoulos-Mihalopoulos, *Niklas Luhmann: Law, Justice, Society* (Oxon: Routledge-Cavendish, 2010), 157.
152. Similarly, Hope and others conclude that since each theory for allocation of health resources faces difficulties, it is more important to concentrate on the procedure to reach the decisions. See Hope, Reynolds, and Griffiths, 'Rationing Decisions', 144.

Index

ABC News 53
accountability 2–3, 16, 40, 47–64, 94, 113, 158
Aceves, W. 92, 95
Action Programme on Essential Drugs 150
advocacy 54, 56
Afghanistan 49, 53
Afghanistan (United Nations Sanctions) Order 11
Africa 1, 74, 115, 118, 123–4, 145, 151, 153
African Commission 152
Agamben, G. 146, 153, 155–7
aggregate health 153–5, 157–8
Agreement on Sanitary and Phytosanitary Measures (SPS) 110
Ahmed case 16
AIDS virus 117, 151
Albania 85
Alfei Menashe 68
all hazards approach 127
Alston, P. 148
anaesthetic gun system 86
anti-terrorism *see* counterterrorism
Apartheid 85
Arabs 73
Arbel, Judge 73
Argentina 57
armed conflict 48–51, 56, 59, 66, 68, 83, 89–92, 95–6, 109, 112, 114
armed forces 30, 89
Asia Pacific China Police Expo 86–7
asset freezing 10–13
Attorney General, UK 18
Attorney General, US 51, 53
Australia 91–2, 111
Authorisation for Use of Military Force (AUMF) 8
autonomy 130, 135, 152

Bagram 49, 51
balance 1–3, 7–9, 13, 17, 19; Council of Europe 27, 37–40; freedom of expression 26–46; Israel 65–82; public health 106–22; WHO 125, 130
Banisar, D. 37–8
bans on disclosure 32–4
Barak, Judge 69–70, 72
Basel Convention on the Control of Transboundary Movements of Hazardous Wastes 112
Basic Laws 65, 74
BBQ-901 anaesthetic gun system 86
BBQ-901 narcosis gun 86
Beinisch, Judge 70
Beit Sourik case 67–9, 72
Bennoune, K. 18
Bentham, J. 108
Benvenisti, E. 10
Berman, P. 154
biobanks 114, 116
biological weapons *see* chemical and biological weapons
Biological Weapons Convention 112
biomedical research 114, 116–17
biopower 146, 155–8
bioregulators 85
Black, C. 49
black sites 49–51
blanket bans 32–4
Body of Principles for the Protection of All Persons under Any Form of Detention or Imprisonment 95
Bonner, D. 10
Brauman, R. 154
Brazil 57
Brennan, J. 55
Britain 108
British Medical Association 85
Bucur v. Romania case 31, 34–5
Buergenthal, Judge 68
Bulgaria 114
Bush, G.W. 8, 48–56, 58, 75
Bybee, J. 47, 50, 54

calmative gas flows 88
Cameron, I. 35
Canada 34, 75, 110
cancer 145, 151
carfentanil 88

case law 1–2, 7, 12, 14–17, 27; chemical weapons 93, 97; Council of Europe 29–30, 33, 35; human rights 113, 115–16; Israel 67
Central America 151–2, 154
central nervous system (CNS) 88, 91–2
Chadwick, B. 108
Charter of the United Nations 4, 8, 11–14, 18, 128
Chayes, A. 90
Chechens 88
checks and balances 6–25, 126, 133
chemical and biological weapons (CBW) 87–8, 109, 112
chemical weapons 3, 83–105
Chemical Weapons Convention (CWC) 3, 83, 85, 87–92, 94, 96, 112
Cheney, R. 53, 55, 58
Chile 57
China 85–7, 96
China North Industries Corporation (NORINCO) 86
cholecystokinin B agonists 96
chronic diseases 109, 111
CIA 2, 7, 48–55, 58
citizenship 3, 66, 70–4
Citizenship Law 71–2, 74
civil liberties 65–6
civil rights 4, 7, 109–10, 112, 114–19, 125, 128–33, 135, 152, 157
civil servants 33
civil society organisations 38, 40, 97, 107
class 57, 108
climate change 106, 112, 118
clinical trials 116–17
cloning 116
cluster bombs 86
Code Monétaire et Financier 11
commerce 3, 108–11
Commission on Macroeconomics and Health 153, 157
Committee against Torture 59
Committee on Economic, Social and Cultural Rights 4, 146–8, 150–2
Committee of Ministers 27, 30
Common Position 2001/931/CFSP 12
communism 35
compensation 48, 56, 93–4, 132
Conference of State Parties 91
confidentiality 28, 32, 36–7, 130
conflicts 2, 4–5, 8–10, 17–19, 48–51; armed 56, 59, 66, 68, 83, 89–90, 92, 95–6, 109, 112, 114; authorities 10–12, 14–17; counterterrorism 6–25; resolution 12–13
Congress 50–1
consent 95, 110, 112, 116, 134–5
constitutionalism 3, 65–82
Constitutions 50, 108–9, 111, 151
contestation 48, 55
Convention Against Torture (CAT) 50–1, 59, 95
Convention on Biological Diversity 112
Convention on Civil Aviation 112
cordon sanitaire 133
corruption 31, 37–8, 40
Costa Rica 154
Council of Europe (COE) 2, 10, 15, 17, 26–46, 108, 116
counterinsurgency 84, 92
counterterrorism 2, 6–25, 30, 48, 75, 83–4, 91–2
Court of First Instance (CFI) 12–14
Crowley, M. 3, 83–105
cruel treatment 49–51, 59, 92, 94–6
Cuba 111
cultural rights 4, 109, 117–19, 129, 146–52, 154–5, 157–9
Czech Republic 87

damage tests 32, 34–7
Dando, M. 3, 83–105
De Wet, E. 15
Decision 2011/487-CFSP 11
Defence Research and Development Organisation (DRDO) 87
Defence Science and Technology Laboratory 88
degrading treatment 49–51, 59, 92, 94–6
delistings 16, 18
democracy 2, 5–7, 10, 17, 19; Council of Europe 29–31, 35; Israel 66, 75; medicines provision 158; public health 116–18; US 48–9, 52, 55–8, 60; WHO 125
democratisation 48
Denning, Lord 7
depression 96
derogation 4, 7, 9, 65, 73; chemical weapons 95; human rights 107, 114–15, 119; model 125–7, 129–30, 135
Detainee Treatment Act (DTA) 50–1
detention 48, 51–2, 54–5, 73–5, 95–6, 114, 116, 129, 132, 134–5
developing countries 106, 111, 113, 116–17, 129, 151, 153
dictatorship 57
digital media 40
dignity 3, 65–7, 72, 74–5, 110, 128–9, 134–5
dirty tricks 88
disability-adjusted life-years (DALYs) 153
disclosures list 37–40
Doha Declaration 111
Dominican Republic 111
double jeopardy 153
drinking water 109
dual-use research 86, 88–9, 96
due process 14, 16, 130, 134–5
al-Dulimi case 18
Dupuis case 35
Durbin, R.J. 47
Dworkin, T. 38

Ebola virus 1, 3, 115, 117–18, 123–4, 127–9
EC Regulation 881/2002 11–13

EC Regulation 1286/2009 16
EC Regulation 2580/2001 12
EC-Asbestos case 110
ECCR v Bulgaria case 114
economic rights 4, 109, 117–19, 129, 146–55, 157–9
education 4, 135, 149
Elements of Crimes 95
Elster, J. 56
Emergency Committee 124
emergency measures 9, 50, 65, 73, 115, 119, 123–35
England 108
enhanced interrogation techniques (EITs) 49–51, 58–9
Enhorn v. Sweden case 116
environment 106–8, 112–14, 118, 123, 127, 147, 149
epidemics 112, 119, 123, 129, 147, 149
epidemiology 154
equality 72, 129, 135, 147, 153, 155
Eritreans 72–4
espionage 27
essential medicine lists (EMLs) 150
essential medicines 109, 117, 145–52, 157–8
ethics 37, 54, 108, 116, 146, 153–4, 157–9
European Commission 10, 13, 16, 18, 110
European Committee of Social Rights 113
European Convention on Human Rights and Biomedicine 116
European Convention on Human Rights (ECHR) 7, 9, 17–18, 27–9, 31, 37, 40, 93–5, 114–16
European Court of Human Rights (ECtHR) 12, 15, 17–18, 27, 29–35, 40, 93–4, 115–16
European Court of Justice (ECJ) 2, 6, 12–18
European Social Charter (ESC) 113–14
European Union (EU) 2, 9–18, 27
exceptionalism 1–5, 49, 58, 130
executive 9–10, 15, 18, 27, 32; Council of Europe 36, 39; Israel 75; measures 2, 5, 7, 12, 17, 19; US 50, 52, 55, 58–9
extraordinary rendition 58

Feinberg, M. 1–25
fentanyl 87–8
Fidler, D. 91–2, 96, 127
Focal Point 16
Fogelman, Judge 73
food and beverages industry 106, 111
foreign policy 10, 15–16
Foucault, M. 146, 153, 155–7
Framework Convention on Climate Change 112
Framework Convention on Global Health (FCGH) 107
Framework Convention on Tobacco Control (FCTC) 110–11
France 11, 35, 40, 110, 148
freedom of expression 26–46
freedom from torture 7, 92, 135
freedom of information 2
Freedom of Information Act (FOIA) 49
freedom of movement 1–2, 4, 73, 107, 130, 132–3, 135
freedom of speech 2, 4, 27–30, 32–8, 40
further research 97, 110, 113, 119

Galenkamp, M. 113
gas-phase techniques 86
Gaza 69–71
General Agreement on Tariffs and Trade (GATT) 110
General Court 13, 16
general purpose criterion (GPC) 90
genetic testing 116
Geneva Conventions 49–51, 69, 112
Germany 75, 91
global health security 107, 109, 114, 118–19, 124
globalisation 109, 113
golden shield 50
Goldsmith, J. 50
good faith 27, 29–31, 34, 36, 50, 53, 55
Gostin, L. 109, 123, 127
governance 9, 127, 156
Greece 114
Grootboom case 152
Guantanamo 49–52, 58, 75
Guatemala 57
Guinea 129
Guja v. Moldova case 31, 35

habeas corpus 132
Hafetz, J. 2–3, 5, 47–64
Hamas 69–71, 88
Hamdan v. Rumsfeld case 51
Hammer, J.S. 154
Hampson, F. 94
Health Organisation of the League of Nations 108
health security 107, 109, 114, 118–19, 124
health security threats 107, 109, 119
hegemony 72
Heinisch case 34–5
Hestermeyer, H.P. 148
HIV virus 116–17, 151
Honduras 111
Horwitz, P. 56
hostages 84, 88, 93
House Intelligence Committee 53
human rights 3, 31, 34, 38, 48–50; balance 7–9; chemical weapons 83–5, 92–7; Council of Europe 26–46; counterterrorism 6–25; exceptions 1–5; fundamentalism 155–7; Israel 65–82; medicines provision 145–65; public health 106–22; role 106–22; US 52, 55–9; WHO 123–44
Human Rights Committee 12, 93, 97, 128, 131

Human Rights Watch (HRW) 118–19
human security 8
humanitarian model 154
Hunt, P. 148

identity 130
ideology 72
Imam Hossein University (IHU) 87
imminent public risk 134
incapacitating chemical agents (ICAs) 3, 83–94, 96–7
India 74, 87
indigenous population 57, 113
individual rights 29, 75, 107, 113–18, 146, 149–52, 155–8
Indonesia 111
inequalities 107, 109, 113–14, 118
infectious diseases 107, 109, 112, 114, 116–18, 123–4, 127–9, 131–3, 147, 152
influenza 123, 128
inhuman treatment 49–51, 59, 92, 94–6
Institute of Advanced Legal Studies, London 1
intellectual property 3, 106, 109–10, 113
intelligence community 2, 7, 26–9, 31–4, 36, 39–41, 52–3, 56, 88
International Committee of the Red Cross (ICRC) 85, 91, 94
international community 3, 13–14, 17, 40, 84, 97, 124–35
International Court of Justice (ICJ) 10, 12, 67
International Covenant on Civil and Political Rights (ICCPR) 4, 7, 12, 59, 114–16, 125–6, 128–33, 135
International Covenant on Economic, Social and Cultural Rights (ICESCR) 4, 115, 117–18, 129, 146–55, 157–9
International Criminal Court 95
International Health Regulations (IHR) 4, 109–10, 115, 123–44
international humanitarian law (IHL) 50, 56, 66, 69, 83, 108
international law 2–3, 10, 12–15, 49–50, 55–6; chemical weapons 83–4, 91–7; Israel 65–7, 69–70, 74; medicines provision 146, 148–9; public health 107–13, 116, 119; WHO 124–35
International Principles for Whistleblower Protection 38
International Sanitary Conferences 108
International Union of Pure and Applied Chemistry 86
interrogation 2, 48–55, 57–9, 75
Iran 87
Iraq 49, 53, 85
Ireland 91
Israel 2–3, 65–82, 85, 87–8, 96
Israel Institute for Biological Research 88
Israeli Arabs 71
Israeli Defence Force (IDF) 70

Jaffer, J. 49
Janes Intelligence Review 88
Japan 37
jihadis 1
Jordan 88
journalists 30, 35
judiciary 2, 7, 10, 29, 33; chemical weapons 96; Council of Europe 35–7, 40; Israel 65, 67, 75; judicial review 5, 9, 13–15, 17–19, 50, 66, 72–3; medicines provision 151; public health 113–14; US 55, 57; WHO 132
jus in bello 71
jus cogens 13–14
Justice Department 47, 50, 53–4, 56

Kadi case 2, 6–7, 12–18
Kadi II case 13, 15–16
Kadi, Y.A. 12–14, 16
Kagiaros, D. 2, 4, 26–46
Kalkilya 68
ketamine 87
Khadr case 75
Kiriakou, J. 53
Krutzsch, W. 90–1
Kyoto Protocol 112

Labour Law Code 40
Bin Laden, O. 58
land mines 86
last resort 28, 39, 116
Latin America 57, 151–2, 154
law enforcement 3, 83–105, 129, 133
League of Nations 108
Leahy, P. 56
Lebanon 148
legislation 1–2, 8–10, 14–15, 27–32, 34–40, 51, 73–4, 107, 124
legislature 35, 39, 74–5
Lester, S. 110
Levin, D. 50
Levy, Judge 72
Lewis, D. 36
Liberia 129
liberty 8, 18, 30, 68, 74, 107, 114–16, 118–19, 130–2, 134–5
life sciences 83, 86
limitations model 125–7, 129–31, 135
Lisbon Treaty 11, 16
listings 13–18
Lockerbie case 12
London 1
Luban, D. 50
Luhmann, N. 146, 153, 155–8

malaria 151
man-made disasters 109
Mara'abe case 68
margin of appreciation doctrine 29–31
Margolis, D. 54

Médecins Sans Frontières (MSF) 154
medetomidine 87
media 27–8, 30, 33, 35, 38, 55, 87
medical examination 93, 130–2, 134–5
medical experimentation 129, 135, 154
medicines provision 4, 106, 111, 113, 130, 145–65
Meier, B.M. 113
Meselson, M. 90
midazolam 87
migration 3, 66, 70, 113, 118
Milanovic, M. 18
military 27, 38–9, 50–1, 53–4, 57, 67–71, 84, 87–92, 106, 126, 133
Military Commissions Act (MCA) 51
Minister of Health v TAC case 151–2
Mishal, K. 88
Model List of Essential Drugs 150
Moeckli, D. 8
Moldova 35
monism 15, 111
Montreal Protocol on Protection of the Ozone Layer 112
Mori, L.M. 113
Morse, M. 32
Mossad 88
motor-vehicle safety 109
Mukasey, M.B. 51

Nada v. Switzerland case 12
nanotechnology 85–6
narcosis gun 86
National Health Service (NHS) 145
National Institute for Health and Clinical Excellence (NICE) 145, 153
National Research Council (NRC) on Emerging Cognitive Neuroscience 85–6
national security 1–5; balance 7–9; chemical weapons 83–105; Council of Europe 26–46; counterterrorism 6–25; human rights 106–22; Israel 65–82; medicines provision 145–65; public health 115, 117; US 47–64; WHO 123–44
National Security and Public Health: Exceptions to Human Rights Conference 1
nationalism 11
natural disasters 109, 114
Neil, D. 91
Netherlands 111
neuroscience 85, 95
nevirapine 151
Niada-Avshalom, L. 1–5, 145–65
non-government organisations (NGOs) 49, 111, 113, 151
noradrenaline antagonists 96
normalisation 157
norms 2–3, 6–25, 56–8, 60, 65–8, 74, 92, 129, 146
Norway 91
nuclear disasters 109, 127

Obama, B. 8, 48, 52–6, 58–9
occupational health 109, 113–14
Office International d'Hygiène Publique (OIHP) 108
Office of Legal Counsel (OLC) 50–3, 58
Office of the Ombudsperson 16–18
Office of Professional Responsibility (OPR) 54
official secrets 27, 29, 32, 37–40, 53
Official Secrets Act 27, 32
offshore/secret prisons 50, 52, 58
opioids 87–8
Organisation des Modjahedines du peuple d'Iran v. Council of the European Union and UK case 12
Organisation for the Prohibition of Chemical Weapons (OPCW) 84, 86–7, 89, 91–2, 96
OSCE 38
Oval Office 52
Oviedo Convention 116
Owada, Judge 68

Padilla, J. 54
Palestinians 68, 70–1
pandemics 123, 127–8, 149, 151
panic attacks 96
Parliamentary Assembly 27, 29–30, 38–40
particle engineering 85
patents 111, 151
Patriot Act 8
People's Liberation Army 87
Perry Robinson, J. 90
Peru 57
Petraeus, D.H. 53
pharmaceuticals 84, 87
pharmacology 85–6
Philippopoulos-Mihalopoulos, A. 158
policy-making organisations (PMO) 92, 96
poliovirus 128
political rights 4, 7, 109–10, 112, 114–16; medicines provision 146, 152–3, 157; role 118–19; WHO 125, 128–33, 135
pollution 106, 112, 118
polycentrism 127, 135
Poole, Thomas 8
Poor Law Commission 108
Popelier, P. 36
Porton Down 89
poverty 154–5
prisoners of war 112
privacy 31, 75, 107, 114–16, 118–19, 130, 134–5, 152
private sector 27, 34
profit 106
Project 'Gas Flow' 88
property rights 13, 149
prophylaxis 130–1, 134–5
proportionality 2, 8, 17, 33–6, 115–19, 125–6, 130–1, 133
propranolol 96

Prosecutor General's Office 35
protectionism 113
public health 1–5, 106–21, 123–43, 145–65
public health emergency of international concern (PHEIC) 124–35
Public Interest Disclosure Act 27
public interest (PI) 26–9, 31–40
public opinion 35
public sector 27, 34, 151
punishment 53, 94–5

al-Qaeda 11, 49–52, 54
al-Qaeda Sanctions Committee 11
quality-adjusted life-years (QALYs) 153
quarantine 114, 117–19, 131–2, 134–5
Quinn, G. 148
3-quinuclidinyl benzilate (BZ) 89

Rapporteurs on Freedom of Expression 38
rationing 4
receptor research 85, 88
refugees 65–82
Refugees' Convention 73
refuse 108
regime change 48, 57
remifentanil 88
repression 47, 56–7
Republicans 54, 59
resistance 2, 48–51, 54–6, 60
Resolution 1214 11
Resolution 1267 10–12, 14–18
Resolution 1373 11–12, 14
Resolution 1551 29
Resolution 1729 29–30
Resolution 1838 30
Resolution 1877 30
Resolution 1904 16
Resolution 1954 30, 38–9
Resolution 2177 1, 124
Resolution 2178 1, 18
Resolution on National Security and Access to Information 38
Review Conferences 91
Revolutionary Guard 87
right to dignity *see* dignity
right to family 71–2, 75, 114–15, 118–19, 132, 135
right to health 106–7, 110–14, 117–19, 129, 133, 145–65
right to life 38, 69, 92–3, 114, 131
riot control agents (RCAs) 84, 86, 90–1, 96
risk within rights 125
Rogers, M. 53
Roma 114
Romania 27, 31, 35, 91
Romney, M. 59
Rosen, G. 108
Rotterdam Convention on the Prior Informed Consent Procedure for Certain Hazardous Chemicals and Pesticides in International Trade 112
Royal Society 84, 95
rule of law 3, 17, 35, 48, 52, 55, 57, 60, 65–6, 126
Russian Federation 83, 88, 93–4, 96

Safe Water Drinking Act 38
Sagar, R. 33
sanctions 2, 6–7, 9–12, 15–18, 27, 29, 37, 54, 95
Sanctions Committee 12–13, 16, 18
sanitation 108, 110, 112
Saudi Arabia 12
Scarry, E. 57
second opinions 132, 135
secret services 30
security 27–9, 32, 35, 39, 55, 65–82, 126, 155–8
Security and Information Act 34
Senate Select Committee 2, 7, 48–9, 52, 54–5, 58–9
separation of powers 17
September 11 2001 2, 5, 7–8, 10, 47–64, 66
severe acute respiratory syndrome (SARS) 123, 127
Sheaff, R. 154, 158
Shevchenko, Y. 88
sieges 84, 88
Sierra Leone 129
Siracusa Principles 115–16, 125
slavery 114
sleep deprivation 49
Slovakia 91
Slovenia 34
social rights 4, 109, 113, 117–19, 129, 146–55, 157–9
socio-economics 109, 148
sociology 146
Solomon, S. 3, 5, 65–82
South Africa 37, 56, 85, 151
sovereignty 9, 73, 156
Soviet Union 85
Spain 75
Special Procedures 97
Special Rapporteur on Extra-Judicial, Summary or Arbitrary Executions 93
Special Rapporteur on the Right to Health 148, 150
Special Rapporteur on Torture 95
State 9616 Plant 86
Stockholm Convention on Persistent Organic Pollutants 112
stockpiles 87–91, 96
Sturken, M. 58
sub-Saharan Africa 145, 151
subsidiarity 15
Subsidiary Organs Branch 16
substance P agonists 96
Sudan 73
Sudanese 72–5

Supreme Court, Canada 75
Supreme Court, Israel 3, 66–8, 70–5
Supreme Court, UK 16
Supreme Court, US 51, 70
surveillance 1, 31, 35, 38
SWAT units 86
Sweden 27, 116
Swedish Defence Research Institute 87
Switzerland 91
synthetic biology 85
Syria 89
systems biology 85

Taliban 11, 49
targeted killings 69–70
taxpayers 30, 145, 149
Teitel, R. 47
television shows 51
terrorism 1, 3, 6–25, 30–1, 48–52, 57–8, 66–75, 96, 109
Thiessen, M. 58
Time 88
tobacco industry 106, 110–11, 118
Tobacco Plain Packaging Act (TPPA) 111
Toebes, B. 1–5, 106–22, 148, 152
Tomasevski, K. 149
torture 3, 5, 7, 38, 48–60, 85, 92, 94–6, 114, 129, 135
torture memos 47, 52, 54–5, 58
trade 3, 106–14, 129
trademarks 111
training 4, 40, 135, 151
transitional justice 2, 47–64
transparency 5, 38, 52
Transparency International 38
transplantation 116
transportation 3, 68, 108, 110, 112
Trapp, R. 85, 90–1
travel 110, 112, 129–31, 133–5
Treatment Action Campaign (TAC) 151–2
Treaty on the Functioning of the European Union 11, 15
TRIPS Agreement 110–11, 113
Truth and Reconciliation Commission 56
Tsakyaris, S. 8
Tshwane Principles on National Security and Access to Information 38–9
tuberculosis 151
Turkel Committee 71
Turks 71
Tzanakopoulos, A. 15

Ukraine 111
United Kingdom (UK) 7, 11, 16, 18, 26–7, 32, 84–5, 88–91, 145, 153
United Nations (UN) 2, 9, 19, 38, 50; Charter 4, 11–14, 18, 128; chemical weapons 93, 95, 97; General Assembly 10, 67, 146; public health 108, 112, 115; Secretary-General 16, 115, 126; Security Council 1, 8, 10–16, 18, 124
United States (US) 2–3, 5, 26, 70, 74; accountability 47–64; Army Field Manual 52; chemical weapons 85, 89, 91; Council of Europe 37–8, 40; counterterrorism 7–8, 12
Universal Declaration of Human Rights (UDHR) 4, 14, 125, 128, 131, 133
urbanisation 118
Uruguay 57
utilitarianism 4, 49, 58, 108

vaccination 109, 114, 116, 130–1, 134–5
Van De Heyning, C. 36
Verdirame, G. 8
vested interests 111–14
Vienna Conventions for the Law of Treaties 7
violence 47, 56, 67, 96
Von Schirnding, Y. 112
Von Wagner, A. 90
Voskuil v. Netherlands 35

war crimes 48–9, 51, 95
War Crimes Act 49–51
war on terrorism 3, 8, 31, 48, 50–1, 54, 58, 66, 69–71
warfare 50, 57, 66, 69, 74; chemical weapons 84–5, 88, 91; counterterrorism 7; exceptions 3–4; human rights 106–7, 110, 112–13
waterboarding 49–53, 58
weaponisation 84–5, 87–9, 91–2
weapons of mass destruction 38
West 116
West Africa 115, 118, 123
West Bank 67–9
Whistleblower Protection Act 27, 37
whistleblowers 2, 26–46
White, M.J. 51
wiretapping 35
World Bank 153
World Health Organisation (WHO) 4, 107–10, 115, 123–45, 149–51, 153, 157
World Trade Organisation (WTO) 110–11, 113
wrongdoing 2, 26–41, 47, 56

Yoo, J. 47, 50, 54
Youth Smoking Prevention Foundations 111
Yugoslavia 85

Zalaquett, J. 57
Zidar, A. 4, 109, 123–44
Zubaydah, Abu 50